Human Rights, the Citizen and the State

SOUTH AFRICAN AND IRISH APPROACHES

AUSTRALIA

LBC Information Services
Sydney

CANADA and USA

Carswell

NEW ZEALAND

Brookers
Wellington

SINGAPORE AND MALAYSIA

Thomson Information (S.E. Asia)
Singapore

Human Rights, the Citizen and the State

South African and Irish Approaches

Jeremy Sarkin and William Binchy

Editors

DUBLIN
ROUND HALL SWEET & MAXWELL
2001

Published in 2001 by
Round Hall Ltd
43 Fitzwilliam Place
Dublin 2

Typeset by
Gough Typesetting Services
Dublin

Printed by
MPG Books, Cornwall

ISBN 1-85800-240-0

A catalogue record for this book
is available from the British Library.

TABLE OF CONTENTS

INTRODUCTION

Ireland and South Africa, though far removed from each other geographically, share some broad similarities in their legal history. Both have experienced the superimposition of a new constitutional dispensation on an earlier legal system which had much sophistication but also associations with a rejected political order. Both countries are increasingly concerned to test their domestic law by the standards of contemporary international human rights norms. In this regard, South Africa had the advantage of being able to absorb many of these norms when drafting its 1996 Constitution. That privilege naturally was not available to Ireland, whose Constitution is now well into its seventh decade. Nevertheless the Irish Constitution remains vibrant through judicial activism and the possibility of enlightened amendments to the Constitution. Thus, for example, the recent abolition of recourse to the death penalty, even in times of national emergency, placed Ireland in the forefront of international human rights standards on that issue. Conversely, the amendment on bail was a step backwards. It is interesting to note that these two themes – the death penalty and bail – have exercised judges and academics enormously in South Africa.

Anyone who wishes to understand their own legal system and to test its values and practical operation will benefit from the study of how other legal systems grapple with the same issues. In that spirit, members of the Law School of Trinity College Dublin and the Law Faculty of the University of Western Cape, in the company of distinguished Judges from Ireland and South Africa as well as other academics and lawyers, met at the University of Western Cape on 15 September 2000 for a Colloquium. This book contains the edited proceedings of that colloquium. It represents the first of what is intended to be a long series of collaborative ventures. As we move from the first encounter to greater familiarity with each other's legal system, we hope that our comparative insights will gradually be deepened. The second Colloquium, which took place on 14 September 2001, was a happy and successful event. Those papers will be published in the coming months.

Jeremy Sarkin
William Binchy

JUDICIAL REVIEW AND SOCIO-ECONOMIC RIGHTS

GERARD HOGAN*

Much of modern legal thinking concerning the proper role of courts, exercising the power of judicial review of legislation, may be said to have commenced with the famous footnote 4 of Stone J.'s judgment for the U.S. Supreme Court in *U.S. v. Carolene Products*.[1] In this celebrated footnote, Stone J. observed that:

> "There may be narrower scope for operation of the presumption of constitutionality when legislation appears on its face to be within a specific prohibition of the Constitution, such as those of the first ten Amendments, which are equally specific when held to be embraced within the 14th. . . . It is unnecessary to consider now whether legislation which restricts those political processes which can ordinarily be expected to bring about repeal of undesirable legislation, is to be expected to more exacting judicial scrutiny under the general prohibitions of the 14th Amendment then are the most other types of legislation Nor need we enquire whether similar considerations enter into review of statutes directed at particular religious or national or racial minorities [or] whether prejudice against discrete and insular minorities may be a special condition, which tends seriously to curtail the operation of those political processes ordinarily to be relied upon to protect minorities and which may call for a correspondingly more searching judicial inquiry."[2]

Carolene Products provided the rationale for a number of U.S. constitutional law theorists – notably Professor Ely in his great book *Democracy and Dis-*

---

* Law School, Trinity College, Dublin

[1] 304 U.S. 144 (1938). For the background to this footnote, see Lusky, "Footnote Redux, A *Carolene Products* Reminiscence" (1982) 82 *Colum.L.Rev.* 1093. Professor Lusky was law clerk to Stone J. at the time and he (Lusky) is generally credited with authorship of footnote 4. For further valuable analysis, see Powell, "Carolene Products Revisited" (1982) 82 *Colum.L.Rev.* 1087 and Perry, "Justice Stone and Footnote 4" (1996) 6 *George Mason University Civil Rights Journal* 35.

[2] 302 U.S. at 152-154. For a superb analysis of the importance of this case, see Pratt, "A New Vocabulary for a New Constitutional Law: *United States v. Carotene Products*" in O'Dell ed., *Leading Cases of the Twentieth Century* (Dublin, 2000), pp. 125-148.

trust[3] – who argued that judicial review ought primarily to be process-based.
By this they meant that judicial review ought to re-inforce the democratic
process by making it work effectively. The thinking was that if the democratic
process worked properly, then an enlightened, responsible legislature would
repeal laws which discriminated against minorities, although it was also recognised – as Stone J. pointed out – that racial and other forms of prejudice
might tend to stultify the operation of that democratic process. The role of the
courts in judicial review ought – according to this theory – to be principally
concerned with invalidating laws and practices which interfered with the proper
working of the democratic system as opposed to invalidating laws on substantive grounds, especially where the courts relied on as the basis for such invali-
dation the vague contours of provisions such as the 14th Amendment's due
process clause.

The context of *Carolene Products* is sometimes overlooked. The defendants in that case had been charged with shipping skimmed milk in inter-state
commerce, contrary to a federal statute, the Filled Milk Act 1923. The defendants pleaded that the statute violated their property rights under the Fifth Amendment, but a majority of the U.S. Supreme Court robustly sustained the
constitutionality of the statute. Along with *West Coast Hotel v. Parrish*,[4]
Carolene Products is regarded as the turning-point in that Court's abandonment of substantive due process in respect of economic and regulatory legislation. Acutely conscious of the traumatic experience of the Court during the
New Deal era, the Court has since paid great deference to legislative judgments and there have been almost no instances of where either federal or state
regulatory legislation has been found to be unconstitutional on this ground.

Of course, the famous footnote 4 in *Carolene Products* charted the path
ahead for the Court.[5] However, in one sense, the task ahead was an easy one
for a liberal such as Stone J. He was well aware that there were plenty of
"discrete and insular minorities" in US society whose rights and interests had
been scandalously infringed by the quasi-apartheid "Jim Crow" regime in the
southern United States. And quite apart from the race issue, the Court had
only begun by the 1930s to develop the law in relation to key matters such as
free speech and criminal due process.

At the risk of a significant over-generalisation, the courts in most countries have more or less come to the end of the route map sketched out in
Carolene Products. It is nowadays very unusual to find legislation that can be
said to restrict "those political processes which can ordinarily be expected to
bring about repeal of undesirable legislation" and cases that neatly illustrate
Stone J.'s argument are so rare as to be something in the nature of collectors'

---

[3] Stanford, 1980.
[4] 300 U.S. 379 (1937).
[5] See Pratt, *op. cit.*, pp. 143–148.

items. Speaking for myself, I can think of only two modern instances from jurisdictions with which I have some familiarity, that might be said to illustrate this point.

In *McKenna v. An Taoiseach (No. 2)*[6] the Irish Supreme Court held that a practice whereby the Government gave public funds to one side in a referendum campaign to the exclusion of other side was unconstitutional.[7] The second case is *Bowman v. United Kingdom*,[8] where the European Court of Human Rights held that a U.K. law that imposed a £5(!) limit on the amount of money a non-party candidate could spend in the course of a general election campaign, amounted to a violation of the right of free speech guaranteed by Article 10 of the European Convention of Human Rights. Nor would one nowadays normally expect to find legislation expressly aimed at religious, national or racial minorities. If, therefore, judicial review was to be confined – or, at any rate, largely confined, to this process-based review, constitutional courts would probably not have a great deal of work on their hands.

This is not in any way to take from the valuable insights provided by *Carolene Products* or from the work of such fine jurists as Ely. It is, rather, first, to make the point that the process-based review theory is largely a product of a particular time and place when there were substantial restrictions on the proper functioning of democracy in the United States. In addition, much more importantly, experience has shown the limitations to the modern democratic process.

In many ways, the *Carolene Products/Ely* theory proceeds on an idealised view of the democratic legislative process, since it is implied by Stone J. that – the special case of racial and ethnic prejudice apart – once the democratic process functioned properly, then it was to be expected that such a process would produce fair and rational legislation respecting fundamental rights. Such is the complexity (and unintelligibility) of much of modern regulatory and economic legislation, however, that legislators simply cannot adequately ensure that such legislation will be fair to all interested parties who might be affected by it. More often that not, the legislation will be a messy compromise after a prolonged "turf war" between various governmental departments who seek to protect their particular favourite interest groups. As often as not the legislation will in practice give rise to issues simply not foreseen in parliament. If, therefore, the *Carolene Products* agenda has been largely fulfilled, what ought to be the role of a modern-day constitutional court? If *Carolene Products* was a form of acceptable "mission statement" for 1938, can something similar be suggested for 2001?

---

[6] [1995] 2 I.R. 10.

[7] This principle has also been extended to party political broadcasts transmitted during the course of a referendum campaign: see *Coughlan* v. *Broadcasting Complaints Body* [2000] 3 I.R. 1.

[8] (1998) 26 E.H.R.R. 1.

4 *Human Rights, the Citizen and the State*

Two possibilities can be suggested. The first is that, having regard to the realities of modern legislative life, the courts should perhaps take a closer look at regulatory and economic legislation when it is challenged on constitutional grounds. The second possibility concerns the protection of social and economic rights.

THE CASE FOR CLOSER SCRUTINY OF ECONOMIC AND REGULATORY LEGISLATION

In some ways, it is surprising that *Carolene Products* has come to signify the desirability of a relaxed approach to judicial review in cases of economic and regulatory legislation. Of course, it is perfectly understandable that the US Supreme Court would have wanted to take this approach at that particular time, given that it wanted to quickly distance itself from the excesses of the "Four Horsemen" and the substantive due process. The attractions of footnote 4, however, have sometimes caused commentators to overlook the particular facts of that case.

In fact, *Carolene Products* had been indicted for selling a form of skimmed milk in inter-state commerce. Such milk is, of course, perfectly healthy. However, the powerful agricultural lobby had persuaded Congress to ban skimmed milk, largely because the emergence of the new skimmed milk was considered to be a major threat to established agricultural interests. Although Stone J. had noted the congressional findings of this form of skimmed milk "as injurious to health and a fraud upon the public", he added (this is the text just before the footnote four):

> "Even in the absence of such [legislative] aids, the existence of facts supporting the legislative judgment is to be presumed, for regulatory legislation affecting ordinary commercial transactions is not to be pronounced unconstitutional unless in the light of such facts made known or generally assumed it is of such a character as to preclude the assumption that it rests upon some rational basis within the knowledge and experience of the legislators. . . ."[9]

Of course, the reality of the situation was that skimmed milk presented no danger to public health whatsoever. The congressional "findings" to the contrary were transparently flawed. In reality, this was old-fashioned special in-

---

[9] 302 U.S. at 154. The Irish Supreme Court has expressed broadly similar views, saying that, in constitutional cases, it is not necessary to search the parliamentary debates to find objective justification for the impugned legislation as "it will usually be possible for the court to make reasonable inferences from the provisions of the statute itself and the facts of the case": *Re Article 26 and the Illegal Immigrants (Trafficking) Bill* 1999 [2000] 2 I.R. 360 at 392, *per* Keane C.J.

terest legislation at the behest of a powerful lobby group, which was designed to eliminate a potential threat to existing vested agricultural interests.[10] Is this not precisely the type of legislation that significantly prejudices the right to earn a livelihood and other ancillary rights that ought to call for a closer scrutiny by the courts?

If this argument is correct, why then should the US Supreme Court have consistently adhered to the *Carolene Products*-type review in the case of economic and regulatory legislation? Part of the reason, of course, is that the Court is simply unwilling to re-fight the battles of the 1930s and it is often readily assumed that any heightened review of economic and regulatory legislation would simply enable the courts to strike down social legislation that they did not like. Of course, a Constitution should not – as Holmes J. famously warned in his celebrated dissent in *Lochner v. New York*[11] – embody a particular economic philosophy. However, this ought not to mean that the courts should adopt an entirely "hands-off" approach in cases of this kind, especially where the regulatory or economic legislation imposes peculiarly unfair burdens.

An Irish example of heightened scrutiny of legislation of this kind may be found in the judgment of Costello P. in *Daly v. Revenue Commissioners*.[12] This case concerning the validity of the operation of aspects of a withholding tax regime for professional persons, which effectively required these taxpayers to pay a sizeable portion of their income tax in advance, thus seriously affecting – among other things – their cash-flow.[13] Section 18 of the Finance Act 1987 (as inserted by section 26(1) of the Finance Act 1990) provided that the tax credit for certain professional persons would be postponed from one tax year to the next, with the result that some taxpayers ended up in effect paying double taxation in one year in respect of payment for professional services from the State. Although this was supposed to deal with a transitional problem caused by the movement of self-employed from a preceding year to a current year basis (and thus to avoid a windfall gain), it operated as a permanent measure. Furthermore, it applied to all such taxpayers and not merely those who would have obtained a windfall gain in that particular tax year.

While Costello P. agreed that simply because the Oireachtas (Parliament) had interfered with property rights, it did not follow that the legislation in

---

[10]One commentator has described the legislation as "an utterly unprincipled example of special interest legislation" (Miller, "The True Story of Carolene Products" (1987) *Supreme Court Review* 398). See further, Pratt, *op. cit.*, pp. 145–148.

[11]198 U.S. 45 (1905).

[12][1995] 3 I.R. 1.

[13]This was especially true of the applicant in this case. He was a doctor in general practice who was substantially dependant on fees from the (state-run) General Medical Services Board. Costello P. found that the operation of the regime had caused him real hardship, as withholding tax was deduced from gross fees (*i.e.* with no allowance at that stage for expenses) and in any given tax year he was liable to suffer a double payment of tax.

question was unconstitutional by reason of this fact alone. The plaintiff was required to show that the infringement of his property rights was disproportionate in the circumstances:

> "But legislative interference in property rights occurs every day of the week and no constitutional impropriety is involved. When, as in this case, an applicant claims that his constitutionally protected right to private property referred to in Article 40.3.2° has been infringed and that the State has failed in its obligation imposed on it by that Article to protect his property rights, he has to show that those rights have been subject to 'an unjust attack.' He can do this by showing that the law which has restricted the exercise of his rights or otherwise infringed them has failed to pass a proportionality test."[14]

Costello P. agreed that the applicant had established that the section in question operated in two respects as a disproportionate interference with his property rights and was therefore an unconstitutional attack on his property rights. First, the tax operated as a form of double taxation, which was "manifestly unfair". Secondly, although the section was designed to deal with a transitional problem, the Oireachtas had imposed a permanent measure that involved a permanently unfair method of collecting tax. As this measure affected property rights "in a manner out of proportion to the objective which the measure is designed to achieve", it was to that extent adjudged to be unconstitutional. While Costello P. approached this case on proportionality grounds, I would prefer to characterise the case as an example of legislation that placed an unusual burden on a particular class of taxpayers and was subjected to heightened judicial review.

If a fresh look was taken at much modern economic and regulatory legislation, one suspects it would be seen that, as often as not, it is based on compromises and assumptions that would not withstand close scrutiny if subjected to judicial analysis. The Irish courts have, for example, recognised the right to earn a livelihood, but they have as yet to do any more than pay lip service to the right in question. Our regulatory legislation permits the placing of limits on the number of taxi licences that may be granted and the number of pharmacies that may be opened. This legislation – like the Filled Milk Act in *Carolene Products* – is really designed to appease two powerful special interest groups and the public interest justifying these restrictions seems to me to be very doubtful. Yet if this legislation were challenged on constitutional grounds (ignoring for present purposes all competition law issues), the courts would probably regard the challenge as a weak one. In all probability the courts would uphold the constitutionality of the statutes on the grounds of some hypoth-

[14][1995] 3 I.R. 11.

esized public interest rationale in the course of applying a weak standard of constitutional review along the lines of *Carolene Products*. If the right to earn a livelihood is not to be emptied entirely of substance, does it not at least mean that the courts should subject this hypothesized rationale to closer scrutiny and that the right of a suitably qualified applicant to earn a livelihood should not be frustrated by entry quotas which are a testament to the lobbying power of interest groups?

This line of thinking prompts one to consider other examples of pervasive practices that have been unthinkingly accepted and have not been subjected to closer scrutiny, least of all by the courts. The Irish newspapers recently reported that the final places in many university departments are filled by the random selection of equally qualified student applicants. Why should a university be allowed to make a choice like that – which could so dramatically affect the student's subsequent career – on essentially arbitrary criteria, especially where entry places in some subjects (*e.g.* medicine, pharmacy) have been curtailed as a result of an agreement between the Department of Health and the professional bodies in question? The Irish newspapers are also full of stories about waiting lists for certain types of operations and treatments. No Irish court has got involved in this area, but I suspect that in some instances the criteria for the allocation of scarce resources and the admission to waiting lists have never been subjected to close scrutiny by outsiders. Should we also make benign, *Carolene Products*-type assumptions about the way these criteria have been formulated and applied?

SOCIO-ECONOMIC RIGHTS

The issue of criteria and scarce resources brings us directly to the issue of socio-economic rights. In its avant-garde Constitution, South Africa has led the way in expressly recognising such an extensive list of socio-economic rights. By contrast, the draft Charter of Fundamental Rights of the European Union is nothing as brave. Thus, Article 33 of the draft Charter somewhat tentatively states that:

> "Everyone has the right of access to preventive health care and the right to benefit from medical treatment under the conditions established by national law and practices."

When this issue was considered by the Irish Constitution Review Group[15] in 1996, it recommended against the express protection of socio-economic rights, chiefly on the ground that it would tend to distort the separation of powers,

---

[15] Pn. 2326.

with yet further powers accruing to the judiciary. In that regard it is interesting to note that the South African Constitutional Court addressed – and rejected – the separation of powers argument in its *First Certification Judgment:*

> "It is true that the inclusion of some socio-economic rights may result in courts making orders which have implications for budgetary matters. However, even when a court enforces civil and political rights such as equality, freedom of speech and the right to a fair trial, the order it makes will often have such implications. A court may require the provision of legal aid, or the extension of state benefits to a class of people who formerly were the beneficiaries of such benefits. In our view, it cannot be said that by including socio-economic rights within a bill of rights, a task is conferred upon the court so different from that ordinarily conferred upon them by a bill of rights that it results in a breach of separation of powers."[16]

It is difficult to disagree with this analysis, save to observe that if the socio-economic rights are made justiciable and are vindicated by the courts, it will tend to distort the traditional balance of the separation of powers between the judiciary and other branches of government, in that more power will flow to the judiciary. One might also observe by way of comment that the socio-economic rights are, by definition, resource dependent, whereas this is not true (at least not generally) of the classic civil and political rights. Sometimes the protection of classic civil and political rights will have budgetary implications, but this is usually an indirect consequence of the courts' order.[17] In these respects there are still significant differences between civil and political rights on the one hand and socio-economic rights on the other, and these differences are greater than the Constitutional Court might be thought to have allowed.

What, then, is the position in other jurisdictions? In their excellent textbook, *Bill of Rights Handbook*[18] de Waal, Currie and Erasmus comment that:

> "It is somewhat difficult to find comparable foreign case-law to assist in the interpretation of socio-economic rights. This is because South Africa is the only jurisdiction to incorporate an extensive list of directly enforceable socio-economic rights in their constitutions (for example, Brazil, India, Portugal and Ireland) do so in the form of Directive Principles of State Policy. These principles are not directly enforceable but

---

[16] *Certification of the Constitution of the RSA, 1996, ex p. Chairperson of the Constitutional Assembly, 1996,* 1996 (10) BCLR 1253 (CC).

[17] The court-directed provision of legal aid is probably the exception which proves this particular rule.

[18] (Juta, 1999), 2nd ed.

may influence the interpretation of those rights by being read into' those rights or are relevant in the interpretation of legislation."[19]

This is a substantially accurate statement regarding the status in Irish constitutional law of socio-economic rights, but the position in Ireland is somewhat more complex than so presented. In particular, the right to education and the State's corresponding duty to provide that education are part of the fundamental rights recognised by Articles 40-44 of the Irish Constitution (*i.e.* it is not simply one of the – largely non-justiciable – Directive Principles of Social Policy recognised by Article 45).

In the last five years there has been a huge increase in litigation in this area and we have seen how, so to speak, a full-blown socio-economic right would work in practice. Since that time it is not an exaggeration to say that the Irish courts have been almost overwhelmed with hundreds of actions dealing with a huge range of educational issues, ranging from the treatment of children with special needs (such as dyslexia, attention deficit disorder and mental handicap) to the construction of special regimes for disruptive and unruly children.

It probably suffices to cite *D.B. v. Minister for Justice*[20] to illustrate the breadth of the jurisdiction recently being assumed by the courts in cases of this kind. In this case Kelly J. granted an order directing the Minister for Justice "to provide funding and to do all things necessary for the building, opening and maintenance of a high support unit" for young offenders. The applicant was a young offender who required secure accommodation in a high support unit, but who had failed to obtain it due to a shortage of facilities. It is, of course, true that this case turned on the fact that the constitutional rights of the young persons in question under Articles 41 and 42 would otherwise have been infringed, and Kelly J. only made the order after reciting how plans to remedy the rights of these children had been "bogged down in a bureaucratic and administrative nightmare."[21] Nevertheless, *D.B.* is just one example from a long line of cases where very elaborate orders have been made: orders from the High Court directing the provision of special teachers and special classes are now quite common.

Suppose the State pleaded that it lacked the resources to comply with these orders: what would be the position? *D.B.* seems to go quite far in the direction of compelling the executive to obtain the necessary monies, if necessary by securing appropriation of monies from the Dáil (lower House of Parliament).

Yet it may be thought that on this issue of resources the Irish Supreme Court leant in the opposite direction in *Brady v. Cavan County Council*.[22] In this case local residents sought mandamus to compel the local county council

---

[19]p. 420.
[20][1999] 1 I.R. 39.
[21]*ibid.* at 44.
[22][2000] 1 I.L.R.M. 81.

to repair roads, which were in an admitted state of total disrepair, in accordance with a statutory (but not, of course, constitutional) duty. In the High Court,
Carroll J. granted the order sought, but a majority of the Supreme Court reversed her decision. The evidence was that by reason of the small rating base
and the (then) inadequacy of the rate support grant,[23] the Council could not
tackle the some 600 roads then in very poor condition without giving this
particular strip of road "unjustified priority in their road repair programme".

Keane J. noted that the Houses of the Oireachtas (Parliament) were not a
party to these proceedings and "presumably, having regard to the separation
of powers, could not be". While these bodies might well vote appropriation of
monies following an order of the Court, there was "no guidance as to what is
to happen if they do not". He thus concluded that he would not grant mandamus
as against a public authority:

> "where it is acknowledged that they have not the means to comply with
> the order and that its successful implementation depends on the co-op-
> eration of other bodies not before the Court."

Keane J. agreed with the statement of Lord Browne-Wilkinson in *R. v. East
Sussex CC, ex p. Tandy*,[24] where the latter had said that:

> "To permit a local authority to avoid performing a statutory duty on the
> grounds that it prefers to spend the moneys in other ways is to down-
> grade a statutory duty to a discretionary power."

In *Tandy* the House of Lords had held that a Council could not avoid its statutory obligation to provide certain essential services to the young applicant by
pleading lack of resources. However, Keane J. distinguished *Tandy* on the
ground that there was no suggestion in *Brady* that the Council could meet the
huge financial costs of the road repair programme by diverting resources from
other purely discretionary programmes (as would have been possible in *Tandy*);
closing a library, for example, would not release sufficient funds to enable the
huge road repair programme to be completed.

An interesting clue to the possible reconciliation of *D.B.* with *Brady* may
be found in the judgment of the South African Constitutional Court in
Soobramoney v. Minister for Health.[25] In this case a patient with chronic re-
nal failure claimed that the authorities failed to provide him with the dialysis
treatment he needed to keep him alive. Unfortunately, the relevant departmen-

---

[23] At that time, finance for local authorities came from rates (a form of local business tax) and
rate support grant (payments from the central Government).
[24] [1998] 2 All E.R. 769.
[25] 1998 (1) S.A. 765 (C.C.).

tal budget was seriously over-stretched and there was a severe shortage of dialysis machines, not only in the district, but throughout South Africa. Guidelines had been developed to enable those working in the clinics "to make the agonising choices which have to be made in deciding who should receive treatment and who not". These guidelines were applied in the present case, but the patient did not qualify thereunder:

> "By using the available dialysis machines in accordance with the guidelines more patients are benefited than would be the case if they were used to keep alive persons with chronic renal failure and the outcome of the treatment is also likely to be more beneficial because it is directed towards curing patients, and not simply to keeping them alive in a critically ill condition. It has not been suggested that these guidelines are unreasonable or that they were not applied fairly and rationally when the decision was taken by the Anderton Hospital that the appellant did not qualify for dialysis. . . . The provincial administration which is responsible for health services . . . has to make decisions about the funding that should be made available for health and how such funds should be spent. These choices involve difficult decisions to be made at the political level in fixing the health budget and at the functional level in deciding upon the priorities to be met. A court will be slow to interfere with rational decisions made in good faith by the political organs and the medical authorities whose responsibility it s to deal with such matters."

Perhaps what distinguishes *Brady* and *Soobramoney* from *D.B.* is that the former cases both involve guidelines[26] and the rational allocation of scarce resources. This is really at the heart of *Brady*, where the Irish Supreme Court was unwilling to give unjustified priority to one road out of 600. It did not, of course, directly concern a constitutional right. This is in contrast to *D.B.* where the bureaucracy had come up with no coherent plan to tackle the problems of troubled young persons.

Impressive as the reasoning is in *Soobramoney*, there is a deference in the judgment to values and assumptions made by political organs and administrators which may, perhaps, not be entirely justified, especially when measured against constitutional values. It must be borne in mind that the applicant in that case was (presumably) going to die if he were denied access to the dialysis machine. We would have no difficulty in saying that the State must pay for legal aid in the case of a person facing a criminal charge. Why should the Constitution ordain any differently in the case of a dialysis machine? Moreover, at the heart of the guidelines at issue in *Soobramoney* is the assumption

---

[26] In *Brady* the County Council could demonstrate that it had guidelines for road repair and had a rational order of priority for the road repairs.

that it is better that dialysis is used to cure rather than simply keep alive the chronically ill. That is a perfectly understandable judgment for doctors and medical administrators to make, but is such a distinction between the curable and the chronically ill justifiable when judged from a constitutional standpoint?

CONCLUSION

There is no doubt but that excessive judicial review probably saps at the sinews of the democratic order, especially where the judiciary uses this powerful instrument as a mechanism for imposing its own social mores and economic beliefs on the population at large. This, after all, was the sobering lesson which the US Supreme Court learnt painfully during the 1930s. In learning that lesson, however, they went too far in the opposite direction, all but avoiding judicial review of economic and regulatory legislation. Moreover, Stone J.'s famous footnote 4 proceeds on an idealised vision of how the democratic system might work in a world freed from unjustified constraints on the working of that system. Now that these constraints have been lifted, we know that legislatures the world over work in a far from idealised fashion, by achieving messy compromises with competing interest groups, often acting on the basis of conventional wisdom and untested and glib assumptions.

A constitution should not, of course, embody a particular economic philosophy; but why should the courts not take a closer look at much economic and regulatory legislation to see if there is, in fact, a rational and defensible basis for these assumptions? The philosophy underlying *Carolene Products* has been hugely influential in contemporary legal thought. Why should we, in turn, pay such deference to a decision that says that the courts will not think twice about ascribing an hypothesized rationale to justify legislation that banned a perfectly healthy product such as skimmed milk?

THE ROLE OF NATIONAL HUMAN RIGHTS INSTITUTIONS IN POST-APARTHEID IN SOUTH AFRICA

JEREMY SARKIN*

INTRODUCTION

Before 1994 South Africa was a highly polarised and divided society.[1] Many people had been dispossessed of their land, had had their language and cultures marginalised, and had suffered gross human rights violations.[2] The majority of South Africans had been denied access to an enormous variety of amenities, institutions and opportunities, including many places and types of employment, particularly in state institutions. The South African state systematically violated the rights of black people and subjected them to socio-economic deprivation.[3] Black South Africans were disenfranchised and many were forcibly removed from where they lived and deprived of their citizenship.[4] State employees, and others acting with state sanction and assistance, routinely carried out torture, assaults and killings.[5] Many detentions[6] and deaths in custody occurred.[7] Freedom of expression and association were severely limited. As a result of

---

* Professor of Public Law and Deputy Dean, Law Faculty, University of the Western Cape, South Africa; B.A., LL.B. (Natal), LL.M. (Harvard), LL.D. (UWC); attorney of the High Court of South Africa, attorney at law in the State of New York, USA.
[1] See Jeremy Sarkin and Howard Varney, "Traditional Weapons, Cultural Expediency and the Political Conflict in South Africa: A Culture of Weapons and a Culture of Violence" (1993) in 6 *South African Journal of Criminal Justice* 2.
[2] See Jeremy Sarkin, "The Development of a Human Rights Culture in South Africa" (1998) in 20(3) *Human Rights Quarterly* 628, 644.
[3] Jeremy Sarkin, "Can South Africa Afford Justice? The Need and Future of a Public Defender System" (1993) 4 (2) *Stellenbosch Law Review* 261.
[4] See D.D. Mokgatle, "The Exclusion of Blacks from the South African Judicial System" (1987) in 3 *South African Journal on Human Rights* 44.
[5] See Howard Varney and Jeremy Sarkin, "Failing to Pierce the Hit Squad Veil: An Analysis of the Malan Trial" (1996) 10 *South African Journal of Criminal Justice* 141.
[6] See Jeremy Sarkin, "Preventive Detention in South Africa" in *Preventive Detention and Security Law: A Comparative Survey* 209 (Andrew Harding & John Hatchard, ed., 1993), p. 271.
[7] Max Coleman, *A Crime against Humanity: Analysing the Repression of the Apartheid State* (1998).

parliamentary supremacy, Parliament could enact law over which the courts played no oversight role.[8]

South Africa's dire record of human rights under apartheid thus forms the backdrop to discussing the human rights situation in South Africa. After nearly six years of democracy, South Africa's human rights situation is far better than it was under apartheid. This does not mean that a human rights culture is firmly established,[9] but rather that major progress has been made. However, while the promotion of human rights was on the top of the agenda for the first three years of the transition, this is no longer the case. Human rights now occupies a less important place on the nation's agenda. In fact, the promotion and advancement of human rights has suffered major setbacks over the last three years.

The creation of independent institutions[10] to support democracy, to promote the observance of human rights, and to protect people from abuse of government power is a significant achievement in the country's transition to constitutional democracy.[11] While most of the institutions were founded in the interim Constitution of 1993, under the title "State Institutions Supporting Constitutional Democracy", Chapter 9 of the 1996 Constitution[12] provides for the Public Protector,[13] the South African Human Rights Commission (SAHRC),[14] the Commission for the Promotion and Protection of the Rights of Cultural, Religious and Linguistic Communities, the Commission for Gender Equality (CGE),[15] the Auditor-General[16] and the Electoral Commission.[17]

---

[8] See Jeremy Sarkin, "The Common Law in South Africa: Pro-Apartheid or Pro-Democracy" (1999) 23(1) *Hastings International and Comparative Law Review* 1.

[9] "Human Rights in South Africa: Constitutional and Pan-African Concept" in *The Principle of Equality* (Sarkin, Vander, Lanotte and Haeck, eds.), pp. 89–114.

[10] For a general analysis on the importance of these institutions, see Commission on Human Rights. 1999. *Effective Functioning of Human Rights Mechanisms: National Institutions for the Promotion and Protection of Human Rights: Report of the Secretary-General submitted in accordance with Commission on Human Rights resolution 1998/55*, 3 February.

[11] On an earlier discussion of the creation of a human rights culture, see Jeremy Sarkin, "The Development of a Human Rights Culture in South Africa" (1998) 20(3) *Human Rights Quarterly* 628.

[12] Section 181. On the drafting process of the final Constitution, see generally Jeremy Sarkin, "Innovations in the Interim and 1996 South African Constitutions" *The Review* (June 1998) 57; Jeremy Sarkin, "The Drafting of the Final South African Constitution from a Human Rights Perspective" *The American Journal of Comparative Law* (1999) 254 and Jeremy Sarkin, "The Effect of Constitutional Borrowings on The Drafting of South Africa's Interim Bill of Rights and the Role Played by Comparative and International Law in the Interpretation of Human Rights Provisions by the Constitutional Court" (1998) *Journal of Constitutional Law* 1. See further Jeremy Sarkin, "The South African Constitution and the Politics of Memory: Narrating and Authoring a Nation's History and Future Potential" (2000) (4) *South African Law Journal* (forthcoming 2002).

[13] See also Public Protector Act 23 of 1994.

[14] See also Human Rights Commission Act 54 of 1994.

[15] See also Commission on Gender Equality Act 39 of 1996.

[16] See also Auditor-General Act 12 of 1995.

[17] See also Electoral Commission Act 51 of 1996.

Other constitutional and statutory institutions also play a role. These include the Truth and Reconciliation Commission,[18] the Office of the Inspecting Judge,[19] the Legal Aid Board,[20] the Commission on the Restitution of Land Rights,[21] the Constitutional Court,[22] the Independent Complaints Directorate (ICD),[23] the Commission for Conciliation, Mediation and Arbitration (CCMA),[24] the Judicial Service Commission,[25] the Pan South African Language Board (PANSALB),[26] the National Youth Commission[27] and the Heath Special Investigating Unit.[28]

In general, the role of many of these structures in the promotion of human rights has been of limited impact and often problematic.[29] Numerous issues have diminished the effectiveness and credibility of these institutions. There have been internal problems on issues such as direction and policy formulation. This paper evaluates the role and effectiveness of the ICD, the Office of the Inspecting Judge, the Legal Aid Board, the SAHRC, the CGE, the Auditor-General, the Public Protector and the Truth and Reconciliation Commission to determine the effect, both positive and negative, that these institutions have had on the promotion and protection of human rights and the development of a human rights culture. The article also makes some recommendations on how a human rights culture could be promoted, and how these institutions could become more effective in achieving their mandated goals and improving human rights in the areas in which they work.

DEVELOPING A HUMAN RIGHTS CULTURE

A human rights culture[30] is dependent on the knowledge and acceptance of

---

[18]Promotion of National Unity and Reconciliation Act 34 of 1995.

[19]Correctional Services Act 111 of 1998.

[20]Legal Aid Act 22 of 1969.

[21]Restitution of Land Rights Act 22 of 1994.

[22]ss. 97 to 100 of the Constitution of the Republic of South Africa Act 200 of 1993; Section 167 of the Constitution of the Republic of South Africa Act 108 of 1996; Constitutional Court Complementary Act 13 of 1995.

[23]Police Service Act 68 of 1995.

[24]Established in terms of section 112 of the Labour Relations Act 66 of 1995.

[25]In terms of section 178 of the 1996 Constitution.

[26]Created in terms of section 6 of the 1996 Constitution and the Pan South African Language Board Act 59 of 1995.

[27]National Youth Commission Act 19 of 1996.

[28]Created in terms of the Special Investigations Units and Special Tribunals Act 72 of 1996.

[29]See further Jeremy Sarkin, "Reviewing and Reformulating Appointment Processes to Constitutional (Chapter Nine) Structures" (1999) 15(4) *South African Journal on Human Rights* 587; Jeremy Sarkin, "Appointment Processes to Constitutional Structures" *Konrad Adenauer Foundation Seminar Series* 1999.

[30]See further Jeremy Sarkin, "The Development of a Human Rights Culture in South Africa" (1998) 20(3) *Human Rights Quarterly* 628.

human rights in a society. As far as knowledge and attitudes among the general public in South Africa on human rights are concerned, research was conducted in 1998 by the Community Agency for Social Enquiry (CASE). CASE assessed the knowledge of human rights among the general public and specified target groups: children, prisoners, refugees, disabled people, people with HIV/AIDS, and dispossessed people. In their November 1998 report,[31] the researchers found that only just over half of the population (55 per cent) had heard of the Bill of Rights. They found this knowledge more common among whites (80 per cent), than among Indians (58 per cent), coloureds (51 per cent), and Africans (50 per cent). Major provincial variations were also found: 70 per cent in Gauteng had heard of the Bill compared with 62 per cent in the Western Cape, 55 per cent in the Free State and the North-West, 54 per cent in KwaZulu-Natal, 49 per cent in Northern Province, 47 per cent in Northern Cape and 32 per cent in the Eastern Cape. Taking into account the major community outreach of the Constitutional Assembly during the drafting of the Constitution in 1995 and 1996, this is a major indictment of South Africa's progress towards achieving a human rights culture.

To ascertain levels of knowledge about the various Chapter 9 institutions, CASE investigated where people would go with certain problems. Reporting on their findings, CASE researchers state:

> "watchdog bodies such as the Public Protector's office, the South African Human Rights Commission, and the Commission for Gender Equality rarely if ever receive a mention in responses to the series of questions ... This is the case probably because they are not that well known, but also because they have yet to prove their efficacy in defending rights, in a way that would make these bodies obvious channels for assistance."[32]

Referring to the various specific groups, CASE found no knowledge of the various national human rights institutions. For example in relation to the "dispossessed" target group CASE states:

> "In addition to lack of awareness regarding rules, procedures and processes, participants were in the dark regarding the organisations and structures that were available to assist them. No mention was made of human rights bodies such as the Commission for Gender Equality, the South African Human Rights Commission, or any relevant NGO[33] (National Land Committee, Surplus People's Project) working in this field. Al-

---

[31] Piers Pigou, Ran Greenstein and Hahla Valji, *Community Agency for Social Enquiry: Assessing Knowledge of Human Rights Among the General Population and Selected Target Groups* (1998).
[32] *ibid.*, p. 18.
[33] Non-governmental organisation.

though this may reflect the limited operational scope of these organisations, it is evident that such organisations must strive to make themselves more accessible to vulnerable and marginalised communities."[34]

Clearly, one of the major weaknesses in the development of a human rights
culture is the absence of widespread human rights education. At present, generally, statements by politicians and government officials do more to undermine human rights than to promote them. Much work remains for them to
inform and educate the general public about rights and why the rights of all
deserve protection.

Emphasis should therefore be placed on developing an understanding of,
and respect for the Constitution and the Bill of Rights and the process and
mechanism of their enforcement. Unfortunately, the SAHRC and other institutions such as the CGE, whose constitutional mandate is to educate the public on human rights, have not adequately fulfilled this task.

While December 1998 saw the launch of the National Action Plan for
Human Rights[35] – the government's five-year plan to improve, protect and
promote human rights in South Africa[36] – little has been done by government
or other institutions to bring the plan to life. The plan suggests how the state
will deal with human rights, but was made with little civil society involvement. Most of the statements are set out in theoretical terms, with little or no
detail as to how they are to be implemented. An enormous amount of work on
the ground will need to occur for the plan to succeed.

THE INDEPENDENT COMPLAINTS DIRECTORATE

The issue of human rights abuse committed by the police is a major problem
in South Africa.[37] About 700 people a year die in police custody[38] and about
3000 have died in police custody since 1994.[39] As a result, during 1996, civil
claims against the South African Police Services (SAPS) amounted to R409.6

---

[34] *ibid.*, p. 140.

[35] *The Star*, December 11, 1998.

[36] *The Pretoria News*, December 10, 1998.

[37] ICD (1996–1997) (1997–1998) (1998–1999) *Annual Reports*. See also report on the work-
shop "The Prevention of Deaths as a Result of Police Action and in Police Custody" hosted by
the CSVR and the ICD, April 14, 2000. See also *Business Day*, July 13, 2000.

[38] See this author's comments in relation to the systemic problems in policing that cause huge
numbers of deaths in "No Easy Walk For District Surgeons" (2000) 90(6) *South African
Medical Journal* 575.

[39] The Minister of Safety and Security, Steve Tshwete, noted in the National Assembly on May
18, 2000 that deaths in custody decreased from 756 in 1998–1999 to 681 in 1999–2000. See
address by the Minister for Safety and Security, Mr S.V. Tshwete, Independent Complaints
Directorate Budget Vote, National Assembly, May 18, 2000.

million[40] and during the 15-month period ending July 1996, the SAPS paid out R66 million in civil claims.[41] A report based on statistics from the Ministry of Safety and Security found that the likelihood of police being involved in crime was three times higher than that of the general public.[42] It also found that of the 17,500 complaints lodged against the police under investigation, only 1,355 cases have resulted in convictions, an extremely high number in any case, and 4,300 in disciplinary measures.[43] According to the report, authorities fail to prove criminal action against police officials in 94 per cent of the cases. The number of police officers convicted of crimes did, however, increase from 793 cases in 1998 to 1,551 in 1999.[44] There are at least 14,000 criminal cases against police officers currently, the Minster of Safety and Security announced in Parliament in June 2000.[45] He reported that the cost of these cases to the state was R29 million in the 1998–1999 financial year.[46] Human rights abuse by the police and other crimes and misconduct is unacceptably high in South Africa. Corruption is also a major problem.[47] As a result, the image of the SAPS continues to be tarnished.[48]

It is in the light of these circumstances that provision for the creation of the Independent Complaints Directorate (ICD), an independent mechanism under civilian control, was provided for in section 222 of the interim Constitution[49] and in Chapter 10 of the South African Police Service Act.[50] The ICD, according to its mandate, considers complaints or allegations relating to :

1. deaths of persons in police custody or deaths which are as a result of police action;

2. the involvement of police members in criminal activities;

3. police conduct or behaviour which is prohibited by the Police Regula-

---

[40] *Pretoria News*, March 20, 1997.

[41] *The Star*, January 21, 1997.

[42] Piers Pigou, "Cop Monitoring Needs Serious Rethink" in *Mail & Guardian*, August 18-24, 2000.

[43] Human Rights Committee report reported in *Mail and Guardian*, May 22 to 28, 1998.

[44] *Sowetan*, April 17, 2000.

[45] *Saturday Star*, June 24, 2000.

[46] *Saturday Star*, June 24, 2000.

[47] Taleh Sayed and David Bruce, "Inside and Outside Police Corruption" (1998) 7(2) *African Security Review* 3.

[48] Jeremy Sarkin, "The Development of a Human Rights Culture in South Africa" (1998) 20(3) *Human Rights Quarterly* 628.

[49] Act 200 of 1993.

[50] Act 68 of 1995. See Bronwen Manby, "The Independent Complaints Directorate: An Opportunity Wasted?" (1996) 12(3) *South African Journal of Human Rights* 419; David Bruce, Kate Savago and Johan de Waal, "A Duty to Answer Questions? The Police, the Independent Complaints Directorate and the Right to Remain Silent" (2000) 16(1) *South African Journal on Human Rights* 71; N.J. Melville, *The Taming of the Blue: Regulating Police Conduct in South Africa* (1999).

tions, such as neglect of duties or failure to comply with the Code of Conduct.

While the ICD endeavours to register, investigate and/or monitor all complaints regarding alleged offences and misconduct committed by members of the SAPS, the directorate has adopted a strategy of prioritising complaints by classifying them into four categories – the most important being deaths in custody – to ensure the efficient use of scarce resources.

The ICD was allocated a budget of R27,760,000 for the 1998–1999 financial year.[51] This shows an increase of R 12,269,000 from the 1997–1998 financial year's budget of R15,491,000.[52] A lack of resources is a major reason for the difficulties facing the ICD as its tries to achieve its objectives.[53] It is unable to handle the approximately 30,000 cases reported each year. It has not had much impact on the problems in the police as its investigative capacity is greatly strained – there are only 45 investigators for the entire country.[54] In 1999 the ICD referred more than 70 per cent of its cases to the police to investigate.[55] The ICD is also aware that not many of its stakeholders are aware of its existence, including members of the SAPS and the public. Another serious problem is that the ICD is normally only accessible in urban areas.[56]

In 1997 alone more than 5,300 complaints of assault were lodged against the police.[57] By 31 December 1998, the ICD had dealt with a total of 3,891 complaints and inquiries.[58] Of this number, 1,292 were complaints of deaths in custody or as a result of police action.[59] This figure accounts for 32 per cent of all the complaints received by the ICD.[60] A total of 778 complaints, (about 20 per cent) were complaints of serious criminal offences ranging from ordinary assault to assault with intent to cause grievous bodily harm. The remainder, that is 1,478 (38 per cent), were complaints of misconduct and less serious offences committed by the members of the service. A total of 222 complaints (about six per cent) related to matters falling outside the scope of the functions of the ICD. Such matters were referred to appropriate organisations, such as the Public Protector. The remaining 121 complaints (about four per

---

[51] ICD *Annual Report* 1998–1999.
[52] ICD *Annual Report* 1997–1998.
[53] Independent Complaints Directorate: Report of the Independent Complaints Directorate to the Parliamentary Committee on Safety and Security, May 19, 1998
[54] Presentation of the ICD to the Parliamentary Medium Term Expenditure Framework Committee meeting: 2000–2001—2002–2003.
[55] *Saturday Argus*, March 11/12, 2000.
[56] Presentation of the ICD to the Parliamentary Medium Term Expenditure Framework Committee meeting: 2000–2001—2002–2003.
[57] "Human Rights Abuses Continue in South Africa" *Mail & Guardian*, June 17, 2000.
[58] Media statement by the ICD on the tabling of the Second Annual report of the ICD, February 16, 1999.
[59] *ibid*.
[60] *ibid*.

cent) were referred to the ICD by the Minister for Safety and Security and members of the Executive Councils (MECs – the provincial equivalents of Cabinet ministers). In 147 completed complaints, the ICD made recommendations to the Directorate of Public Prosecutions to prosecute certain members of the police service. Prosecutions were instituted in 57 cases and in 55 cases, directors of public prosecutions ordered the holding of inquests. With regard to the rest, the prosecuting authorities declined to institute prosecutions. In 64 cases the ICD recommended that the disciplinary action be taken against certain members of the police service. Disciplinary action was taken in 19 cases and this resulted in nine convictions for misconduct.[61]

In the first four months of the year 1999, the ICD dealt with a total of 1,566 new complaints – up by about 45 per cent.[62] During this time about 962 cases were finalised and, in 211 of these, recommendations were made to prosecute the SAPS member concerned.[63] Only in 18 cases were prosecutions instituted. Of the matters referred to the SAPS for internal discipline, only about five were successfully concluded.[64] This is a highly problematic state of affairs. The goals of the ICD ought to be to develop public confidence in the efforts of the SAPS and the ICD to prevent inappropriate police conduct, as well as to facilitate the criminal prosecution of those members found to have engaged in criminal conduct.

While the number of complaints submitted to the ICD has increased dramatically, the directorate is only touching the tip of the iceberg of human rights abuses being perpetrated by the police. As a result of limited personnel and resources, the unit has reviewed its investigative priorities and disregarded a number of complaints.[65] It has also used mediation techniques as a cost-cutting measure. It is also problematic that the ICD is referring a substantial number of complaints back to the police.[66] As the directorate itself states, this upsets the members of the public concerned, and results in disillusionment with the process. While the ICD recognises that this is not a desirable course of action, resource constraints seem to necessitate such a course of action.

The ICD recognises that the complaint system in the SAPS is inadequate and needs to be improved. An adequate complaints mechanism is needed to permit the ICD rather than the police to do investigations. In spite of the inevitably high cost, such a system will ensure that there is an adequate system of police scrutiny. This will have a dramatic impact on the current situation in which many police members commit human rights abuses with impunity.

---

[61] *ibid.*
[62] Presentation of the ICD to the Parliamentary Medium Term Expenditure Framework Committee meeting: 2000–2001—2002–2003.
[63] *ibid.*
[64] *ibid.*
[65] ICD Report to the Parliamentary Portfolio Committee on Safety and Security, April 5, 2000.
[66] ICD returns 71 per cent of all cases to the South African Police Services to investigate. See *Pretoria News*, March 10, 2000.

The public at large does not know about the role and mission of the ICD. A larger problem is the lack of awareness of human rights within the police and the failure of the SAPS to apply disciplinary procedures, prosecutions or other steps to prevent abuses from occurring. While the ICD has made contributions to the curricula for SAPS training programmes, especially in the area of human rights and disciplinary issues, much more is necessary to inculcate awareness of the ICD and build a human rights culture within the SAPS. The ICD ought therefore to start educating the public and the police on what constitutes acceptable conduct. This could be done in collaboration with other institutions, such as the SAHRC, the CGE, as well as various NGOs, using existing networks of cultural, religious, sporting groups and others.

Such work could be accompanied by the wide distribution of a booklet, which would educate the public on what the police can legitimately do in a democracy and educate the police about what is acceptable conduct. ICD documentation ought to be more widely available. Its website is quite well maintained, but more systematic and regular information would enhance the role and profile of the institution.

Often nothing is done when the ICD recommends criminal prosecution or disciplinary steps be taken against an individual. Steps should therefore be taken to boost the powers of this directorate to enable the ICD itself to institute whatever steps it deems appropriate. Research must be undertaken and a strategy developed to change the relevant legislation. The necessity of carrying out research into the nature and reasons for complaints must not be overstated – without doubt, the reasons for many of the problems in police conduct are already well known.

ICD director advocate Neville Melville has recently resigned to take up a post with the Banking Council. Hopefully his place will be taken by a fearless and robust person if the ICD is to be an institution that has a major impact on the promotion and protection of human rights in policing.

OFFICE OF THE INSPECTING JUDGE

The situation in prisons is desperate. South Africa has a daily prison population of about 175,000 individuals in 231 prisons under the care of 3,000 prison officers, even though the system has been designed for only about 100,000 prisoners.[67] Prisons are bursting at the seams as prisons become more overcrowded,[68] and the numbers continue to rise.[69]

---

[67] *Sowetan*, June 8, 2000.

[68] The number of sentenced prisoners has grown slowly from 92,581 in January 1995 to 109,930 in May 2000, *i.e.* up to 19 per cent. However, the number of un-sentenced prisoners has more than doubled from 24,265 in January 1995 to 61,950 in May 2000, *i.e.* up 155 per cent. Of the number of un-sentenced prisoners 14,759 were juveniles.

[69] Opening and Welcoming Address by the Minister of Correctional Services, Mr Ben Skosana, at the National Symposium on Correctional Services 1 August 2000.

Violence levels in prisons are very high.[70] As a remedial measure, the state has taken to releasing those whose bail has been set below R1,000 but cannot afford to pay.[71] However, there are still about 50,000 people awaiting trial in sometimes atrocious conditions. Corruption is extremely high[72] and other human rights concerns in the prisons include the keeping of children in prison,[73] as well as inadequate health care.[74] At present, South African prisons do more to promote criminality than to assist the fight against crime, and they do very little rehabilitate offenders.[75]

In 1997, in an attempt to be seen to be doing something to address the crime problem, the Department of Correctional Services announced harsher conditions for prisoners, including the possibility of turning mine shafts into prisons. The use of prison ships were also mooted, as well as proposals to privatise prisons.[76] There was little public opposition to these proposals. The first privatised prisons are already under construction.

A major development in this regard was the sudden appearance of super-maximum security ("C-Max") prisons in South Africa.[77] In a blow to parliamentary and public oversight and accountability, the building of the first C-Max prison was kept secret until a week before it opened. While prison authorities say C-Max prisons are intended to stop escapes and ensure that dangerous prisoners are unable to injure others, they are a misguided attempt to deter crime by showing how harsh prison can be. These prisons also help to satisfy a vengeful public by providing very harsh punishment for certain prisoners. However, many of the people being confined in these institutions do not fall into the categories of offender for which they were built. On at least one occasion it has been found that prisoners awaiting trial are being held in these

---

[70] Jeremy Sarkin, "The Development of a Human Rights Culture in South Africa" (1998) 20(3) *Human Rights Quarterly* 628.

[71] About 11,000 prisoners awaiting trial who could not afford bail were released in September 2000. On the question of new bail laws and the constitutional interpretation of these, see Jeremy Sarkin, Esther Steyn, Dirk van Zyl Smit and Ron Pachke, "The Constitutional Court's Bail Decision: Individual Liberty in Crisis? *S v. Dlamini*" (2000) 16(2) *South African Journal on Human Rights*. On the role of the Supreme Court of Appeal, the highest court in the land for non-constitutional or human rights matters, in developing the common law, see Jeremy Sarkin, "The Common Law in South Africa: Pro-Apartheid or Pro-Democracy" (Winter 1999) *Hastings International and Comparative Law Review*.

[72] *Business Day*, April 17, 2000.

[73] *Argus*, June 18, 1997.

[74] Jeremy Sarkin, "The State of Health and Human Rights in Post Apartheid South Africa" (1999) 89(12) *South African Medical Journal* 1259 and Jeremy Sarkin, "A Review of Health and Human Rights after Five Years of Democracy in South Africa" (2000) 19(2) *Medicine and Law* (forthcoming).

[75] Jeremy Sarkin, "Panic Over Crime Could Poison South Africa" (March 1996) *Democracy in Action* 17.

[76] See further Hugh Corder and Dirk van Zyl Smit, "Privatised Prisons and the Constitution" (1998) *South African Journal of Criminal Justice* 475.

[77] See T. Legget, "Cmax: Incapacitation or Retribution?" (1997) 10 *Crime and Conflict* 29 and *Argus*, June 3–4, 2000.

institutions. Another problem is that the number of prisoners, their names, and the crimes they are alleged to have committed are being kept secret. This is being done to limit scrutiny of these highly problematic institutions.

While new legislation in 1998 restructured the prison service and brought prison law into the constitutional era, many sections affecting the treatment of prisoners did not come into force immediately.

On the positive front, prisoners have had some success in promoting their rights. However, this has not happened because the state has given credence to these rights, but rather because the courts have come to their assistance. While the Independent Electoral Commission attempted to bar prisoners from voting in the June 1999 national and provincial elections, the Constitutional Court ruled that they had the right to vote. In August 1999, a High Court decision restored various privileges to prisoners awaiting trial that the Department of Correctional Services had taken away.[78]

While the new Correctional Services Act 1998[79] conforms largely to the Constitution as well as domestic and international human rights obligations, the present practice of the Department of Correctional Services falls well short of these commitments and obligations.

A positive innovation is the provision of a Judicial Inspectorate, an Inspecting Judge and independent prison visitors (IPVs). Section 90(2) of the Act provides that the Office must "inspect or arrange for the inspection of prisons in order to report on the treatment of prisoners in prisons and on conditions and any corrupt or dishonest practices in prisons". The legislation also provides for a number of officials to assist the Inspecting Judge. Nine inspectors, 10 administrative support staff and 22 IPVs have been appointed.

IPVs are lay people appointed by the Inspecting Judge under section 92(1) of the Act. There must be a call for nominations and consultations with community organisations before these appointments are made. In April 1999, an IPV Pilot Project was established for a period of three months.[80] The Office of the Inspecting Judge consulted with community organisations in the Western Cape before appointing 15 IPVs. These people were trained with the assistance of the United Nations High Commissioner for Human Rights, which pledged R394,800 to the project. In terms of section 94, the Inspecting Judge approved the establishment of Visitors' Committees at Cape Town and the Boland districts. Visitors' committees will be established in other provinces when IPVs are appointed there. About 1,000 complaints have been received from prisoners by the Office of the Inspecting Judge. These complaints were investigated by members of the Judicial Inspectorate as no IPVs had yet been appointed at the prisons concerned.

---

[78] In *Blanchard v. Minister of Justice, Legal and Parliamentary Affairs* 1999 (4) SA 1108 (ZSC)
[79] Act 111 of 1998.
[80] Inspectorate Pilot Project: Appointment of Independent Prison Visitors: Judicial

Judge John Trengrove was the first appointee to the position, but he resigned in 1999 and Judge Johannes Fagan was only appointed on April 1, 2000 to fill the vacancy.[81] The Office is in the process of setting itself up, appointing staff, drawing up policy, drafting manuals and so on. At present, staff members have very little experience or skill in the work they will be doing. They are unaware of the individuals or groups doing work in their fields of operation and are largely unaware of other such institutions in other parts of the world. They also are not really knowledgeable on human rights or intervention strategies. It is problematic that training on issues such as treatment of prisoners and conditions in prisons is done by the Department of Correctional Services, and the training on the new Correctional Services Act 1998 is being done by the legal services section of the department. A training scheme for the Office of the Inspecting Judge should therefore be developed, drawing on well-qualified academics and leaders of human rights NGOs.

Some inspections of prisons by the Office have taken place.[82] The Office has reported that, with the assistance of the IPVs, by mid-2000 it had dealt with approximately 8,500 complaints, covering a wide spectrum: alleged assaults, hunger strikes, treatment, food, etc.[83] Investigations of assaults by correctional officials on prisoners at Witbank and East London prisons were conducted, and reports on these findings submitted to the Minister of Correctional Services, but the reports have not been made public. The Inspecting Judge conducted the first Commission of Inquiry in terms of the provisions of section 90(5) of the Act into allegations of mass assaults upon prisoners at the Johannesburg Medium B prison, but its results have also not been made public.

The development of the IPV scheme will assist in the monitoring and reporting of the treatment of prisoners in prisons as the Office does not have the resources itself to do regular unannounced visits all over the country. The appointment of the right individuals – independent and fearless people who will not be co-opted by the system, and who receive good training from skilled and independent human rights workers – could play a dramatic role in advancing the protection of human rights in the prisons.

The Office of the Inspecting Judge is one of the most unknown human rights protection institutions in South Africa at present. It is sorely needed in a prison system where human rights abuses abound. It is, however, not entirely independent, as the Inspecting Judge, already a judge of the High Court, is appointed by the President. In addition, reports are delivered to the Minister of Correctional Services. The Office should ensure that it is perceived to be

[81] *Business Day*, April 7, 2000.
[82] Inaugural Annual Report submitted by the Inspecting Judge of the Judicial Inspectorate of Prisons for the period 1 June 1998 to 1 February 2000.
[83] J.J. Fagan, "The Role of the Inspecting Judge in dealing with Human Rights in Prisons" delivered at the UWC Crime and Human Rights Conference (July 28–29, 2000).

independent by making its reports widely available. Support could be provided for this by producing plain-language publications in a variety of languages.

THE LEGAL AID BOARD

Although democracy was meant to level the playing fields as far as access to justice is concerned, the exorbitant cost of legal services in South Africa still renders it the privilege of the few who are wealthy. The vast majority of accused are still indigent and often unrepresented.[84] In combination, these factors result in the vast majority of people being denied justice.[85] The Legal Aid Board in its 1995–1996 Annual Report indicated that approximately 700,000 people charged with serious offences were not legally represented.[86] Anyway, the provision of criminal and civil legal aid to the indigent in South Africa is in a shambles. It is under enormous pressure and has huge debts.[87] The number of private lawyers opting out of legal aid work is growing because the Legal Aid Board (LAB) has a backlog of unpaid fees dating back many years and because the tariffs paid to lawyers have recently been significantly reduced.[88] One effect of this is that cases involving unrepresented accused are being thrown out of court because people are constitutionally entitled to legal representation in serious cases.

Traditionally, legal aid in South Africa has been provided by private lawyers in terms of the Legal Aid Act 1969, which created the Legal Aid Board and empowered it to provide legal aid to indigent persons at state expense using a means test. In 1972, 4,500 legal aid applications were granted. In 1982, the figure rose to 9,100 and in 1992, 67,100 defences were provided. Since 1994, the number of legal aid applications granted has grown. Thus, 196,749 people received legal aid during the 1997–1998 financial year at a cost of R210 million to the state. Private lawyers represented 193,177 of them.[89] Part of this number are those deemed to fall within the constitutional provision for legal services to be made available to persons where the interests of justice seem to necessitate this.

In 1991 and 1996, the Legal Aid Act was amended to address the inde-

---

[84] The Constitutional Court had an opportunity to delineate, and ensure compliance with, the constitutional right to representation in certain cases in the case of *S v. Vermaas* . It failed to do so. See Jeremy Sarkin, "The Constitutional Court's Decision on Legal Representation: *S v. Vermaas and S v. Du Plessis*" (1996) 12(1) *South African Journal on Human Rights* 55.

[85] See further J. Sarkin, "Can South Africa Afford Justice? The Need and Future of a Public Defender System" (1993) 4(2) *Stellenbosch Law Review* 261.

[86] Legal Aid Board Annual Report (1996) 6.

[87] *Business Day*, October 4, 1999 and *Business Day*, August 31, 1999.

[88] *Cape Argus*, July 31, 2000.

[89] *Business Day*, February 16, 1999.

pendence, aims, objectives and composition of the Board to make it more representative of the South African population. The LAB is now an independent body run by an 18-member board of directors and an executive committee. The LAB receives money from the government, via an allocation to the Department of Justice, and reports to the Parliament and the Auditor-General annually.

Besides using private lawyers, the LAB operates a small public defender's office and also uses a network of university law clinics to provide legal services. Each of these clinics receives funding to employ articled clerks and supervising attorneys.

Private lawyers have not always provided the best service. The financial implications and effectiveness of the salaried versus the judicare systems of legal aid has been debated world-wide. The lower salaries, higher caseload and special expertise of salaried lawyers, in addition to the economies of scale enjoyed by their offices, all contribute towards making a salaried programme more cost-effective than a judicare programme. Weaknesses inherent in a salaried programme include a restriction on the choice of a lawyer, the use of young and less experienced lawyers, and the pressure of heavy caseloads leading to staff "burnout". However, to service the legal needs of South Africans, a comprehensive salaried public defender and civil legal aid programme is seen by many as the appropriate vehicle to meet these needs.

Plans are being made to provide an effective legal service to indigent litigants across the board by creating justice centres around the country[90] and moving away from the use of private lawyers[91] will make legal aid far more accessible to the poor in all areas. The centres will provide a range of services, including defence in criminal trials and representation in civil matters. This approach will ensure a much better and more widely available service, but a number of problems must be solved to appropriately meet the needs of the indigent in both criminal and civil law. The continued use of the university law clinic network should be an important feature of the new system, as the interests of students, candidate attorneys and the poor converge at these places.

Many of the clinics are at historically black universities, servicing areas (often rural) where there are currently no justice centres, or in places where justice centres may never be established. Law students and graduates need training in this type of work before going into practice. The strength of the legal clinics is that they provide a useful, economical service. However, adequate and continuing training is necessary to ensure a high quality of service. The LAB should therefore provide financial support to these clinics.

---

[90] "NGOs and LAB to Moot New-Look Legal Aid System" *De Rebus*, March 2000, 11.
[91] Department of Justice, *Draft White Paper on Legal Aid – Transformation of Provision of Legal Aid Services in South Africa: Challenges and Solutions*, May 26, 1999.

Recently, the LAB and Lawyers for Human Rights (LHR) embarked on a collaborative scheme to place candidate attorneys, mainly from disadvantaged backgrounds, with attorneys in private practice. The LAB pays their salaries as well as a contribution to the overhead costs of the firm where they work. These candidate attorneys are obliged to take on 10 cases per year on a legal aid basis and spend one afternoon a week in a community (mainly para-legal advice centres run by the LHR). The LAB and LHR hope to bring more lawyers into rural areas to maintain a reasonable numbers of attorneys to work on cases such as farm worker evictions and other rural matters. The LAB intends to expand this project. This project will have a profound effect on black lawyers being able to find employment and the availability of legal services in the rural areas. It will also assist in the provision of aid and training to para-legals and advice centres operating all over the country. Promoting the link between the para-legal movement and the advice offices would improve access to justice for a broad range of people.

The LAB has already established one centre in Kimberley and is planning to open a second one soon. In the Kimberley centre, 13 lawyers are paid to provide mostly free criminal legal assistance to the people falling within the criteria of the LAB. The LAB could consider assisting other justice centres in places such as the Transkei by paying rent and some operational expenses. Promoting the establishment of these centres all over the country would ensure wider-scale access to justice. This would be an expensive initiative but would assist millions of South Africans currently without access to legal services.

The staff of the LAB is in dire need of training on almost everything. In order to deal with the changeover to a new system, a number of training schemes are needed to impart skills in such areas as business administration, communication, information technology, and management. The number of public interest lawyers has fallen since 1994, and skills in the sector have declined. Sensitising and human rights education is necessary to make staff more sympathetic to the clients' issues. It is also necessary to provide human rights and other training to lawyers in the employ of the LAB as well as lawyers doing legal aid work. This will become more important as more justice centres are opened and the number of lawyers employed by LAB increases.

A training unit could be established, using expert public interest lawyers in an ongoing way to provide training in the areas necessary for the general work of the LAB as well as in specific skills necessary to promote human rights and public interest law in general. For a relatively small amount of money, such a unit could make a dramatic long-term impact on the type of service offered all over the country by providing ongoing training at university legal aid clinics, advice offices, para-legal offices and other places.

A proposal to largely replace the system of articles of clerkship with a Community Legal Services Programme for all graduating law students has been on the table for many years.[92] This programme, similar to the one that requires medical graduates to perform community service for a period of time, would require all law graduates to work in a civil legal aid office or in a public defenders' office. This type of programme is being investigated by the Department of Justice.[93] However, there are potential pitfalls. Because legal aid resources are limited and the number of cases overwhelming, lawyers in the field may be inclined to become impersonal and bureaucratic. These lawyers are also likely to be newly qualified and therefore inexperienced, and the turnover rate will be high. The quality of service may be lower than the ideal, but this can be mitigated by taking steps to constantly supervise and train these emerging practitioners.

An important advantage of the community legal services programme is the educative function that it would provide to many future corporate lawyers and prosecutors. Their legal skills would be honed within a short period of time while they provide a much-needed service. This type of legal practice would also quickly expose and orientate these lawyers to areas of the law with which they may never otherwise become acquainted, and may result in some of them continuing to work in such fields. A public defender programme should not be viewed in isolation, but in conjunction with other, complementary, programmes.

One possibility could be to employ more para-legals and to utilise existing para-legal services more effectively, thereby providing more comprehensive legal services than are currently being delivered through the legal aid system.[94] By incorporating para-legals into the public defender programme and the provision of legal aid, scarce resources would be used more effectively.

Adequately trained para-legals, who should have some nationally certified training, possibly established in conjunction with the law societies,[95] could make a further impact by staffing the advice offices that already exist in many parts of South Africa. These advice offices, set up to address grievances of the poor that are not necessarily specific to law, could also be partially utilised as legal education agencies which promote legal rights awareness. Also, because many advice offices are located in rural areas where there are few lawyers, such a scheme would increase the access of people to the law.

The legal profession could also play a role through the provision of free legal aid work, whereby each lawyer would be required to perform a stipulated

---

[92] See J. Sarkin, "Can South Africa Afford Justice? The Need and Future of a Public Defender System" in 4(2) *Stellenbosch Law Review* (1993) 261.

[93] *Cape Argus*, July 31, 2000.

[94] National Community-Based Paralegal Association, "Position Paper to the National Legal Aid Forum on the Restructuring of the Legal Aid Board" (January 1998). See further National Paralegal Institute, "Position Paper on the Recognition and Regulation of the Practice of Paralegals in South Africa" (November 1999).

[95] "Law Society Seeks to Define the Role of the Paralegal" *De Rebus* March 2000.

number of hours of free legal work for the indigent. Firms could devote time to *pro bono* work each year, or offer a certain financial contribution to legal aid organisations. Duty lawyers' offices constitute another avenue of encouraging lawyers to engage in *pro bono* work. Such offices could be set up in the courts for criminal matters and elsewhere to handle civil cases. They could be staffed by lawyers on a rotation basis and provide free legal advice to indigent people throughout the year.

These programmes can be co-ordinated by means of a certification procedure, whereby the annual issuing of an admission to the bar licence would be contingent upon the lawyer providing proof of fulfilment of the statutorily required minimum hours of *pro bono* service to the community. A number of the steps suggested here require Parliament to urgently review the laws relating to legal aid as well as those relating to legal professionals.

THE SOUTH AFRICAN HUMAN RIGHTS COMMISSION

The establishment of the Human Rights Commission in terms of the 1993 Constitution was an important step towards the promotion of human rights in South Africa. In terms of the of the 1996 Constitution,[96] the Human Rights Commission must promote respect for human rights and a culture of human rights, promote the protection, development and attainment of human rights, monitor and assess the observance of human rights in the Republic. The method of appointing commissioners has been the subject of much debate and is seen to undermine the work of the Commission.[97] Criticism of the role of the SAHRC has been widespread.[98]

The SAHRC has the powers, as regulated by national legislation,[99] necessary to perform its functions, including the power to investigate and to report on the observance of human rights, to take steps to secure appropriate redress where human rights have been violated, and to carry out research and education. Each year, the SAHRC must require relevant organs of state to provide it with information on the measures that they have taken towards the realisation of the rights in the Bill of Rights concerning housing, health care, food, water, social security, education, and the environment. The major function of the Commission is to promote human rights through a variety of methods: education and raising community awareness; making recommendations to Parliament; reviewing legislation; and, importantly, investigating alleged violations

---

[96] S. 184(1).
[97] *Financial Mail*, January 14, 2000.
[98] See, for example, Claire Bisseker, "Toothy Bulldogs With No Bite" *Financial Mail*, October 3, 1997 and Vuyo Mvuko, "Pityana Faces Court Challenge" *Business Day*, April 2, 1999.
[99] The Human Rights Commission Act 54 of 1994.

of fundamental rights and assisting those affected to secure redress.

The SAHRC also has the power to resolve disputes through mediation, conciliation and negotiation, and may take issues and disputes to court. Powers of the Commission are far-reaching, including controversial powers of search and seizure. In conducting investigations, the Commission may enter and search premises and gain access to information relevant to any investigation. It may compel any person to produce any document and to answer questions under oath.

The Commission receives money from the state for rent, salaries of staff and Commissioners, and other administrative expenses, as well as for a number of operational expenses. International donors provide funding for programme work; for example, the US Agency for International Development funds public awareness of human rights and Rädda Barnen (Save the Children Sweden) funds work on children's rights.

As has been noted above, knowledge of human rights is limited in South Africa. Very little human rights education takes place and what does is either of a limited nature or having a very limited impact. Very few people attend human rights education workshops and seminars, and little, if any, follow up occurs. Critically, the goals and outcomes of the workshops are unknown.

To develop human rights in the country, the SAHRC should embark on a massive education and information programme to foster public knowledge, awareness and acceptance of human rights. While the SAHRC has developed plans around the achievement of equality, especially in the areas of racial discrimination and the rights of people with disabilities, much more must be done to put these plans into action to ensure that the general development of human rights for the person in the street. This should be done in partnership with NGOs who have the skill, commitment and expertise to carry out such a programme. A range of national seminars, courses, meetings, debates, mock trials and conferences on human rights should be developed to promote human rights. A programme such as the community education undertaken by the Constitutional Assembly between 1994 and 1996 is required to implement a sorely needed and long overdue massive intervention on human rights.

To develop an understanding and acceptance of human rights in the country, the SAHRC has promoted human rights education in partnership with the UN/S.A. Technical Co-operation Project based at the SAHRC. Such a programme could use all types of religious, cultural, sports and community groups as well as trade unions, advice offices, police forums, political structures and others to educate people at grassroots level about these issues. In addition, the SAHRC has been co-ordinating human rights education programmes in the country and, in partnership with the Department of Education, is developing human rights curricula and programmes for schools. While policy and plans are in place, little has been done to implement them. The longer implementation takes, the more difficult it will be to achieve the end goal. In addition to general human rights education, there is a need for specific education around crime and human rights, xenophobia, firearms and issues around violence, refugees, prisons and others.

A national programme in schools ought to be developed and run by the SAHRC in collaboration with NGOs. This would ensure that people are inculcated with a respect for human rights from a young age. Although there are approximately 100,000 schools to get to, the schools network is easily accessible and could be reached by training people across the country, who in turn would do training in schools.

SAHRC has assisted government departments to develop human rights education training manuals and has trained some people, but not very much has been done to make this practical. Critical departments to focus on include home affairs, welfare, justice, correctional services, defence and police so that the people who work in these places are more likely to treat vulnerable groups in a more sympathetic manner. Such a programme could be developed in partnership with appropriate NGOs.

The SAHRC has a constitutional duty to monitor and report on the realisation of the socio-economic rights in the Bill of Rights. So far, much of the reporting work is based on information obtained from government departments. However, the Commission refuses to release the information it has received from government for NGOs to scrutinise and comment on. Rather than simply report on socio-economic rights, the Commission should work with NGOs to highlight the lack of attention given to this vital area and to ensure greater public support for the achievement of these rights. More intensive work should be done when reporting on the implementation of socio-economic rights in South Africa as well as when preparing reports to other bodies to which the country has international obligations. For example, as a party to the International Covenant on Civil and Political Rights, the Convention on the Rights of the Child, and the Convention on the Elimination of all Forms of Discrimination Against Women (CEDAW), South Africa must report on its implementation of these treaties.

In the area of developing human rights in the region, a useful mechanism is the Co-ordinating Committee of African National Institutions for the Promotion and Protection of Human Rights. The SAHRC serves as the secretariat and convenor of this body. In this role, the Commission has the task of encouraging and equipping national institutions in Africa to be effective in protecting human rights, to acquire skills for human rights advocacy, to share resources among themselves, and to establish models for good and effective delivery of human rights programmes at national level. To this end it is critical that the expertise and knowledge of the SAHRC is developed. Many of these institutions are in need of support, and a way to enhance their roles and their capacity could be provided. This must however be done in very specific ways, with projects being specifically aimed at developing understanding, skill, expertise and experience.

Finally, and crucially, the human rights agenda of the SAHRC must be examined and redirected. The present focus has been criticised for focusing on the "softer" human rights issues and ignoring core, major and difficult human rights issues with major relevance for South Africa. For example, the United States State Department in its South Africa Country Report on Human Rights Practices for 1998,[100] noted that the SAHRC's "operations have been hampered by red tape, budgetary concerns, the absence of civil liberties legislation, several high-level staff resignations, and concerns about the Commission's broad interpretation of its mandate". The agenda of the SAHRC ought, therefore, to be re-prioritised to tackle far more pressing issues than are presently focused on.

THE COMMISSION OF GENDER EQUALITY

Much progress has been made in gender issues since South Africa's first democratic elections in April 1994.[101] The participation of women in political decision-making structures has increased significantly over the past six years.[102] In the National Assembly and the National Council of Provinces, women make up about 30 per cent of representatives. In the nine provinces, women representatives make up about 28 per cent of the total.[103] Women representatives at local government level total about 18 per cent, with some of these women holding non-traditional portfolios. Also, women are now in charge of key ministries: foreign affairs (Nkosazana Zuma), the public service (Geraldine Fraser-Moleketi), minerals and energy (Phumzile Mlambo-Ngcuka), and communications (Ivy Matsepe-Casaburri).

As far as transformation of the legal system as a whole is concerned, before 1994 the system was staffed overwhelmingly by white men. At the end of 1988 all of the 144 regional court magistrates were white, while of 782 district court magistrates, 768 were white, 10 were Indian, four were coloured and none was black.[104] Attorneys and advocates were almost all white.

Looking at how the system has changed in terms of having more women and people of colour in the courts, the statistics reveal that in 1994 there were 229 women magistrates and 977 men. At the same time there were 534 women prosecutors and 740 men prosecutors. In 1997 the magistracy had 34 male chief magistrates and two female chief magistrates. Among senior magistrates,

---

[100] U.S. Department of State Report 1998 released by the Bureau of Democracy, Human Rights, and Labor on February 26, 1999.
[101] Statistics South Africa, "The People of South Africa Population Census, 1996: Census in Brief" (1998); Central Statistics, "Women and Men in South Africa" (1998) 3.
[102] *The Citizen*, June 14, 1999.
[103] *The Citizen*, July 12, 2000.
[104] *Hansard*, April 28, 1989 cols. 7097-8.

167 were men while there were only seven women holding this position. In addition, there were 1,119 male magistrates and only 56 women. As far as race is concerned, there were 745 white male magistrates, 197 white women, 489 black men and 86 black women. By 1998, 46 per cent of all magistrates were white men, 32 per cent black men, 15 per cent white women and seven per cent black women. Overall, 78 per cent are men and 62 per cent of the total are white.[105]

In 1998, there were 7,173 white male attorneys, 1,400 black male attorneys, 1,612 white women attorneys and 389 black women attorneys. For advocates, the number in 1998 was 1,055 white men, 175 black men, 121 white women and 31 black women. The figures for prosecutors indicate that 24 per cent were white men, 36 per cent black men, 22 per cent white women and 18 per cent black women. Thus, 46 per cent of the total are white and 60 per cent are men.

Despite these important changes, widespread violence against women continues to occur across all socio-economic and racial groups in South Africa. While some legal measures have been taken to protect women, including amendments in relation to domestic violence and maintenance, little has been achieved on the ground and in women's daily lives. Lack of education, unemployment, inadequate health care, and poverty remain major problems for women. While many governmental departments have committed themselves to focusing on issues of concern to women within their policies and programmes, not a great deal has been achieved practically speaking.

To ensure gains in the area of gender, both the 1993 Constitution and the 1996 Constitution provide for the establishment of a Commission on Gender Equality. Its stated objective is to promote gender equality and to advise and make recommendations to Parliament or other legislatures on laws or proposed laws that affect gender equality and the status of women.

The 1993 Constitution, however, made little provision for the structure, composition and appointment of the CGE, leaving much to be determined by Act of Parliament.[106] The composition, powers and functions of the institution are set out in the Commission for Gender Equality Act 1996. The functions include monitoring and evaluating the policies and practices of government, the private sector and other organisations to ensure that they promote and protect gender equality, as well as public education and information, reviewing existing and upcoming legislation from a gender perspective, investigating inequality, commissioning research and making recommendations to Parliament or other authorities.[107]

The Constitution provides that the CGE must promote respect for gender

---

[106] Statistics South Africa, "The People of South Africa Population Census, 1996: Census in Brief" (1998); Central Statistics, "Women and Men in South Africa" (1998) 3.
[107] The Commission for Gender Equality Act 1996.
[108] See further *Insight*, March 31, 2000.

equality and the protection, development and attainment of gender equality.[108] The Commission has the power, as regulated by national legislation, necessary to perform its functions, including the power to monitor, investigate, research, educate, lobby, advise and report on issues concerning gender equality. The CGE has the additional powers and functions prescribed in the founding Act. Powers and functions can be summarised under the following heads: education, research, monitoring, investigation, lobbying, advising and reporting.

The CGE also has a specific role to play in law reform. The Commission's function is to deal with not only Acts of Parliament, but also indigenous and customary law. Powers to take remedial action are also granted. The Gender Commission has the power to resolve disputes through mediation, conciliation and negotiation.

As far as the work of the CGE is concerned, the Commission has noted that it "had to establish itself in an often cynical and hostile external environment, brought about by the mismanagement of some independent bodies, leading to the blanket public perception that all such bodies are just more wagons on the gravy train; debate over the need for all the separate institutions in support of democracy prescribed in the Constitution; and the tendency – common the world over – for gender structures to be marginalised and accorded less importance".[109]

Although the CGE is doing some useful work, its reach and impact is not sufficiently felt. This shortage is partly because, as the CGE states, "negative attitudes also limit the potential of institution like the CGE to operate as efficiently as they otherwise could. The treatment from some quarters in government sometimes begs the question 'Is government committed to gender equality?'"[110]

To some extent the CGE has been responsible for its problems and low profile. Recently it has been racked by internal controversy, about half of its staff resigned and the Commission was embroiled in a court case and sacked CEO Colleen Lowe-Morna and Commissioner Farid Esack.[111] In April 2000, the CGE asked Parliament to remove Esack as a commissioner.

As far as its role in promoting gender equality is concerned, the CGE's audit of remaining discriminatory legislation, launched in March 1999, indicates a useful function it can perform together with other institutions, such as the Auditor-General and NGOs. The CGE has indicated that it wants to produce an annual report card on the Government's performance towards the achievement of gender equality. If done well, this could be a valuable tool in promoting gender equality. It would, however, mean co-ordination of all information and a greater focus on analytical research. While the Office on the

---

[108] s. 187(1).
[109] CGE *Annual Report 1997–1998*.
[110] CGE *Annual Report 1997–1998*, Part Six.
[111] *Esack v. Commission on Gender Equality* 2000 (7) BCLR 737 W.

Status of Women in the President's Office is currently conducting a gender audit of all government departments and all the provinces, this will in all likelihood not be sufficiently detailed or sufficiently independent to be useful. In any case, this information can feed into a well-researched and independent detailed annual audit of gender advancement in government and government departments. Such an audit would be an extremely valuable tool for promoting gender equality in government and should be published in plain language and in a variety of languages for the public. The information derived in the research could also be used as an advocacy tool in promoting a range of issues.

There is also a need to promote knowledge of, and access to, the procedures in the Maintenance and Domestic Violence Acts 1998 as well as the about-to-be amended Sexual Offences Act 1998. It is also critical to monitor the implementation of these Acts on the ground. This detailed and thorough research would have a huge impact on indicating what is actually happening and what can be done to rectify problems. While the cost of doing such research would be quite high, the benefits for the millions of women affected would be dramatic.

A useful tool for promoting gender equality is the use of South Africa's mandatory reporting to international bodies in terms of its commitments under various international human rights instruments. By becoming a signatory to the Convention on the Elimination of all forms of Discrimination Against Women (CEDAW), the South African government agreed to introduce measures to help protect the basic rights of women and to improve the status of women. CEDAW requires countries to report every four years on their implementation of the convention. South Africa presented its first report in June 1998. Part of the process allows people in a country to comment on the government's report and, in fact, draft a shadow report. Here the CGE, in collaboration with a range of others, such as NGOs, can play a vital role in ensuring that the report is meaningful and that South Africa complies with the spirit of CEDAW. The research used to gather the information can also be used as an advocacy tool. This process is broadly supported and such mechanisms would ensure that the state would be more willing to ensure compliance with the human rights standards that they have committed themselves to.

THE PUBLIC PROTECTOR

The office of the Public Protector was created by the 1993 Constitution,[112] which delineated many aspects of the office, including the process of estab-

---

[112] The forerunner in South Africa to the Public Protector was a National Ombudsman, a post that evolved out of the Advocate-General's office. These were part-time posts that were concerned with the spending of public money.

lishment and appointment, the imperative of independence and impartiality, powers and functions, staff and expenditure, and which provided for the establishment of provincial public protectors.

The 1996 Constitution provides that the Public Protector has the power to investigate any conduct in state affairs or in the public administration in any sphere of government that is alleged or suspected to be improper or to result in any impropriety or prejudice, to report on that conduct, and to take appropriate remedial action.[113] The Public Protector has additional powers and functions prescribed by national legislation. The Public Protector may not investigate court decisions. Any report issued by the Public Protector must be open to the public, unless exceptional circumstances, to be determined in terms of national legislation, require that a report be kept confidential. The Public Protector Act, promulgated on November 25, 1994, adds to the powers and responsibilities of the office.

According to the Constitutional Court in its certification judgement on the 1996 Constitution,[114] the powers of the Public Protector are to "investigate any conduct in state affairs, or in the public administration in any sphere of government, that is alleged or suspected to be improper or to result in any impropriety or prejudice, to report on that conduct and to take appropriate remedial action".[115]

Thus, the functions of the Public Protector are threefold. The incumbent's first duty is to investigate any conduct in state affairs, or in the public administration in any sphere of government, that is alleged or suspected to be improper or to result in any impropriety or prejudice. Secondly, the Public Protector must report on that conduct. Finally, the Public Protector must take appropriate remedial action. The Public Protector is also empowered to investigate, report, and take remedial action in relation to improper prejudice, maladministration, dishonesty or improper dealings with respect to public money, improper enrichment, and receipt of improper advantage. The office is concerned not only with ensuring the honesty of those working for the state, but also with ensuring that they treat people with respect. The power of the office is made clear by the rights of search, seizure, and *subpoena* conferred on it. The role of the Public Protector has at times been perceived to be political and less than robust.[116] He has investigated many issues relating to government departments, nepotism, roles of cabinet ministers and other issues; but the findings have often been that there has been no wrongdoing or that any wrongdoing has not been significant. For example, in "The Investigation of

---

[113] s. 182.

[114] *Certification of the Constitution of the RSA, 1996, Re ex p. Chairperson of the Constitutional Assembly, 1996,* 1996 (10) *BCLR* 1253 (CC).

[115] para. 161.

[116] See for example Claire Bisseker, "Kicking the Watchdog Before He Barks" *Financial Mail,* November 20, 1998.

Allegations of Nepotism Pertaining to Several Appointments in the Public Service", in which at least 20 charges of nepotism were investigated, the Public Protector found no nepotism.[117] This enhanced the perception in some quarters that the Public Protector is not always independent.[118] The National Institutions Project of the Human Rights Committee have also commented that:

> "many fear the office will be used as a political tool, as elections get closer. . . . Although the allegations are not proven, it is this kind of scepticism of the PP's non-partisan role that the office wishes to be free of."[119]

It does seem, however, that the Public Protector's office has recently been asserting greater independence. For example, the Public Protector made a finding that the statement made by the Premier of Mapumalanga that politicians are allowed to lie was wrong. More recently, in an inquiry into statements made by former Minister of Minerals and Energy Penuell Maduna about the Auditor-General, the Public Protector criticised the former Minister's conduct; but the report has been faulted for not going far enough in terms of findings and recommendations on sanctions to be imposed on the Minister.[120]

Cases received and finalised by the Public Protector's office

Period	New Cases Received	Cases Finalised	Cases Carried Over
30 September 1995 (Office of the Ombudsman)	—	—	544
Oct – Dec 1995	408	127	825
Jan – Dec 1996	2,369	764	2,430
Jan – Dec 1997	3,341	2,367	3,404
Jan – Dec 1998	3,559	1,974	4,989
*Jan – Dec 1999	10,680	6,183	9,486

* includes North West and Eastern Cape offices.

(Information provided by the Public Protector's Office, March 2000)

---

[117] See further press release from the Office of the Public Protector, "Allegations of Nepotism in Government Without Substance" May 1, 1999.

[118] Claire Bisseker, "Baqwa Wields Wet Noodle" *Financial Mail*, November 28, 1997.

[119] Human Rights Committee National Institutions Project 1(3) *Access*, March 1999.

[120] See Public Protector *Report No 13 Report on the Alleged Irregularities With Regard to the Affairs and Financial Statements of the SFF Association, and on the Relevant Reports of the Auditor-General to Parliament* (December 1999).

While the number of cases has grown, it is unknown whether this indicates greater public knowledge of the office or that there are more problems in the areas dealt with by the Public Protector. Also unknown is the extent to which the office is vigorous and affecting the operations of government departments and other organs of state. More research is required to be able to answer these and other questions.

To enhance the operations of the office, greater training and expertise development is required. Increased capacity for dealing with complaints will ensure greater compliance with the law and the standards that ought to be complied with. A few training workshops or conferences every year could be very beneficial to support these efforts.

A critical problem is the fact that the office operates mainly out of Pretoria. An office is operating in North West province, funded by the North West Provincial Government, and a regional office is operating with the assistance of the Eastern Cape Provincial Government. It is clear that the limited number of offices compromises the availability and accessibility of the office, and ways need to be found to improve this situation.

THE AUDITOR-GENERAL

Misappropriation, corruption, financial mismanagement and wastage of public funds are a serious problem in South Africa.[121] While these occur in both the public and private sector, the problem is most serious in the public sector, where taxpayers' money is affected.

Serious allegations of corruption have been made against officials in a number of government departments[122] as well as in regional government.[123] In the Department of Justice, hundreds of officials are facing charges of misconduct, corruption or fraud.[124] High-ranking officials in the Department of Correctional Services are also facing corruption charges[125] and already the Auditor-General has found that the former Commissioner of Correctional Services gave himself undeserved bonus payments, wasted money on unnecessary overseas trips, used public money to fund a scholarship programme in the U.S. named after himself, and hired members of his professional soccer team to work in the Department.[126] The Minister of Welfare told Parliament in No-

---

[121] Constanze Bauer, "Public Sector Corruption and its Controls in South Africa" in Kempe Ronald Hope Sr. and Bornwell C. Chikulo, *Corruption and Development in Africa* (2000) p. 218.
[122] Taleh Sayed and David Bruce, "Inside and Outside Police Corruption" (1998) 7(2) *African Security Review* 3.
[123] Tom Lodge, "Political Corruption in South Africa" (1998) 387(97) *African Affairs* 157.
[124] *Pretoria News*, May 10, 2000.
[125] *City Press*, March 19, 20000.
[126] *Business Day*, April 17, 2000.

vember 1998 that, of the R6 million worth of welfare cheques stolen in South Africa between 1996 and August last year, more than 90 per cent were lost through fraud or staff negligence. The Heath Special Investigating Unit is also investigating huge amounts of fraud and corruption.[127] It is not surprising, therefore, that in Transparency International's 1998 report South Africa scored 5.2 out of a possible 10 on a scale of corruption.[128] It was placed 32nd out of some 120 countries. There is a need to reverse the degeneration of ethics and morality. A culture of bribery and the corruption of public officials undermines stability, democracy, good governance, the rule of law and development.

While many accused of corruption and fraud within the public sector are exposed, there is little formal process to follow up on these incidents. Tolerance for this state of affairs in a democratic state will have long-term negative effects for the society.

The two institutions created to fulfil the function of ensuring clean and properly administered government are the Public Protector and the Auditor-General. In the words of the Constitutional Court, "where the focus of the Public Protector's attention is efficient and proper bureaucratic conduct, the Auditor-General is concerned with proper management and use of public money".[129] Chapter 9 of the Constitution provides the functions of the office, its tenure and provisions for appointment and removal from office of the Auditor-General.

The Constitution provides that the Auditor-General must audit and report on the accounts, financial statements and financial management of all national and provincial state departments and administrations, all municipalities, and any other institution or accounting entity required by national or provincial legislation.[130] In addition to these duties, the Constitution provides that the Auditor-General may audit and report on the accounts, financial statements and financial management of any institution funded from the National Revenue Fund or a provincial Revenue Fund or by a municipality, or any institution that is authorised in terms of any law to receive money for a public purpose. The Auditor-General must submit audit reports to any legislature that has a direct interest in the audit, and to any other authority prescribed by national legislation. All reports must be made public.[131]

The Auditor-General has the additional powers and functions prescribed by national legislation. The statutory mandate of the functions of the Auditor-General is found in the Auditor-General Act.[132] The legislation does not specify

---

[127] *Saturday Star*, August 22, 1998.
[128] *1998 Corruption Report*, Transparency International.
[129] para. 164.
[130] s. 188.
[131] s. 188.
[132] Auditor-General Act 12 of 1995.

how the office should be involved with the public, other than that its reports must be public documents. The Auditor-General performs the functions assigned by law, with the assistance of staff appointed in the office of the Auditor-General in terms of the Audit Arrangements Act, and with persons appointed in term of section 6 of the Auditor-General Act, that is, people contracted in to do audit work.[133]

The Auditor-General thus promotes the goals of clean and efficient financial administration and the accompanying goal of good governance, which is linked to development and the maintenance of human rights. Although the Auditor-General cannot claim a direct effect on human rights, effective service delivery is vital to the objective of socio-economic rights delivery. He or she assists by providing access to financial information and uncovering corruption.

The office of the Auditor-General has done some excellent work. While much goes to examine financial issues alone in terms of correct and allocated expenditure, the Auditor-General has usefully audited the planning, resource management and control of the National Crime Prevention Strategy. The Auditor-General has found that cells at certain police stations were built with inadequate material, which contributed to their poor condition as well as to the number of escapes.

The office is seen to be fearless and robust in its work. The new Auditor-General Shauket Fakie[134] is proving to be more vigorous and energetic than his predecessor, Henri Kleuver, who was subjected to virulent criticism by government and a range of government ministers. Public awareness of the role of the Auditor-General has come about mainly because of such comments, although the profile of the office has also increased recently because of its various reports to Parliament of gross underspending by government departments on a range of social services.[135] There is still a need for the broader public to be more aware of the work of the Auditor-General in taking care of public money.

The performance reports of the Auditor-General are crucial to identify problems in the supply of services by government departments. Service supply clearly affects the realisation of socio-economic rights, and the public must get value for its money. The vital questions include, how accessible is information about these rights? what information is available on how the Government is performing in providing them? what is the government department's score card on delivery?

While it was noted above that socio-economic rights fall within the man-

---

[133] Shauket Fakie, "The Role of the Auditor-General in Promoting and Developing Good Governance and Human Rights Culture in South Africa", delivered to the Law Faculty at the University of the Western Cape (April 4, 2000).

[134] *Burger*, November 19, 1999.

[135] *Argus*, February 28, 2000.

date of the SAHRC, this institution has barely made any progress in monitoring and ensuring delivery of these rights. In contrast, there was outrage when the audit report on the Department of Welfare was made public by the Auditor-General recently: almost all of the department's poverty alleviation budget remained unspent. Accountability and transparency of government departments would be enhanced if good analytical information on their activities was available to the public. Such information should include analysis of what was and what was not delivered, departmental policy, business plans and budgets. A spin-off of making available this information to the public would be that there would be a greater understanding of, and value for, the role of the Auditor-General.

A dimension of performance audit should be the incorporation of gender analysis. A women's budget audit would advance an important cluster of women's rights. Research is necessary to support an investigation of a women's budget and to assist the CGE and others to promote the agenda of gender equality.

Performance audits ought to be given the prominence they deserve. This will have a major effect on public knowledge and government accountability as far as the realisation of socio-economic rights is concerned. Producing the general and audit reports of the offices of the Auditor-General nationally and translating them into reader-friendly documents for the general public will enhance the work of the office. This will also enable the public to apply more pressure for steps to be taken against those individuals whose misdeeds have been uncovered by the office, or for steps to be taken to deal with problems in government service delivery.

THE TRUTH AND RECONCILIATION COMMISSION

A critical question for the new democracy in South Africa in 1994 was how to deal with gross violations of human rights in the past. Issues raised include whether there ought to be criminal trials,[136] who should to be tried, and whether there ought to be a truth commission or similar process.[137]

The starting point for any examination of the process in South Africa is the fact that a number of factors necessitated compromises in the political settlement that ushered in the new South Africa.[138] These included the fact that those

---

[136] On the problems associated with the use of trials in a country in transition, see Jeremy Sarkin, "Transitional Justice and the Prosecution Model: The Experience of Ethiopia" 1999 (2) *Law, Democracy and Development* 253.

[137] Jeremy Sarkin, "The Truth and Reconciliation Commission in South Africa" (1997) *Commonwealth Law Bulletin* 528.

[138] See generally Jeremy Sarkin, "The Trials and Tribulations of the South African Truth and Reconciliation Commission" (1996) 12 *South African Journal of Human Rights* 617.

who were in power had not been defeated and therefore remained in control; that the security forces were still controlled by the old government; and that the concerns of both local communities and the economic community abroad had to be accommodated.[139] In the negotiation period before 1994, many members of the old government opposed dealing with the past and called for a blanket amnesty. As a result of the need to compromise, the 1993 "interim" Constitution, which came into force on April 27, 1994 provided for a process enabling amnesty to be granted to individuals who had committed politically motivated crimes.[140] Amnesty would not be granted on an automatic or blanket basis.

The first post-apartheid government saw the task of confronting past abuses of human rights as crucial. It argued that a process of public truth-telling was necessary to bridge the bitter divisions of the past in the interests of peace and national unity.[141] Ignoring history would lead to collective amnesia, which would result in the unresolved past returning to haunt all South Africans in the form of anger, resentment and revenge. Only by publicly and collectively acknowledging the horror of past human rights violations could the country establish the rule of law and a culture of human rights. Atrocities had to be exposed, and human rights abuses acknowledged.

The Truth and Reconciliation Commission (TRC) was identified as the appropriate mechanism for coming to terms with the past. It would provide a process for hearing applications for amnesty by individuals who had committed politically-motivated crimes. Months of debate, compromise and delay preceded adoption of the legislation establishing the Commission.[142] A selection panel composed of members of civil society and government was appointed to consider nominations for TRC commissioners.

The primary task of the TRC was to develop a complete picture of the cause, nature and extent of the gross human violations committed from March 1, 1960 to May 10, 1994. It had to facilitate the granting of amnesty to persons who make a full disclosure of all the relevant facts relating to criminal acts associated with a political objective. It had to establish and make known the

---

[139] See Richard Wilson, "Manufacturing Legitimacy: The Truth and Reconciliation Commission and the Rule of Law" (1995) 13 *Indicator* 41.

[140] The Postamble to the interim Constitution (Chap. 15, General and Transitional Provisions, National Unity and Reconciliation) states that, "in order to advance such reconciliation and reconstruction, amnesty shall be granted in respect of acts, omissions and offences associated with political objectives and committed in the course of the conflicts of the past." Interim South African Constitution. (1993), Chap. 15.

[141] On the necessity for such a process in Rwanda, see Jeremy Sarkin, "Preconditions and Processes for Establishing a Truth and Reconciliation Commission in Rwanda – The Possible Interim Role of Gacaca Community Courts" (1999) 3(2) *Law, Democracy and Development* 223 and Jeremy Sarkin, "Promoting Justice, Truth and Reconciliation in Transitional Societies: Evaluating Rwanda's Approach in the New Millennium of Using Community Based Gacaca Tribunals to Deal With the Past" (2000) 2(2) *International Law Forum* 112.

[142] Promotion of National Unity and Reconciliation Act 34 of 1995.

whereabouts of victims, to restore the human rights and civil dignity of survivors of abuse by granting them an opportunity to relate their own accounts of the violations they suffered, and to recommend reparation measures. In addition, the TRC had to compile a report that detailed its activities, findings and recommendations for preventing future violations of human rights.

The establishing Act limited the TRC to investigating "gross violations of human rights". "Gross violations" included killing, abduction, torture or severe ill-treatment of any person, or any attempt, conspiracy, incitement, instigation, command or procurement to commit any of these acts.

More general injustices, such as the detention without trial of at least 78,000 people over the 30-year period under examination, the jailing of about 18 million people for pass law offences, and the forcible removal of millions of people, did not fall within the jurisdiction of the TRC.

As well as an investigation unit the Act provided for three committees to achieve the objectives set out for the Commission:[143] the Committee on Human Rights Violations,[144] the Committee on Amnesty[145] and the Committee on Reparation and Rehabilitation.[146] The Committee on Human Rights Violations gathered information and evidence about human rights violations, and recorded them. The committee also made recommendations for preventing future violations of human rights. The Committee on Reparation and Rehabilitation considered matters referred to it by other committees. It also gathered evidence concerning the identity of victims, their fate, whereabouts and the type of harm suffered by them.

The report of the TRC, containing over 40 pages of recommendations, was handed to President Mandela in October 1998. The Reparation and Rehabilitation Committee (RRC)[147] proposed a comprehensive and innovative scheme based on the recognition that reparations and rehabilitation are essential to build national unity and reconciliation, especially when amnesties are granted. The RRC's proposed policy contains five parts.[148] Firstly, urgent interim reparations will be given to human rights abuse survivors in "urgent need, to provide them with access to appropriate services and facilities". Secondly, individual reparation grants are recommended to each survivor of gross human rights violation. This is a financial grant, determined according to various criteria, to be paid over six years. Thirdly, the RRC proposed that symbolic measures such as a "national day of remembrance and reconciliation,

---

[143] The task of the investigation unit in its objective of comprehensively investigating at least some of the major human rights violations perpetrated was enormous, particularly in view of the limited period in which it had to operate.

[144] s.12.

[145] s.16.

[146] s.23.

[147] See further Lovell Fernandez, "Reparations Policy in South Africa For the Victims of Apartheid" (1999) 3(2) *Law, Democracy and Development* 209.

[148] para. 24.

erection of memorials and monuments, and the development of museums"
would "facilitate the communal process of remembering and commemorating
the pain and the victories of the past". Fourthly, community-based services
and activities should be established with the goal of "promoting the healing
and recovery of individuals and communities that have been affected by human rights violations".[149] Fifthly, the RRC's "proposals include legal, administrative and institutional measures designed to prevent the recurrences of
human rights abuses".[150] In addition, the RRC stated that "[t]he services developed as a result of [the] policy should be responsive to the religious and
cultural beliefs and practices of the community in which the services are provided".[151]

The RRC also stated that there was a "need to provide an environment that
supported and respected the dignity of all who approached it". The RRC recommended training for all who would be involved in the process, such "briefers
and statement takers", as well as "those outside the Commission who would
assist in providing support". The RRC recognised and understood the pain
and trauma inflicted upon the people who would be coming forward to seek
reparations, and noted that to be able to effectively provide for these people,
skill and sensitivity training would be required.[152]

The RRC recognised that reparations are essential to national healing and
unity. It said when a country had been through a period of unrest and conflict,
and had experienced a transitional period from one government to another,
there are often numerous human rights abuses. It acknowledged that international criminal bodies are useful in prosecuting those offences, and that these
prosecutions can help achieve national reconciliation. The prosecution of an
individual in an international court can relieve the need for a domestic court to
try the case, thereby avoiding many of the problems of domestic courts. The
RRC decided on both monetary and non-monetary reparations. While monetary reparations are important, in the case of rape survivors, non-monetary
reparations are also important and may be more feasible.

However, while it seemed that government had been involved in estimat-
ing compensation, it now seems that the state is backing away from granting
any money to victims.

As the Amnesty Committee had not completed its work by the final deadline for completion of the work, it released an interim report of its findings in
October.[153] This committee continues to operate. The Amnesty Committee
reported that at that point it had granted 171 amnesties[154] out of a total of

---

[149] para. 30.
[150] para. 32.
[151] para. 49.
[152] *ibid.*
[153] Truth and Reconciliation Final Report, Volume 5, Chapter 3: Interim Report of the Amnesty.
[154] Truth and Reconciliation Final Report, Volume 5, Chapter 3.

7,127 applications.[155] Of the 4,443 applications finalised as of June 30, 1998, most had been denied for a variety of reasons. Some had been denied administratively, prior to the hearing stage, and others had gone through the entire process.[156] Applications were refused for a variety of reasons: defects in the application; that the applicant had been acquitted in a trial; that no offence had been specified on the application form; or that the act was outside the Commission's jurisdiction. A total of 283 people fell into these categories. Amnesty was denied to 158 applicants because they denied guilt. The applications of 138 people were turned down because they did not fully disclose the details of the act they were applying for. Amnesty was denied to 2,629 individuals as the act they had committed had no political motive. A total of 211 people were refused amnesty because their acts were not politically motivated and the applicants denied guilt. Amnesty was refused in 275 cases because the act had no political motive and the applicant committed the act for personal gain, while 564 cases were refused because the act was committed after the cut-off date. Another 45 people were refused amnesty because the act had been done for personal gain.[157]

The TRC also probed the role of various sectors, including the judiciary, business and the South African Defence Force (SADF). It also probed the role of the health sector in "colluding with, perpetrating and resisting human rights abuses" during the period of its mandate.[158] The intention of this investigation was to examine the context of such violations in order to make recommendations for preventing similar violations in the future.

The relevance and role of the TRC process is the subject of much debate,[159] highlighting the positive or negative role of the TRC in the discovery of the truth (or parts of it) and the role the TRC in promoting reconciliation. Both the process and the report that the TRC produced have been controversial.[160] It is being scrutinised by proponents and opponents of the process, from the left and right, perpetrators and victims,[161] groups and individuals, black and white, those who benefited from apartheid and those who were subjected to its abuse and still live in abject poverty. Without doubt, the process has had a positive effect. The crucial question is "how much?"

The process of establishing the TRC is the starting point of some people's

---

[155] *ibid.*
[156] *ibid.*
[157] *ibid.*
[158] See H. Varney and J. Sarkin, "Failing to Pierce the Hit Squad Veil: An Analysis of the Malan Trial" (1997) 10 *South African Journal of Criminal Justice* 141.
[159] See, *e.g.*, Charles Villa-Vicencio, "Living in the Wake of the Truth and Reconciliation Commission: A Retroactive Reflection" (1999) 3(2) *Law, Democracy and Development* 195.
[160] Jeremy Sarkin , "Reconciliation Through Truth: A Reckoning of Apartheid's Criminal Governance" (November 1999) *Human Rights Quarterly* 1129.
[161] See further Gabriel O'Malley, "Respecting Revenge: The Road to Revenge" (1999) 3(2) *Law, Democracy and Development* 181.

critique of the process. On the one side, some victims believe that there should not have been amnesty. On the other side, there are those who maintain that there should have been a blanket amnesty as the TRC process reopens wounds, causing more pain and bitterness. Those who hold this latter view allege that the TRC was biased – that certain political parties have not been treated fairly and members of those groups have not, and will not, be treated in an unbiased, neutral way.

Reactions to the TRC have been disparate and polarised. Public opinion was often divided along racial lines. For example, the *Business Day* newspaper published a survey that found that the TRC had harmed the state of race relations in South Africa. The controversial survey, conducted by Market Research Africa (MRA) among 2,500 people,[162] found the TRC had worsened relations.[163] It reported that an equal amount of people surveyed (39 per cent) agreed and disagreed that the hearings would help the people of South Africa live together more easily. It further reported that only 18 per cent of people said that race relations had not been worsened by the hearings. Interestingly, it was found that while 70 per cent of whites and about 50 per cent of Indians and coloureds found that the commission had worsened race relations, the percentage for black South Africans was just above 20 per cent. The political editor of *Business Day*, Drew Forrest, responded to the survey,[164] claiming that a more accurate perception of the survey results was that although blacks and whites agree that the Commission has angered people, they differ profoundly on whether the TRC's efforts advanced the cause of reconciliation.[165] Forrest found that whites were not facing the outrageous crimes the previous government did in their interests.[166] He alleged that "[whites] are projecting fear and moral discomfort at the anticipated rage of black people".[167] According to Forrest, the Commission's findings have narrowed the gap in perceptions of apartheid between the white and black communities, and that whites can no longer hide in the notion that apartheid was only a "moral crusade for western values".[168]

Despite the many criticisms, the TRC has helped to uncover at least some truth about what occurred in South Africa. It has helped to piece together some of the many human rights abuses that occurred. It has also imbued the new government with a degree of human rights respectability.

---

[162] Press Release, South African Press Association, July 27, 1998, "TRC Has Harmed Race Relations: Survey."
[163] *ibid.*
[164] Drew Forrest, "Body Has Served Reconciliation" *Business Day*, August 3, 1998.
[165] *ibid.*
[166] *ibid.*
[167] *ibid.*
[168] *ibid.*

CONCLUSION

While South Africa has come long way in developing a human rights culture, movement over the last few years has been regressive in comparison to the major progressive steps taken immediately after the democratic transition that began in 1994. The more recent past has seen the emergence of more obstacles than positive steps in the development of a general climate of human rights acceptance and promotion.

While Parliament has passed many human rights-friendly laws, there has been a trend in the more recent past to enact laws countering this trend. In addition, the state has shown little commitment to enact key pieces of legislation to prohibit discrimination in most areas of South African life, promote access to information and provide a framework for administrative justice.[169] The group of laws on these issues was hurried through Parliament only because a constitutional imperative demanded that these laws be enacted by February 4, 2000, a full three years after the 1996 Constitution came into force. The Employment Equity Act,[170] which came into force late in 1999, eliminated unfair discrimination in the workplace and implemented affirmative action measures for black people, women and people with disabilities. However, it is particularly surprising that the first democratic government introduced no legislation to forbid discrimination in all other areas where discrimination has extensively occurred, such as housing sales, rentals and the use of amenities. In short, too little has been done by Parliament to impact on the private lives of the majority of South Africa's citizens.

The fact that these laws were drafted and enacted in a hurry means insufficient debate and revision took place. For example, the Promotion of Equality and Prevention of Unfair Discrimination Bill's clauses prohibiting discrimination on the basis of HIV/Aids status and nationality have been removed.

Crime and criminal violence are probably still the most important obstacles to public acceptance of human rights issues and continue to undermine the achievement of a human rights culture.[171] While it is crucial to reduce the crime rate, respecting the rights of accused persons is not being "soft on criminals", but rather a matter of protecting all South Africans, because anybody could be accused of a crime. Apart from flouting the human rights norms protected in other democracies by other international human rights instruments and by the Constitution, some new laws do not take into account the state of the legal system. Many accused individuals may be innocent, and have no understanding of the legal system or the language and procedures of the courts.

---

[169] Promotion of Access to Information Act 2 of 2000, Promotion of Administrative Justice Act 3 of 2000, Promotion of Equality and Prevention of Unfair Discrimination Act 4 of 2000.

[170] Act 55 of 1998.

[171] See for example Judge Kees Van Dijkhorst, "The Criminal Justice System in Jeopardy: Is the Constitution to Blame?" (November 1998) *Consultus* 136.

They certainly have no legal skills. Yet, they are now required to prove to a court that they should be granted bail and they may be incarcerated if they are simply accused of a serious offence for which they may not even be any evidence.[172]

For a human rights culture to develop, substantive meaning must be given to the socio-economic rights contained in the Constitution.[173] Improving the lives of the millions of destitute South Africans, particularly in relation to housing and employment, is critical, not only because it is a constitutional imperative,[174] but because without these rights little progress will be made in ensuring public acceptance of civil and political rights.[175] In an extremely critical speech[176] in May 2000, Judge President of the Constitutional Court, Arthur Chaskalson stated:

> "Millions of people are still without houses, education and jobs, and there can be little dignity in living under such conditions. Dignity, equality and freedom will only be achieved when the socio-economic conditions are transformed to make this possible. This will take time. In the meantime government must give effect to its obligations under the Constitution to show respect and concern for those whose basic needs have to be met. The courts must give meaning to and apply the Bill of Rights and other provisions of the Constitution in the context of our history, the

---

[172] See Jeremy Sarkin, Esther Steyn. Dirk van Zyl Smit and Ron Paschke, "The Constitutional Court's Bail Decision: Individual Liberty in Crisis? *S v. Dlamini*" (2000) 16(2) *South African Journal of Human Rights* 291.

[173] See Ettienne Mureinik, "Beyond a Charter of Luxuries: Economic Rights in the Constitution" (1992) 8 *South African Journal of Human Rights* 465.

[174] See further Geraldine van Bueren, "Alleviating Poverty through the Constitutional Court" (1999) 15 *South African Journal of Human Rights* 52.

[175] The first case to give meaning to socio-economic rights is *Irene Grootboom v. Oostenburg Municipality and others* 2000 (3) BCLR 277 (C). This decision, dealing largely with the right to shelter, could be one of the most important cases to have been decided in South African judicial history. It may set a trend towards a far more robust role for the courts in the determination of policy and resource allocation. The case went on appeal to the Constitutional Court with argument being heard by this court in May 2000. On September 21, 2000 the court ordered the municipality to carry out an undertaking it gave during legal argument four months previously to supply water taps and toilets. The municipality was ordered to temporarily install these by the first week of October and permanently by December. See *Cape Times* (September 22, 2000). The decision on the merits of the case was handed down by the Constitutional Court on October 4, 2000. The court found that the national housing programme fell short of the obligations imposed by the Bill of Rights and ordered the state to devise and implement a programme to provide relief for people who have no access to land, no roof over their heads, and intolerable living conditions. How far-reaching this decision is will be determined by future cases in which the courts will be asked to determine whether government has put into place policies and programmes that measure up to the obligations found in the various socio-economic rights contained in the Bill of Rights.

[176] Arthur Chaskalson, "The Third Bram Fischer Lecture: Human Dignity as a Foundational Value of our Constitution" delivered in May 2000.

conditions prevailing in our society, and the transformative goals of the Constitution. . .

The Constitution offers a vision of the future. A society in which there will be social justice and respect for human rights, a society in which the basic needs of all our people will be met, in which we will live together in harmony, showing respect and concern for one another. We are capable of realising this vision but in danger of not doing so. We seem temporarily to have lost our way. Too many of us are concerned about what we can get from the new society, too few with what is needed for the realisation of the goals of the Constitution. What is lacking is the energy, the commitment and the sense of community that was harnessed in the struggle for freedom."

While the delivery on the socio-economic rights contained in the Bill of Rights is probably the most important issue to focus on, another critical need is for the state to focus on human rights education to a far greater extent. At present, in general, statements by politicians and government officials do more to undermine human rights than to promote them. Emphasis should be placed on developing our understanding of, and respect for the Constitution and the Bill of Rights and the process and mechanism of their enforcement.

Unfortunately, the SAHRC and the CGE, whose constitutional mandate is to educate the public on human rights, have not adequately fulfilled this task. Much work remains for them to inform and educate the general public about rights and why the rights of all deserve protection.

Critically, the role of these structures in the promotion of human rights has been problematic. Numerous issues have negatively affected the effectiveness and credibility of these institutions.[177] Problematic appointment processes have been at the root of many of these problems.[178] There have thus been numerous internal problems on issues, such as direction and policy formulation, leading

---

[177] See Bonnie Berkowitz, "Public Institutions" *Nadel Research Report No 7* (1999).

[178] For an evaluation of these problems and suggestions for a new process that would lead to independent appointments, see Jeremy Sarkin, "Reviewing and Reformulating Appointment Processes to Constitutional (Chapter Nine) Structures" (1999) 4 *South African Journal on Human Rights* 587; Jeremy Sarkin, "Appointment Processes to Constitutional Structures" in *Konrad Adenauer Foundation Seminar Series* 1999.

It is, however, important to note recent statements by the chairperson of the SA Human Rights Commission. Barney Pityana noted:

"The Commission was first brought together on the basis of people espousing different ideological persuasions. The result was that the Commission became a battleground, with people bringing their party political agendas in the work of the Commission contrary to our agreement. . . . The first Commission was marked by clear political allegiances of Commissioners. In that sense the original Commission was a battleground, where political parties were the reference points."

Interview with Pityana printed in Human Rights Committee 2(3) *Access* (July 2000) 18 and 21.

to many resignations and a huge turnover of staff. On the issue of the SAHRC human rights agenda, some commentators have criticised the Commission for focusing on the "softer" human rights issues and ignoring human rights issues with major relevance for South Africa. For example, the United States State Department, in its 1999 South Africa Country Report on Human Rights Practices for 1998,[179] noted that the SAHRC's "operations have been hampered by red tape, budgetary concerns, the absence of civil liberties legislation, several high-level staff resignations, and concerns about the Commission's broad interpretation of its mandate". Thus, a critical issue to be addressed before the next round of appointments is the process by which individuals are appointed. Without revising the appointment procedures, many of the present problems will continue to occur in the future.

In addition to the appointment issues, wider questions relating to the independence of these institutions ought to be tackled. While the CGE and the SAHRC have continually raised the question of independence, they have raised this largely in the context of the budgets that they receive from government, rather than from Parliament. Too much has been made of this issue. While the Commissions have asked for greater budgets, problematically, much of their budgets are spent on salaries and other benefits. Additionally, their annual reports reflect unspent allocations, which in the case of the CGE was more than R2 million.[180]

Civil society therefore has a continuing key role in the human rights field, and human rights education in particular.[181] To date, it is fair to say that it is largely NGOs that have played a significant role in promoting human rights. However, human rights NGOs are in decline even though there is a need for critical independent monitoring of the public institutions charged with safeguarding human rights. The largely simple and factual reporting of these bodies needs to be improved. Networking and strategic alliances within the human rights NGO sector must also be encouraged. The formation of a human rights network that is well-resourced in terms of skills, vision, capacity and finance is crucial. This forum could manage the overall identification of core issues and collate information. Some of the individuals involved at this level need to be high-profile people in the human rights field, since they would need to engage in strategic political lobbying. NGOs that have criticised the state for its shortcomings regarding human rights have found themselves coming under vociferous attack by the state. Instead of tackling the issues raised by these groups or individuals, the state is "shooting the messenger". For example, human rights groups focusing on abuses by the police have been publicly ad-

---

[179] *US Department of State Report 1998* released by the Bureau of Democracy, Human Rights, and Labor on February 26, 1999.

[180] See Commission for Gender Equality *Annual Report* April 1999 to March 2000.

[181] See H. Cawthra and G. Kraak. "Annual Review: The Voluntary Sector and Development in South Africa 1997–1998" in *Development Update* (1999).

monished and told that they should spend equal energy on putting criminals behind bars. Safety and Security Minister Steve Tshwete stated that there was an emerging pattern among such groups to pillory the police as villains with no respect for human rights.[182]

In a strongly-worded criticism of the ruling African National Congress in 1998, Dr Mamphela Ramphele, former vice-chancellor of the University of Cape Town and now a senior World Bank official, said "derogatory labels are becoming a way of silencing criticism". In 1999 she warned that South Africa's democracy is at risk because too many people, white and black, are afraid to criticise the new "liberation" establishment. She said "white academics do not speak out on issues of national concern anymore because they are afraid that they will be labelled racist".[183] In her view, black academics did not criticise the government because of misplaced loyalty born out of a comradeship with its roots in the struggle against apartheid – they cannot be seen to be criticising their own – and that these misguided loyalties and a culture of silence are putting South Africa's democracy at risk. Thus, while freedom of expression is a right enshrined in the Constitution, and is not really limited by law, governmental practice and societal pressure is limiting this freedom. While civil society, in general, remains strong, the human rights NGO sector is in decline. Many groups that successfully survived the transition are now having difficulty finding funding and personnel with experience and commitment to replace those who are leaving.

Since 1994, therefore, South Africa has made significant progress towards developing a human rights culture. The outlook for the promotion and protection of human rights was initially very rosy – prospects looked extremely promising. However, the honeymoon period of South Africa's transition has worn off. Many obstacles now stand in the way of the further development of the human-rights-based democracy. Tackling these issues is going to take a lot more effort than was initially thought.

---

[182] "'Back off' Tshwete Tells Rights Groups" in *Daily Mail and Guardian*, November 5, 1999.
[183] *Pretoria News*, December 8, 1999.

THE IRISH CONSTITUTION – AN OVERVIEW

BRIAN McCRACKEN*

HISTORICAL BACKGROUND

While the Irish Constitution was enacted and approved by a referendum in 1937, and has indeed been amended on a number of occasions since by further referenda, nevertheless it must be seen in the context of the previous several hundred years. I propose therefore to introduce this paper with a short historical account.

Prior to 1922 Ireland was governed and controlled from England for many centuries, and by the Act of Union 1801 Ireland formally became part of the United Kingdom of Great Britain and Ireland. For the next 122 years members of parliament were elected from various constituencies in Ireland and sat in the House of Commons at Westminster, and certain Irish bishops and lords became members of the House of Lords. Throughout this time Westminster legislated for Ireland as well as for the rest of the United Kingdom. However, although legally part of the United Kingdom, Ireland (and indeed Scotland) was treated as a separate entity for many purposes in the Westminster legislation. A considerable volume of this legislation did not apply to Ireland and equally considerable legislation applied only to Ireland.

In the late nineteenth and early twentieth century there was a strong movement in Ireland known as the Home Rule Movement, which advocated a form of semi-independence for Ireland, although still within the United Kingdom, and which would permit Ireland to be governed generally by a parliament of its own. There was in fact a considerable support for the principle of Home Rule both in Great Britain and in Ireland, but there was well-organised opposition on two fronts. One faction believed that Home Rule did not go far enough, and wanted a complete break from Great Britain with an independent republic being set up in Ireland, while the other faction, largely centred in the north-eastern part of the island, strongly opposed any form of Irish Parliament whereby they would be ruled from Dublin.

The historical background to each of these factions goes back a long way, and religious beliefs or traditions played a large part in their existence. There is no doubt that, at least until the middle of the nineteenth century, Roman Catholics were treated as second-class citizens, and were seriously prejudiced

---

* Judge, Member of the High Court.

in the practice of religion, in education, in employment and even in land holding. While many of these matters were remedied in the mid and late nineteenth century, nevertheless there remained a residue of the feeling of ill will, and indeed hatred, towards the English. The Roman Catholic Church established itself in a very strong position and had begun to exert a very strong influence over the lives of a large majority of the population by the early part of the twentieth century.

On the other hand, the majority of people living in the northeastern part of the island, in what is now Northern Ireland, came from a strong Protestant tradition. Many of them were descendants of families who had been given land in that part of Ireland in the seventeenth century or who had come from Scotland and settled in that part of Ireland. Again religion played a very big part in these peoples' lives, and the Protestant Churches, both Anglican and Presbyterian, had considerable influence. Furthermore, a number of institutions or organisations developed among the Protestant community, the best known of which of course is the Orange Order, and these still exist to the present day. The Northern Ireland Protestants feared, possibly with some justification, in the early twentieth century, that if they were ruled from Dublin they would forever be a minority being governed by a Roman Catholic Government, which would not acknowledge the Protestant traditions.

In 1914 the United Kingdom Parliament passed a Government of Ireland Act, with a view to setting up an Irish Parliament; but this was never implemented, due to the First World War. During Easter week in 1916 there was an armed uprising by Irish Republicans, largely centred in Dublin, which sought total independence from England; while this rising was initially a complete failure, it gave rise to a large upsurge in support for independence from England. In the years that followed there was considerable guerrilla activity against the British Army and the Police, and in 1920 the United Kingdom Parliament passed a further Government of Ireland Act, which proposed two Irish Parliaments, one in Dublin and one in Belfast, and effectively supported the partition of Ireland into two separate entities. However, armed resistance remained in the Southern part of Ireland until December 1921, and a *de facto* Irish Parliament was set up. In December 1921 a treaty was signed between Great Britain and representatives of the Irish Parliament, under which Ireland was to become substantially independent although it would remain as part of the British Commonwealth. There was also provision for what is now Northern Ireland to opt out of the settlement, which in fact happened, and a separate Parliament was set up in Northern Ireland along the lines envisaged by the Government of Ireland Act 1920.

The *de facto* first Irish Parliament then became the *de jure* governing body of what was then known as the Irish Free State and is now the Republic of Ireland. In October 1922 it adopted a written Constitution, which remained in force until 1937, when a new Constitution was adopted by a referendum. This

Constitution is still in force, albeit subject to a number of amendments over the years.

THE 1922 CONSTITUTION

The 1922 Constitution arose from the treaty signed in 1921 and indeed contained a provision whereby it could not be amended in any way that would conflict with the treaty. I only propose to deal with one specific provision, simply because it differed fundamentally from the 1937 Constitution. Article 50 of the 1921 Constitution provided that it could be amended by a resolution passed by both Houses of Parliament by way of ordinary legislation for the first eight years for which it was to be in force and that thereafter any such amendment would have to be approved by a referendum. During the eighth year of its life, the legislature purported to use this provision to amend Article 50 itself, and extended the period during which the Constitution could be amended by the legislature alone for a further eight years. This was in fact challenged in the courts, but by a majority decision of the Supreme Court in *The State (Ryan) v. Lennon* [1935] I.R.170 it was held that using the provisions of Article 50 to amend that Article itself was a valid constitutional amendment, and that the Government of the day had successfully postponed the necessity to amend by referendum for a further eight years. The 16 years had just expired when the 1937 Constitution was passed, and it was voted on by way of referendum. In contrast to the 1921 Constitution, it contains a provision whereby after the first three years the only method of amendment is by way of referendum, thus taking the Constitution out of the control of the legislature.

The administration of the State in 1937

When the Irish Free State was set up in 1922 the Constitution contained a provision whereby all pre-existing Westminster Statutes applying to Ireland would remain in force unless repealed by the new Irish Parliament or unless they were in conflict with the provisions of the 1922 Constitution. There was also in existence a detailed administrative system largely based on the United Kingdom model, most of which again was continued under the control of ministries set up by the new Parliament. By 1937 this administrative system was firmly established on the new basis, and although there had been a considerable amount of legislation since 1921, there still was a large body of statute law dating from the Westminster Parliament. The 1937 Constitution again provided that all existing laws, and this included pre-1922 legislation, should be carried over and remain valid under the new Constitution, unless it conflicted with any provision thereof. Thus there was in fact a reasonably efficient changeover from the British administration to the post-1922 Irish administration, and then to the post 1937 administration.

THE 1937 CONSTITUTION

The preamble to the Constitution

The 1937 Constitution contains a preamble which, while not strictly speaking part of the Constitution, nevertheless reflects the religious and historical background and also reflects what was for the time a very forward-looking view of social justice. The preamble reads:

> "In the Name of the Most Holy Trinity, from Whom is all authority and to Whom, as our final end, all actions both of men and states must be referred, We, the people of Eire, Humbly acknowledging all our obligations to our Divine Lord, Jesus Christ, Who sustained our Fathers through centuries of trial, Gratefully remembering their heroic and unremitting struggle to regain the rightful independence of our Nation, And seeking to promote the common good, with due observance of prudence, justice and charity, so that the dignity and freedom of the individual may be assured, true social order attained, the unity of our Country restored, and concord established with other Nations, Do hereby adopt, enact and give to ourselves this Constitution."

The religious references in the first part of the preamble clearly reflect the general Christian principles which strongly influenced the Constitution, but the Constitution itself is clearly not restricted to safeguarding Christian denominations. Article 44.1 provides that the State shall respect and honour religion, and this provision has been held to cover all religions, whether Christian or otherwise (*Quinns Supermarket Ltd v. Attorney General* [1972] I.R. 1).

The Constitution also contains provisions in further parts of Article 44 guaranteeing the free profession and practice of religion, prohibiting the endowing of any religion by the State, and prohibiting the State from imposing any disabilities or making any discrimination on the grounds of religious profession belief or status. While these were admirable general provisions covering all professions of religion, the Constitution also contained a much more contentious provision, which was frequently cited by the people of Northern Ireland as justifying their fears had they become part of a United Ireland. Portions of Articles read as follows:

> "2. The State recognises the special position of the Holy Catholic Apostolic and Roman Church as the guardian of the faith professed by the great majority of the citizens.

3. The State also recognises the Church of Ireland, the Presbyterian Church in Ireland, the Methodist Church in Ireland, the Religious Society of Friends in Ireland, as well as the Jewish Congregations and the other religious denominations existing in Ireland at the date of the coming into operation of this Constitution."

This acknowledgement of the special position of the Roman Catholic Church reflects the influence that that Church held in 1937, for, interestingly enough, there was no equivalent provision in the 1922 Constitution. However, perhaps due to the weakening of the power of the Church, and in fairness to the liberalisation of the outlook of the Roman Catholic Church, these provisions were deleted in 1972 by a referendum in which the electorate passed the amendment deleting these provisions by a majority of over five to one.

The other forward-looking provision of the preamble that calls for comment is the reference to the promotion of the common good and also to the dignity and freedom of the individual and to the maintaining of true social order. While this provision may not be part of the Constitution, it has been regarded by the courts on a number of occasions as indicating the objectives of the Constitution, and has been considered particularly relevant in the ongoing interpretation of the Constitution, and the relationship of the Constitution to changing values. This was firmly put most clearly by O'Higgins C.J. in *The State (Healy) v. Donohue* [1976] I.R. 325, where he said:

> "In my view, (the) preamble makes it clear that rights given by the Constitution must be considered in accordance with concepts of prudence, justice and charity which may gradually change or develop as society changes accordance with prevailing ideas. The preamble envisages a Constitution which can absorb or be adapted to such changes. In other words, the Constitution did not seek to impose for all time the ideas prevalent or accepted with regard to these virtues at the time of its enactment."

The Institutions of State

The 1937 Constitution provides for the election of a President, which was an office created by that Constitution and which did not exist under the 1922 Constitution. This is largely a ceremonial office, although a number of specific functions of the President are set out in Article 13. Most of these functions are formal, and only exercisable on the advice of the Government. There are really only two matters on which the President has total discretion. The first of these is that he or she may refuse to dissolve the Parliament even thought the Government has lost the support of the majority of members, and the second is that the President may refer any Bill passed by both Houses of Parliament to the Supreme Court for the consideration by that Court as to whether the Bill, or some parts of the Bill, are in conflict with the Constitution. This latter power has been exercised on a number of occasions, at times to the intense embarrassment of the Government, and is a power which has been taken very seriously by successive holders of the position.

The Constitution also provides for two Houses of Parliament, the lower house being elected under a form of proportional representation and an upper house consisting of 60 members, 11 of whom are nominated by the Prime Minister, six of whom are nominated by universities and the remainder of whom are elected in a rather complicated manner from five panels of candidates, each representing certain interests. While the upper house or Seanad has little or no ultimate power, and in this regard is somewhat similar to the House of Lords in England, nevertheless it does at times perform a very useful service in acting as a watchdog over the actions of the lower house, and frequently brings a new and fresh perspective to proposed legislation.

The Constitution also provides for a Government, which exercises the executive power of the State, and for the appointment of an Attorney General as a legal adviser to the Government, but who cannot be a member of the Government. The Attorney General is also seen as the protector of the Constitution, and must be joined as a party in any proceedings in which it is sought to challenge the constitutionality of any legislation or an important point of constitutional interpretation is raised.

The Courts

The Constitution does not attempt to detail the entire court structure but merely provides that justice shall be administered in courts established by law. It does, however, go on to provide that such courts shall include a High Court invested with full jurisdiction and power to determine all matters and questions, whether of law or fact, civil or criminal; it also provides for a Supreme Court as the ultimate court of appeal. There are in fact two strata of courts below the High Court, namely the District Court, which has a very limited jurisdiction both in civil and criminal cases but is a very much a local court, and the Circuit Court, which has a jurisdiction to hear civil actions with claims up to £30,000 and a wide criminal jurisdiction in all matters except murder, rape and treason.

The appointment of judges is also dealt with, as, more importantly, is their independence. All judges are appointed by the President on the advice of the Government, and the President has no power to refuse to make such appointment. Thus, at least initially, it can be said that the appointment of judges is a political act of the Government. However, the Constitution goes on to provide that all judges are to be independent in the exercise of their judicial functions and that no judge may be a member of either house of Parliament. Most importantly, it provides for security of tenure of a judge of the Supreme Court or

High Court, who cannot be removed from office except for stated misbehaviour or incapacity, and then only on resolutions passed by each house, something which has never occurred. There is also a constitutional provision that the remuneration of a judge shall not be reduced during his continuance in office, thus preventing the State from applying financial pressure to a judge, which might influence decisions.

Separation of Powers

While the Constitution refers to three specific types of powers, namely legislative, executive and judicial, it does not expressly provide for a separation of powers. However, it has been frequently stated by the courts that the separation of powers does exist. My own view is that the scales are very much tipped in favour of the courts, in that the courts interpret legislation, although of course the legislature may subsequently pass amending legislation giving a different interpretation. The courts also have the power to declare legislation to be unconstitutional. This is because the courts have been appointed as the guardians of the Constitution to some degree, and the ultimate power in relation to the constitutionality of legislation is undoubtedly vested in the courts. Similarly, the courts have power to review executive functions and actions by way of judicial review and to invalidate them if they are inconsistent with any constitutional right of an individual or with the concept of natural justice. The courts have in fact been very careful not to abuse powers: they have refused to intervene on a number of occasions, and it may well be said that the courts have exercised a self-imposed separation of powers which is considerably greater than that imposed by the Constitution. For example, in *Roland v. An Taoiseach* [1974] I.R. 338 Fitzgerald C.J. said that:

> "The courts have no power either expressed or implied to supervise or interfere with the exercise by the Government of its executive functions, unless the circumstances are such as to amount to a clear disregard by the Government of the powers and duties conferred upon it by the Constitution."

Of course, the introduction of any form of separation of powers into Ireland is an innovation as compared with the pre-1922 situation. For many centuries, the United Kingdom had operated initially on the basis that "the King can do no wrong" and later perhaps more on the basis that the Parliament can do no wrong. There is no doubt that up to 1922 power was ultimately vested in Westminster, and while the courts administered the laws passed by the Parliament, there was no power in the court to invalidate any laws or any actions of the executive, provided those actions were in accordance with the legislative provisions. The idea of the courts as the guardian of the Constitutional rights of a citizen is one which, certainly in 1937, would have found little support in the United Kingdom.

Personal Rights

Finally, the Constitution deals with fundamental personal rights. Two general Articles form the basis of the protection of individual rights, and it is probably worth quoting them in full.

Article 40.3 reads as follows:

> "1. The State guarantees in its laws to respect, and, as far as practicable, by its laws to defend and vindicate the personal rights of the citizen.

> 2. The State shall, in particular, by its laws protect as best it may from unjust attack and, in the case of injustice done, vindicate the life, person, good name and proper rights of every citizen."

Article 43 reads as follows:-

> "1.1 The State acknowledges that man, in virtue of his rational being, has the natural right antecedent to positive law, to the private ownership of external goods.

> 2. The State accordingly guarantees to pass no laws attempting to abolish the right of private ownership or the general right to transfer, bequeath, and inherit property.

> 2.1 The State recognises, however, that the exercise of the rights mentioned in the foregoing provisions of this article ought, in civil society, to be regulated by the principals of social justice.

> 2. The State, accordingly may as occasion requires delimit by law the exercise of the said rights with a view to reconciling their exercise with the exigencies of the common good."

It can be seen that these general provisions do not confer absolute rights on anybody. The use of the words "as far as practicable", "as best it may" and "the exigencies of the common good" make it quite clear that there may be circumstances in which individual fundamental rights will not be enforced. This, of course, is taking a very practical attitude; but it is also leaving it very open to the courts to deal with individual cases in accordance with individual circumstances, and in particular to act in accordance with the social and moral ethos of the times. Indeed, it probably enforces the view that the Constitution was not intended to remain static, but could be interpreted in accordance with changing circumstances.

In addition to these general rights, the Constitution deals with the right to life of the unborn, the right to personal liberties (save in accordance with the law, including the habeas corpus procedure), the inviolability of a dwelling, freedom of expression, freedom of assembly and of association, and religious freedom. There are also interesting Articles dealing with the family and education, which rather reflect the ethos of the 1930s rather than of the twenty-first century. There is, for example a provision that:

> "1. In particular, the State recognises that by our life within the home, woman gives to the State a support without which the common good cannot be achieved.
>
> 2. The State shall, therefore, endeavour to ensure that mothers shall not be obliged by economic necessity to engage in labour to the neglect of their duties at home."

One must wonder whether independent-minded housewives of today are anxious for that sort of protection.

In relation to education, there is an obligation to provide free primary education and, perhaps unusually, a provision that parents are to be free to provide education in their homes.

As the constitutional provisions leave a great deal unsaid as to what is or is not a personal right, the courts have taken it on themselves to give a broad interpretation to Article 40.3 and to Article 43, and to extend their guarantee to a number of unspecified rights. These include the right to bodily integrity, the right to work and earn a livelihood, the right to marital privacy and individual privacy, the right of access to the courts, the right to travel and the right to communicate. However, it has at all times been emphasised by the courts that these rights are limited in the fashion set out in Article 40.3, namely that they are only guaranteed as far as practicable, and that protection is only against unjust attack on the rights of the individual.

While the courts have tended to extend the protection given by Article 40.3, they have by and large given a fairly restrictive interpretation to Article 43, which seeks to protect private property There have been a number of conflicting decisions, for example, in relation to statutory provisions restricting property rights without compensation, and indeed recently the Supreme Court upheld the constitutionality of a statutory provision that a local authority may require that up to 20 per cent of a housing development must be allocated for social housing, that is low-cost housing, although this of course will greatly reduce the value of a development site. The basis for this decision, and a number of others of a similar nature, has been that it may be for the common good that property rights be restricted, and changing views of what is the common good probably explain conflicting decisions under this section over the years.

Indeed, one can be forgiven for thinking that the recent decision is primarily due to the fact that house prices in Ireland have nearly doubled in the last five years, making it impossible for many people on low incomes to purchase houses; therefore it is considered in the common good that affordable housing ought to be built for persons on low incomes. Thus does the Constitution keep pace with the times.

Finally, I do not think that this overview could be complete without a mention of the fairly recent amendment to the Constitution, namely article 40.3.3°, which reads as follows:

> "The State acknowledges the right to life of the unborn and with due regard to the equal right to life of the mother, guarantees in its laws to respect, and, as far as practicable, by its laws to defend and vindicate that right.
>
> This subsection shall not limit freedom to travel between the State and another State.
>
> The subsection shall not limit freedom to obtain or make available, in the State subject to such conditions as may be laid down by law, information relating to services lawfully made available in another State."

This amendment and its subsequent interpretations by the Supreme Court, have been the subject matter of an enormous amount of debate in Ireland. The amendment itself arose out of pressure on the Government of the day to bring in a constitutional amendment absolutely outlawing abortion, which had in fact been illegal in any event since 1861. The amendment, which many consider to be badly thought out and badly worded, was brought into the headlines by a very sad case of *The Attorney General v. X* [1992] 1 I.R. 1, where a 14-year-old girl who was pregnant as a result of an alleged rape was a subject matter of an injunction restraining her from travelling to the United Kingdom in order to have an abortion. The injunction was granted in the High Court, but on appeal to the Supreme Court the injunction was lifted. It was alleged in that case that the girl was suicidal, and therefore there was a serious risk to her life. Finlay C.J. said:

> "Such a harmonious interpretation of the Constitution carried out in accordance with concepts of prudence, justice and charity . . . leads me to the conclusion that in vindicating and defending as far as practicable the right of the unborn to life but at the same time giving due regard to the right of the mother to life, the Court must, among the matters to be so regarded, concern itself with the position of the mother within the family group, with persons on whom she is dependant, with, in other in-

stances, persons who are dependant upon her and her interaction with other citizens and members of society in the areas in which her activities occur. Having regard to that conclusion, I am satisfied that the test proposed on behalf of the Attorney General that the life of the unborn could only be terminated if it were established that an inevitable or immediate risk to the life of the mother existed, for the appointments of which a termination of the pregnancy was necessary, insufficiently vindicates the mothers right to life.

I, therefore, conclude that the proper test to be applied is that if it is established as a matter of probability that there is a real and substantial risk to the life, as distinct from the health, of the mother, which can only be avoided by the termination of her pregnancy, such a termination is permissible, having regard to the true interpretation of article 40, section 3, subsection 3 of the Constitution."

Needless to say, this interpretation has given rise to an enormous amount of controversy, with people absolutely opposed to abortion seeking a further constitutional amendment with an absolute ban on abortion, while others believe that the matter should be controlled by legislation, perhaps defining more clearly the limits of when a mother's life can be said to be in danger. I do not intend to go in to the merits of either argument, but it is sufficient to say that, in the way of most governments, successive governments in Ireland have certainly not assisted the controversy, and have taken the common governmental attitude of sitting on their hands and doing nothing.

I hope I have been able to give some flavour of the background to and contents of the Irish Constitution. There are many who believe that after 60 years it will probably be best if a completely new Constitution were drafted, and there is a parliamentary committee sitting which is considering this matter in some detail. I think we may see a new Constitution, but it will probably not be until somewhere near the end of this decade, and in the meantime I believe that our old Constitution, even if a bit outdated, has served us well.

THE RELATIONSHIP OF INTERNATIONAL LAW AND DOMESTIC LAW IN SOUTH AFRICA AND IRELAND: A COMPARATIVE ANALYSIS

DR CLIVE R. SYMMONS[*]

INTRODUCTION

The Interim South African Constitution contained a general provision (section 96d) similar to that in Article 29(3) of the Irish Constitution ("Ireland accepts the generally recognised principles of international as its rule of conduct in its relations with other States"), namely, that there is to be "respect for international law and treaty obligations" thereunder. As now updated in 1996, it also, like the Irish Constitution, contains detailed provisions on the conclusion of treaties (section 231(2)), a topic which has been rightly stated to have an "international law dimension" because it may have an effect on the validity of a treaty obligation where an internal (constitutional) rule has allegedly not been complied with by South Africa.[1] It is proposed to discuss in this context whether a clash between international treaty commitments on the one hand, and constitutional provisions on the other (*i.e.* South African municipal law), could ever happen in the same way as they might have in the Irish *McGimpsey* case,[2] where the Anglo-Irish Agreement was domestically challenged on such a basis. Lastly, it is proposed to discuss the incorporation of treaty law and

---

[*] Research Associate, School of Law, Trinity College, Dublin. This article is based on a paper given in South Africa in September 2000 (at the University of the Western Cape) during a visit by members of the Trinity College School of Law.

[1] D.J. Devine, "The Relationship between International Law and Municipal Law in the light of the Interim South African Constitution 1993" (1995) 44 I.C.L.Q., 1, 7. There is now a "wealth of literature" on the place of international law in the new South African Constitution: see J. Dugard, *International Law: A South African Perspective* (Juta, 2000), p.50, n.44. As Professor Dugard states (p. 51), the previous South African Constitutions made no mention of this matter, and the 1994 (interim) and the 1996 constitutions "are similar in most respects in their treatment of international law". As will be seen, though, this similarity largely disappears in respect of the finalised provisions relating to implementation of treaties in South Africa, in which case, as Professor Dugard comments (pp. 54-55), these provisions (in section 231), influenced by the Namibian Constitution, "departed radically from the pre-1993 position in respect of the treaty-making power and incorporation of treaties".

[2] *McGimpsey v Ireland* [1990] I.L.R.M. 441, discussed in C.R. Symmons, "International Treaty Obligations and the Irish Constitution: the *McGimpsey* Case" (1992) 41 I.C.L.Q. 311.

international customary law into the respective South African and Irish municipal law systems and to note the significant similarities and differences in the two systems.

THE TREATY-MAKING PROCESS

The procedural constitutional provisions on this matter in the South African context are not dissimilar to those in the Irish Constitution, in that they provide for a (generally) clear role for the democratic arm of government in the treaty-making process. In the South African case, the negotiation and signature of a treaty is the prerogative of the executive (the President under section 82(1)(i) of the Interim Constitution and now the "national executive" under section 231(2) of the new 1996 Constitution),[3] in just the same way as does (albeit by implication) the executive arm, the "Government", in Ireland under Articles 28 and 29 of the Irish Constitution.[4] However, as also in Ireland, the South African Parliament has a vital role in the ratification or accession process here. In this respect section 231(2) of the Interim South African Constitution (1994) stated:

> "Parliament shall, subject to this Constitution, be competent to agree to the ratification or accession to an international agreement negotiated and signed in terms of section 82(1)(I)."[5]

This has now been changed in the new (1996) Constitution to read:

> "An international agreement binds the Republic only after it has been approved by resolution in both the National Assembly and the National Council of Provinces, unless it is an agreement referred to in subsection (3)."

---

[3] s. 231(1) states that "the negotiating and signing of all international agreements is the responsibility of the national executive".

[4] This states, for example, in Art. 28.2, that the "executive power of the State shall, subject to the provisions of [the] Constitution, be exercised by or on the authority of the Government". Art. 29.4.1° states that the "executive power of the State in or in connection with its external relations shall in accordance with Article 28 . . . be exercised by or on the authority of the Government". These two sets of provision were interpreted in *Crotty v. An Taioseach* [1987] I.L.R.M. 400 as indicating that the conduct of foreign affairs was the prerogative of the Government alone, but with Dáil Éireann having the "primary control" over the Government entering into international agreements under Art. 29 (*ibid.* at p. 450). Otherwise, as Walsh J. stated in *Crotty*, (at p. 454), the Dáil has no part to play in the treaty-making process as it is "the Government alone which negotiates and makes treaties".

[5] For the latter provisions, see above n.3.

Subsection (3) (of the same section) in turn states:

> "An international agreement of a technical, administrative or executive nature, or an agreement which does not require either ratification or accession, entered into by the national executive, binds the Republic without approval by the National Assembly and the National Council of Provinces, but must be tabled in the Assembly and the Council within a reasonable time."

Although now only of historical interest, one past commentator on section 231(2) of the Interim Constitution interpreted the word "agree" here as being (in part at least) similar to the process in Article 29.5.1° of the Irish Constitution whereby "every international agreement to which [Ireland] is a party shall be laid before Dáil Éireann".[6] This, however, is only partially so, as in this (more general) instance the Irish legislative body's role is purely consultative[7] and does not even entitle the Dáil to vote for approval of a treaty. The same commentator opined that the word "agree" simply implied that the South African parliament must affirmatively vote on the issue; and that no actual legislative act is required to "arm the executive with the municipal law power to ratify or accede [to a treaty] on behalf of the Republic".[8]

Fortunately, this matter has now been clarified by sections 231(2) and 231(3) of the new (1996) Constitution, as seen above. This requires specific approval (by vote) of the more important types of treaties, that is, "by resolution" in two representative bodies, the National Assembly and the National Council of Provinces. Although it is not specifically stated, it seems to follow logically that such approval should precede rather than follow any act of ratification or accession by the national executive, if only to avoid the embarrassment of a "*McGimpsey*-type" situation in South Africa (see below).

The South African provisions give an enhanced role to the legislature in the treaty process compared to Ireland, as the Irish Dáil is powerless to prevent further executive action for every type of treaty; and indeed, if the treaty is of a "technical and administrative" nature, the Dáil need not even be consulted at all prior (or subsequent) to ratification,[9] even if the treaty makes a charge on "public funds".

Ironically, in the new (1996) Constitution, as seen above, South Africa has adopted a somewhat "copycat" provision to that in existence in Ireland, which

---

[6] Devine, above, n.1 at p.8.
[7] See C.R. Symmons, "Ireland" in P.M. Eisemann, *The Integration of International and European Community Law into the National Legal Order: A Study of Practice in Europe* (Kluwer, 1996), pp. 317, 318, 323.
[8] Devine, above, n.1 at p.8.
[9] See *The People (Attorney-General) v. Gilliland* [1987] I.L.R.M. 287-288 (hereafter the *Gilliland* case) and Symmons, *op. cit.*, above, n.7 at p.322.

dispenses with "approval" by either of the two parliamentary bodies specified bodies – the National Assembly or National Council of Provinces – where a treaty is of a "technical, administrative or executive nature".[10] The new provision also extends this proviso where a treaty does not require "either ratification or accession". This latter wording clarifies the previous position under the Interim Constitution, which omitted to deal with the situation where a treaty is binding simply on signature.[11] Professor Dugard informs us as to the reason for this change: the interim solution "took no account of the fact that many treaties are intended to come into operation immediately and that slow parliamentary ratification would undermine the value of such treaties".[12]

There are some uncertainties in this new South African process relating to the (generally) less important type of treaties (officially described as "agreements of a routine nature, flowing from the daily activities of government departments").[13] Although the word "tabled" seems reasonably clear in this context, implying a simple laying of the proposed treaty before the relevant bodies (in similar fashion to such treaties having to be "laid before [the Dáil]" under Article 29.5.1° of the Irish Constitution),[14] it is not wholly clear whether this must be prospectively or retrospectively done (*i.e.* before or after signature, ratification, etc., as the case may be). On balance, the phrase "within a reasonable time" suggests that this will normally be done retrospectively to any executive action (*i.e.* after – and dating from – the time of signature, ratification or accession as the case may be), though inherent ambiguities reside in the very meaning of "reasonable time".

It is also not wholly clear what the legal effect will be of a failure by the executive to take such consultative action within a reasonable time (or at all). Will such procedural failures prevent any binding effect for a treaty in such an instance where any "approval" process is constitutionally dispensed with? This matter has never been judicially determined in Ireland.[15] On balance, the word "but" placed in the 1996 South African Constitution before the mandatorily worded phrase "*must* be tabled", and the preceding phrase "*binds* the Republic without approval" (emphases added), implies that such omissions will be fatal to any international effect for such treaties.

In fact, in the Irish context, it is only where the treaty creates a "charge upon public funds" that the Dáil must give its actual approval[16] and the *Gilliland*

---

[10]Similar terms used in the Irish Constitution have never been interpreted by the courts. Indeed, they could give rise to ambiguity if only because the phrase "technical and administrative" is used *conjunctively*, and not disjunctively, as in the South African situation.

[11]See below, n.16.

[12]See above, n.1 at p.56

[13]See M. Oliver, "Informal International Agreements under the 1996 Constitution" (1997) 22 S.A.Y.I.L. 63, 64.

[14]See Symmons in Eisemann, *op. cit.* at p.323.

[15]See *ibid.*, at p.326 and M. Forde, *Constitutional Law of Ireland* (1987), p.203.

[16]*cf.* Devine, above, n.1 at p.8

case in 1986[17] has shown what importance this may have. As Article 29.5.2°
says:

> "The State shall not be bound by any international agreement [unless of
> a technical and administrative nature under Article 29.5.3°[18] involving a
> charge upon public funds] unless the terms of the agreement shall have
> been approved by Dáil Éireann."

In this case, the Irish Supreme Court found that a bilateral extradition treaty
between Ireland and the USA had not been approved by the Dáil (as it should
have been) because it was a treaty involving a charge on public funds. I have
discussed elsewhere the question of whether the treaty remained binding on
the State despite this, or whether it merely remained domestically uneffective.[19]
The Supreme Court was unclear on this, but one judge at least stated that
Ireland was "not bound".[20] The subsequent Irish action of passing a (much
later) special motion and submitting the treaty to re-ratification (as was also
done in the case of other similar extradition treaties) implies that the treaty
was considered internationally invalid as it stood.[21] The case also clarifies that
the Dáil must give expression to this by approval in a special motion referring
to the treaty in question. In the context of the new South African Constitution
of 1996, a similar process of voting would presumably apply in section 231(2).

It seems, though, to be unlikely that in the South African context a *Gilliland*-
type situation could arise. Even under the Interim Constitution, the (former)
all-embracing initial requirement of parliamentary agreement to the ratification of, or accession to, all types of (post-constitution[22]) treaties, not just of
select and specified ones as in the Irish context, seemed to rule out such a
possibility. Such a situation might only arise now in South Africa post-1996 in
the case of a mistaken categorisation of those treaties now "excepted" from
the normal "approval" process, (*i.e.* those of a technical or administrative character, etc.).[23] Even so, it may be noted parenthetically that in Ireland, since

---

[17] See above, n.9.
[18] See Symmons, *op. cit.*, above, n.7 at p.322.
[19] *ibid.*, at p.326.
[20] above, n.9 at p.289 (Finlay C.J.).
[21] Symmons, *op. cit.*, above, n.7 at p.327.
[22] See section 231(5) of the new (1996) Constitution, which says "The Republic is bound by
international agreements which were binding on the Republic when this Constitution took
effect". On treaties to which South Africa purported to become a party (prior to April 27,
1994), see Devine, above, n.1 at p.11 ("the 'old' South African law still applies to them").
[23] The other excepted situation – in effect residual agreements such as treaties binding merely on
signature – are unlikely to cause interpretation problems. Treaties binding on mere signature
seemed not to be dealt with under the Interim Constitution: see J. Dugard, in D. Van Wyk, J.
Dugard, B. de Villiers, and D. Davis (eds), *Rights and Constitutionalism: The New South
African Legal Order* (OUP, 1996) pp.171, 192, n.103, citing *S. v. Eliasov* (1967) (4) S.A. 583
(A).

Gilliland, most treaties now tend to be put through the more formal "Article
29.5.2°" procedure, if only *ex abundanti cautela* (in case they should incur
relevant public expense). The recent review of the Constitution[24] has recommended expanding parliamentary intervention in this area; namely, that Article 29.5.3° be amended to make it clear that even technical and administrative
agreements should require prior Dáil approval where they involve a charge on
public funds. It is interesting to note that in South African practice, there has
been a similar official approach suggested, namely, that if there is any doubt
as to whether an agreement falls under section 231((3), "the longer, parliamentary route should be followed".[25]

As potentially in the Irish situation, these types of agreements may give
rise in South Africa to disputes about the meaning of "technical, administrative or executive"; though, as Professor Dugard has commented, whether agreements fall into such categories is ultimately a question of "intention"; and that
where "parties intend that an agreement is to come into force immediately
without ratification at the international level, it would be ridiculous for the
South African Parliament to insist on parliamentary approval".[26]

Under the Interim South African Constitution, serious ambiguities also
resided both in respect of the meaning of the phrase "agreement of Parliament" in section 231(2) thereof and also in respect of the consequential legal
effect of this wording. On this issue, Professor Devine opined that this wording did not require a "legislative act" but merely an affirmative "resolution" of
Parliament;[27] and he stated that such a resolution would not only empower the
South African executive to proceed with the ratification or accession process[28] but would also, following such ratification or accession, make the treaty
"binding on South Africa *as a matter of international law*".[29] It is true that on
this important matter, the subsequent section, section 231(3) of the Interim
Constitution, seemed to add some ambiguity by inserting additional wording
which might, on a loose reading, have interconnected with this process, namely,
that Parliament must "expressly so provide"; and Professor Devine interpreted
the word "provides" as implying a different process, namely, a "legislative
act".[30] So he maintained that this additional provision in the old section 231(3)
meant that "a [further] *legislative* act" might still be required before a treaty
"binds" South Africa internationally.

Although now only of historical interest, a fundamental ambiguity seemed

---

[24] See *Report of the Constitution Review Group*, May 1996, p.119.
[25] See *op. cit.*, above, n.1 at p.57.
[26] *ibid.* at pp. 56-57.
[27] See above, n.1 at p.8.
[28] As seen above, these matters are within the prerogative of the "national executive".
[29] See above, n.1 at p.8. Unfortunately, in the very next sentence, Professor Devine seems to
contradict this by saying that this process alone is "not enough to make the treaty *binding on
South Africa internationally*" (emphasis added).
[30] *ibid.* at p.8.

then to reside in the context of a treaty becoming "binding" in former section 231(3). Professor Devine appears to have interpreted the combined effect of former sections 213(2) and 213(3) as requiring a two-fold parliamentary intervention for international effect[31] and in *two* possibly different forms: first (as seen) through the "agreement" of parliament to ratification and *"thereafter* [through] confirmation by Act of Parliament if [the treaties] are to be *binding in international law"* (emphasis added).[32] On this writer's view as an outside observer, such a suggested two-fold competence was, even then, debatable, as subsections (2) and (3) seemed in large part to merely complement and reinforce each other, with subsection (3) arguably adding no further parliamentary competence relating to the matter of international validity; as the concluding phrases ("provided Parliament expressly so provides" and "such agreement" having to be not "inconsistent with [the] Constitution"), seemed to more qualify the immediately preceding wording as to internal implementation rather than the more detached antecedent wording as to international obligatoriness ("shall be binding"). Much here depended on whether the word "agreement" related back and had the same meaning as the word "agreement" in section 2(2)[33] or whether it qualified the immediately proceeding phrase "so provides" and so meant a different (and secondary) type of "agreement". In this writer's opinion, the latter interpretation was the only viable one.

Professor Dugard seems, in the past at least, to have ostensibly supported my own reading of this Interim Constitution matter; namely, that, even prior to 1996, only one parliamentary act of agreement was constitutionally necessary for giving international effect to a treaty and that this process involved simply prospective parliamentary approval, not retrospective approval as well. For he has commented in the past that treaties will not become binding on South Africa unless "ratified by Parliament" under section 231(2), (*i.e.* not section 231(3)).[34] This process, he said, could, for example, result in South Africa becoming party to the major human rights conventions "without incorporating them into domestic law".[35] Indeed, Professor Devine's statement relating to the Interim Constitution,[36] namely, that the "agreement" of Parliament "is not ... enough *to make a treaty binding on South Africa internationally"*(emphasis

---

[31] *ibid.* at p.7.

[32] See also *ibid.*, at p.7 where he says that "Parliament retains the power to provide that an existing treaty does not bind the Republic" by a *legislative* act.

[33] See Devine who opines that "agreement" and "approval" (*sic*) under the relevant two subsections of s.231 mean the "same thing" (*ibid.* at p.10, n.61); but, in fact the term "approved" or "approval" is not used at all – the critical additional term being, as seen, "provides". The word "agreement" might even be related back to the earlier reference to "*international* agreement" (emphasis added) and be interpreted as a shorthand version of this, so meaning simply a treaty; but, this seems unlikely because of the absence either of the word "an" before it or the qualificatory term such as "international".

[34] In Van Wyk *et al.*, above, n.23 at p.192.

[35] *ibid.* (emphasis added).

[36] above, n.1 at p.8.

added), seems to somewhat contradict a previous statement of his, namely,
that merely on ratification or accession a treaty would become binding on
South Africa "*as a matter of international law*" where Parliament has "armed
the executive authority" with its "agreement" to same[37] (and this seems to be
implicitly reinforced by his later statement[38] that "section 231(3) does prevent
[unconstitutional] treaties from being binding or being translated at the *municipal law* level").

Fortunately, any past academic viewpoints on this matter can now be laid
to rest, as the new section 231(2) in the 1996 Constitution is abundantly clear
on this issue when it says (as seen) that an "international agreement" only
"binds" South Africa "after it has been approved by resolution" in both relevant bodies(emphasis added). Thus, in future a treaty requiring ratification
or accession (and of a non-technical, non-administrative or non-executive nature under section 231(3)(see above)) will only be internationally binding on
South Africa if it has received a majority vote both in the National Assembly
and the National Council of Provinces and seemingly, from a timing perspective, *if* this approval has been given *in advance* of such ratification or accession by the executive, as the phrase "*only* after" (emphasis added) tends to
infer. Professor Dugard has recently commented that although this new provision will "ensure that Parliament will continue to play an active role in treaty-
making", it is nonetheless "unfortunate that the realities of the bureaucratic
process compelled the Constitutional Assembly to require an 'Act of Parliament' or other form of 'national legislation", in addition to the resolution of
ratification, for the incorporation of treaties into municipal law"; and that this
"represent[s] an abandonment of the idealism of 1993 that sought "to bring
international law and domestic law in harmony with each other".[39]

THE POSSIBILITY OF CONSTITUTIONAL CHALLENGE TO (BINDING) TREATIES

Under the Interim Constitution, and the former section 231 parliamentary process which, if followed by executive ratification or accession,[40] made a treaty
internationally binding on South Africa, there might have been even more
obvious scope than in Ireland for a potential clash between international law
and the (then) South African constitutional (*i.e.* domestic) law. For the old
section 231(3) had as one of its two provisos the stipulation that any treaty

---

[37] *ibid.*
[38] *ibid.* at p.10 (emphasis added).
[39] *Op. cit.*, above, n.1 at 56. He adds (*ibid.* at p.55) that the "clear purpose" of the interim
constitution was to facilitate the incorporation of treaties into municipal law, but that Government bureaucracy in terms of scrutiny of treaties prior to submission to Parliament meant that
"few treaties were referred to Parliament expeditiously".
[40] *ibid.* at p.8, fn.57.

provisions should explicitly not be "inconsistent with [the] Constitution". Professor Devine seems to interpret this as meaning that a treaty would not have been "binding" (seemingly internationally) "insofar as it conflict[ed] with the Constitution".[41] Such an interpretation, if true, could also have led to a possible replay in South Africa of the Irish *McGimpsey* case, wherein the Anglo Irish Agreement – a fully consummated treaty (having been signed, ratified and deposited with the UN Secretary-General by both Governments), was thereafter challenged in the Irish courts as being invalid for allegedly infringing certain substantive provisions of the Irish Constitution.[42] The Irish Supreme Court (whilst implicitly accepting (see below) the competence of individuals to make such a late challenge to a binding treaty) in fact found that there was no infringement of the two cited aspects of the constitutional provisions.[43] It seems clear that even under the 1996 Constitution, a treaty that has been actually signed and ratified will be binding "on the international plane", so the *McGimpsey*-type problems might potentially occur.[44]

There is in fact no express provision in the Irish Constitution permitting an individual to challenge a treaty for unconstitutionality,[45] so that in Ireland such a right has been implied on an analogy with a similar challenge to an alleged unconstitutional statute (this also seems to be the South African position: see section 172 of the 1996 Constitution). However, unlike the pre-1996 South African situation, there is nothing in the Irish Constitution that expressly restricts the legislature's powers – limited as they are – in respect of the treaty-making process specifically on the basis that a treaty is contrary to a provision or provisions of the Constitution generally. Nonetheless, in *McGimpsey* the most surprising aspect of the Supreme Court judgment (as this writer has extensively discussed elsewhere[46]) was that, by implication at least, an individual could challenge a ratified – and therefore internationally-binding – treaty. This implication was not on all fours with previous Irish precedent, in particular, the *Boland* case,[47] which concerned merely a non-binding intergovernmental agreement,[48] and the famous *Crotty* case.[49] The latter, a challenge to the Sin-

---

[41] *ibid.* at p.9.

[42] See Symmons, *above*, n.2 at p.311.

[43] *ibid.* at pp.312-318.

[44] See Dugard., *op. cit.*, above, n.1 at p. 58 who says that in this context, South Africa *could* incur responsibility "towards other signatory States".

[45] *ibid.* at p.319, n.45.

[46] above, n.2.

[47] *Boland v. An Taioseach* [1971] I.R. 371

[48] See Symmons, above, n.2 at p.320. It is somewhat unclear whether *non-binding* intergovernmental agreements such as memoranda of understanding are wholly covered by the phrase "of an executive nature" (a phrase not, incidentally, contained in the Irish constitutional version of a similar provision) in s.213(3) of the 1996 South African Constitution and so have to be "tabled" before the relevant bodies. It seems, though, that the use of the word "binds" earlier in this subsection means that such non-binding agreements need not be subjected to such a process.

gle European Act was also very different from the *McGimpsey* situation, as there the final act to make it binding (*i.e.* deposit of ratification) had not yet taken place at the time of legal challenge.

As the writer has stated elsewhere, had the *McGimpsey* challenge succeeded on its (substantive) arguments, the Irish Government would have been in the classic dilemma of choosing between the principle of *pacta sunt servanda* on the one hand or the pre-emptive superior application of its Constitution on the other[50] and so being in technical breach of international law. Such a latter situation would surely be one which the courts of most states would, in any litigated case, tend to peremptorily dismiss because of potentially far-reaching effects on the binding quality of treaty law.[51]

The only "escape routes" from such a legal dilemma would be, in the Irish context, to make the relevant changes to the Constitution by referendum (presupposing the referendum was successful)[52] if the alleged constitutional breach concerned substantive provisions. Or, if the alleged infringements were purely procedural (*i.e.* the omission of Dáil approval for the treaty where a treaty or agreement involved a "charge on public funds", the effect of failure to lay a treaty before the Dáil under Article 29.5.1° having never been determined,[53] an *ex post facto* remedying of the defect by later Dáil motion (accompanied by possible re-ratification or re-deposit of the treaty as happened post-*Gilliland*[54]) could remedy the defect *ex post facto*. Other alternatives include renegotiation (or worse, attempted denunciation) of the treaty to comply with the constitution; or, controversially, it might be possible to rely on Article 46 of the Vienna Convention on Treaties on the basis that the treaty was not binding for allegedly infringing a provision of its internal law regarding competence to conclude treaties where the "violation was manifest and concerned a rule of its internal law of fundamental importance".[55]

It has been suggested in the South African context that a similar dilemma might have arisen under the Interim Constitution,[56] because of the provisions of former section 231(3) and on the basis[57] that the South African Parliament would be "incompetent to make an unconstitutional treaty binding in municipal law *or* to translate such a treaty into South African law".[58] In this instance, the former express blanket-type proviso forbidding inconsistency with South African constitutional provisions did indeed open up the vista of a post-

---

[49]above, n.4.
[50]above, n.2 at p.339.
[51]As, *e.g.* in Colombia in the *Reyes* case (see Symmons, above, n.2 at p.341, n.154).
[52]See Symmons, above, n.2 at p.328.
[53]See Symmons, *op. cit.*, above, n.7 at p.326.
[54]*ibid.* at pp.322, 327.
[55]*ibid.* at 329.
[56]Devine, above, n.1 at p.11.
[57]*ibid.* at p.10.
[58]*ibid.*

ratification challenge to an already binding treaty,[59] on the basis even of alleged breaches of substantive provisions of its Constitution rather than the merely procedurally-oriented aspect in section 231(2). There was, and is now, nothing in the South African Constitution that expressly forbids such a domestic challenge. Indeed, the reference here to inconsistency with the "Constitution" in former section 231(3) might even be interpreted as impliedly allowing it.

Even under the Interim Constitution, however, there might, in the South African context, have been no possibility of *ex post facto* rectifying any such subsequently alleged constitutional defect on a procedural matter alone if the executive organ has already proceeded to ratification following previous parliamentary "agreement" to same. In relation to the time requirement for parliamentary intervention in the treaty process, the former section 231(2) seemed to presuppose that positive antecedent parliamentary consent had happened by this stage and without any reference now to matters of unconstitutionality in this context. This situation is perhaps even clearer under section 231(2) of the 1996 Constitution which, as seen, expressly appears to presuppose that both the National Assembly and the National Council of Provinces have positively approved a treaty prior to ratification or accession.

This would mean that a later remedial parliamentary vote,[60] which attempts to remedy a previous procedural constitutional defect (as effectively happened in the Irish scenario in *Gilliland*, a pure omission situation), might not be legally effective in the South African situation where Parliament (which includes, under section 42(1) the Council of Provinces) has actively assented prior to executive action. As seen, under the Interim South African Constitution, an alleged constitutional defect could have included obviously substantive constitutional provisions as well.[61]

It seems likely now, however, in the light of new and clear wording on the binding effect of a treaty in the 1996 Constitution, that a South African court would refuse *locus standi* to any post-ratification domestic challenger of the treaty itself on *pacta sunt servanda* grounds for fear of finding the actual treaty retrospectively invalid for constitutional reasons. This is particularly so now because the former blanket-type reference to "inconsistency with the Constitution" has been excised in the 1996 Constitution and now only makes an appearance in connection with "self-executing" treaty provisions (section 231(4)).

Even if a domestic challenge to a treaty for constitutional infringement were to be allowed in South Africa and was successful, the courts there would surely (as seems implicit in Irish case law such as *Gilliland*) assume a "half-

---

[59] See above, n.33.

[60] See Symmons, above, n.2 at p.322.

[61] In fact, as Devine points out (above, n.1 at p.9), albeit in the context of Article 46 of the Vienna Convention on Treaties, there could theoretically be a breach of any of 200-plus articles in the Constitution!

way" house position in such a case and simply declare the legislation (or statutory instrument) based on the treaty, if any, as being domestically invalid, so preserving the international obligations of South Africa in the matter. Such an eventuality is implicit in the new subsection 4 of section 231, which says that an international agreement "becomes *law in the Republic*" (emphasis added) (rather than, for example, "binding on the Republic") unless it is "inconsistent with the Constitution or an Act of Parliament".

Indeed, even under the interim constitutional provisions, Professor Devine seemed to come to this conclusion, referring, as seen above, to invalidity in terms of "municipal law". In this context he stated:[62]

> "It would appear to be quite clear ... that [former] section 231(3) does prevent [unconstitutional] treaties being binding or being translated at the *municipal* level. If, therefore, a treaty conflicts with the substantive provisions of the Constitution, it would be possible to *challenge the legislation* incorporating it into municipal law, *and this is so even if the treaty is binding on South Africa as a matter of international law*. This situation is one which creates a dilemma in that respect for international obligations may be incompatible with the Constitution and vice versa." (emphasis added)

With this general interpretation on mere domestic invalidity – which is still of relevance to the post-1996 situation – the present writer agrees, though the problem here discussed under the Interim Constitution does not seem to approximate to the same one that Ireland faced in *McGimpsey*, where the instrument challenged (post-ratification) was the treaty itself and not (as seemingly, in the case of *Gilliland*) the legislation or statutory instruments dependent on such treaty (indeed there was no such Irish legislation in existence at the time relating to the treaty in question, the Anglo-Irish Agreement). In the South African context, especially if, as suggested below, section 231(3) of the Interim Constitution required legislation simply and solely for internal South African implementation of treaty law, surely what would effectively have been challenged on the domestic plane under any (former) section 213(3) proceedings would have been a provision or provisions of the dependant legislation rather than the content of the treaty itself. Assuredly, any litigation resulting in such a "domestic blockage" to what are international commitments – such as in the field of human rights – is destined to make South African implementation of international obligations more difficult (and so possibly lead to a "dilemma"); but such a result is more "fine-tuned" (as compared with the *McGimpsey* situation) in that it theoretically at least keeps alive the international commitment.

---

[62] See above, n.1 at p.10.

It would seem, therefore, both under the old (1994) and new (1996) constitutional provisions, that any internal South African challenge to international validity of an ostensibly "approved" treaty itself – even if based on alleged infringement of the procedural aspects (including now failure to "table" treaties not subject to ratification or of a technical, administrative or executive nature[63]) – would fail because of the international implications of doing so. Here, on the Interim Constitution, Professor Devine rather surprisingly concluded that the whole of (former) section 231(3) of the South African Constitution (as opposed to former section 231(2)) would amount to procedurally "notorious" provisions within the meaning of Article 46 of the Vienna Convention on Treaties. So that, if not observed, "other States cannot hold South Africa to the treaty".[64] This view, however, does not seem to be supported by his also expressed view elsewhere,[65] as seen, that it would be "very doubtful whether section 231(3) could prevent an unconstitutional treaty from operating at the *international* level". Nor, as seen, is it supported by this writer's personal reading of former section 231 as a whole.

Professor Devine's opinion would also seem to have taken international invalidity too far because of the potential breadth of former section 231(3). Although ostensibly procedural in requiring parliamentary "agreement", nonetheless this section – by linkage with the "constitution incompatibility" proviso – indirectly incorporated *all* the constitutional *substantive* considerations into the (essentially) procedural one. Surely another State should not have been put on notice here as regards possible multiple substantive breaches, especially as the legislature itself – unlike in every Irish-based situation – would *ex hypothesi*, at the time of challenge, have affirmatively given the executive the "green light" to proceed with the treaty ratification, with all the trappings of presumptive constitutionality that this entails.

In the case of an alleged "oversight" breach of former section 231(2) alone (*i.e.* simply a procedural breach, whether through absence of the correct form of parliamentary agreement or, more seriously, through breach simply by omission to obtain Parliament's agreement), any discovered constitutional infringement, if retrospectively remediable, might, by contrast, amount to no more than a temporary "blip" to acquisition of binding international effect for a treaty. For in the case of incorrect form of parliamentary agreement, at least,[66] such a defect could possibly have been speedily and retrospectively remedied by a later (correctly performed) parliamentary motion as has happened in Ireland (accompanied by possible re-ratification of a treaty by the executive). Furthermore, such a situation would be unlikely to arise more than once. For once the executive is aware of the exact constitutional requirements (a "once

---

[63] See above, n.10.
[64] *ibid.* at p.9.
[65] *ibid.* at p.10.
[66] *cf.* the different situation discussed above at n.60 and accompanying text.

bitten, twice shy" legal scenario), it is likely to ensure that no such procedural breach by the democratic organ of government will happen again (as has turned out to be the case in Ireland in the *Gilliland*-type situation).

Under the changed wording in section 231(2) of the 1996 Constitution, it appears that there are only two situations – and those both procedural – where Article 46 of the Vienna Convention on Treaties might allow South Africa to invoke "notorious" constitutional provisions to seek to invalidate a treaty internationally: first and foremost, where the National Assembly and National Council of Provinces have not given (seemingly advance) "approval" to a non-technical, non-administrative, or non-executive type of treaty subject to ratification or accession (or have purported to do so, but not in the correct form); and secondly – and more dubiously – where treaties not subject to ratification or accession or of a technical nature, have not been "tabled" before the same relevant bodies. Even the reference in section 231(4) of the 1996 Constitution to "inconsistency with the Constitution" in the case of self-executing treaty provisions would not bring in Article 46 of the Vienna Convention. In fact, this latter situation is the only obvious instance where a domestic constitutional challenge on a substantive issue might now succeed; but this would only result in a possible finding of invalidity of the impugned treaty provisions at the municipal law level.

CONSTITUTIONAL AND COMMON LAW ANALOGIES IN RESPECT OF
INCORPORATION OF INTERNATIONAL LAW

As is usual in the context of any analysis of how international law enters a domestic system, a distinction must be drawn between the two major sources of international law, namely, treaties and custom.

Treaties

In Irish law, as in British practice, the position in respect of internal implementation of treaties is fairly clear: in practice, a legislative act is required to incorporate the treaty law into the respective domestic law. This evidences a strong dualist approach and the necessity for "transformation" before treaty law can be relied upon in domestic courts. Not surprisingly, a very similar rule is to be found also in the South African Constitution, though the wording has here changed between Interim 1994 Constitution and 1996 Constitution.[67]

Formerly, under the Interim Constitution, section 231(3) (which, in a somewhat different context, has been discussed above) stated:

---

[67] See Dugard, *op. cit.*, above, n.1 at p.54.

"Where Parliament agrees to the ratification or accession to an international agreement under subsection (2), such international agreement shall be binding on the Republic *and shall form part of the law of the Republic provided Parliament expressly so provides* and such agreement is not inconsistent with this Constitution." (emphasis added)

On this writer's interpretation of this provision, as seen, the essential thrust was not – in the latter wording at least – towards ensuring the treaty became binding internationally upon South Africa, but merely that it becomes binding internally. As already suggested above, the international binding aspect would have come about prior to this situation, namely, as soon as the executive ratified or acceded to a particular treaty following a former "section 231(2)-type" motion in Parliament. Thus, Professor Dugard has called the provision in question "an additional and separate process for the incorporation of treaties ratified by Parliament for international purposes under section 231(2)".[68] This former subsection was, then, effectively concerned with internal implementation (and so binding effect domestically) in South Africa, despite the somewhat curious set-out of the phraseology therein ("binding on the Republic", rather than, say, "*in* the Republic"). Professor Dugard seems to have come to this viewpoint[69] because it was backed up by the *travaux preparatoires* to the Interim Constitution. Under these, it was originally envisaged that a treaty "ratified" by Parliament would "form part of South African law unless it was expressly excluded by Act of Parliament";[70] but that the final draft of the Negotiating Council was reversed in the version approved by Parliament.

This finalised 1993 version added (as seen) the words "provided parliament expressly so provides". The drafting history – though now of academic interest – seems to confirm what has been argued above, namely, that the latter wording qualified only the immediately preceding words ("shall form part of the law of the Republic") rather than the seemingly separated earlier phrase "shall be binding", which relates to the previous subsection. Furthermore, it may be argued that the use of the same phrase ("inconsistent with the Constitution") in former section 231(4) – here in the sole context of incorporation of international (customary) law into South African domestic law – reinforced this interpretation relating to a similar situation in the preceding treaty-based provision.

Though again largely only of historical interest, if this was the true interpretation of the Interim Constitution, the question, of course, still remained as to what was really meant by the phrase "so provides" (a different verb to that of "agrees" as used earlier) to give treaty law internal force in South Africa.

---

[68] *op. cit.*, above, n.18 at p.192 (emphasis added).
[69] *ibid.*
[70] *ibid.*

Professor Devine has opined that it meant that there must be an Act of Parliament before the treaty became part of domestic law.[71] However, Professor Dugard had a different view.[72] He opined that a statute was not required in this situation; and that "[p]robably an *endorsement of incorporation* will suffice"; but, that it was "not clear how incorporation will take place". Fortunately, this particular ambiguity has never needed to find judicial resolution in a test case because section 231(4) of the 1996 Constitution now states in its place:

> "Any international agreement becomes law in the Republic when it *is enacted into law by national legislation*; but a self-executing provision of an agreement that has been approved by Parliament is law in the Republic unless it is inconsistent with the Constitution or an Act of Parliament." (emphasis added)

Thus, it is now clear that a legislative act is normally required here to give a treaty domestic effect as is the case in most other common law jurisdictions, including Ireland (whether in the text of, or schedule to, a statute, or possibly in an enabling Act which gives the executive power to implement the treaty in domestic law by means of a proclamation, etc.).[73] And, most importantly in this instance, there is no express qualification (as previously) to this effect in terms of inconsistency with the Constitution. This may mean that any such internalised treaty provisions in legislative form will be judicially applied even though they contravene provisions of the 1996 Constitution or prior statutes; so that such treaty-based statutes have, unlike in Ireland, a prioritised status in South African law. It may also be noted in this context (as seen) that section 233 of the 1996 Constitution has (unlike in the Irish Constitution) an express interpretative provision on the prioritised application of international law. This says:

> "When interpreting any legislation, every court must prefer any reasonable interpretation of the legislation that is consistent with international law over any alternative interpretation which is inconsistent with international law."

The fact that legislation is now expressly required for normal internal incorporation of treaty law in South Africa parallels the practised rule under the Irish Constitution. Here Article 29(6) of the Constitution states that "No inter-

---

[71] Though this sits rather uncomfortably with a previous statement of his (*ibid.*, at p.8) that when "the Constitution requires something to be done by Act of Parliament, it says so expressly".
[72] *Op. cit.*, above, n.23 at p.192.
[73] See J.P. Casey, *Constitutional Law in Ireland* (3rd ed., 2000), p. 196. Note, however, that in Ireland the term "Oireachtas" does not just include the two houses of parliament, but also the President: see Article 15.1.2°.

national agreement shall be part of the domestic law of the State save as may be determined by the Oireachtas". Although the word "determined" here could imply treaty law becoming internally binding merely by "simple [parliamentary] resolution" (as possibly also under the Interim South African Constitution), in practice legislation has always been required in Ireland to give domestic effect to any treaty.[74] Ample case law in Ireland[75] indicates that this provision prevents an individual litigant relying directly on a treaty that is not so incorporated (though this may happen indirectly to the extent that the treaty may be found to reflect Irish public policy under the Constitution[76] or where principles of estoppel arise[77]). There is, therefore, under the Irish Constitution, no possibility of any treaty having "self-executing" effect as is now possible in some instances under the 1996 South African Constitution.

In fact, the only point of difficulty in terms of the "legislative" rule in South Africa is what the proviso in the concluding wording of section 231(4) means when it refers to a "self-executing provision" of an agreement which has been "approved by Parliament" as being the "law in the Republic unless it is inconsistent with the Constitution or an Act of Parliament". This seems to throw up various points of difficulty of interpretation, most particularly as to what is meant by a "self-executing" treaty provision.[78] Such distinctions between "self-executing" and "non-self-executing" treaties have already caused difficulties in U.S. practice,[79] and seem likely to do so also in South African future practice unless at the time of parliamentary approval of the initial treaty ratification or access, Parliament expressly indicates whether, and if so which, provisions of any treaty under scrutiny are to be considered as "self-executing". Such "incorporated" treaty law would thus not, by contrast, have any prioritised status.

Another point of doubt arises over what appears to be an apparent *casus omissus* here, namely, whether the less important type of treaty, *i.e.* those of the technical, administrative variety or ones that are not subject to ratification or accession, may ever have domestic effect automatically as "self-executing" treaties. In such cases, as seen above, the new section 231(3) does not require

---

[74] See Symmons, *op. cit.*, above, n.7 at p.330.

[75] See Dugard, *op. cit.*, above, fn.1 at p.57.

[76] *Desmond v. Glackin (No. 1)* [1992] I.L.R.M. 490.

[77] *Fakih v. Minister for Justice* [1993] I.L.R.M. 274.

[78] See, *e.g.* M. Shaw, *International Law* (4th ed., CUP, 1997) pp.118-119 (who comments that the distinction leads to "considerable ambiguity and doubt").

[79] See Dugard, *op. cit.*, above, n.1 at p.58 where he says "Now South African courts will be required to decide whether a treaty is self-executing in the sense that existing law is inadequate to enable to Republic to carry out its international obligations without legislative incorporation of the treaty or whether it is non-self-executing in which case further legislation is required. No general guideline can be given on this matter. Each case ... will have to be decided on its own merits by the courts with due regard to the nature of the treaty, the precision of its language and the existing South African law on that subject".

the process of parliamentary approval, but simply a "tabling" of the treaty in the Assembly and Council within a "reasonable time". Under new section 231(4) of the 1996 South African Constitution, the opening words "[*any*] international agreement" (emphasis added) appear to mean that legislative intervention is the normal rule for any type of treaty; so that prima facie any such less important treaties will also have to be put into statutory form to have domestic effect. The interpretative inference from the words that follow indicates, as seen, that in certain circumstances a "self-executing" treaty provision may, *ipso jure*, be "law in the Republic"; this seems to be confined to those that have previously been "*approved* by Parliament" (emphasis added), *i.e.* solely to those treaties that require ratification or accession. In which case, it seems to follow that treaties in the "excepted" categories mentioned above can never be "self-executing" and so require legislative implementation. This seems a fair rule, bearing in mind that National Assembly "approval" in the case of treaties *needing* ratification or accession is somewhat analogous to the legislative process, whereas mere parliamentary consultation by way of "tabling" treaties leads to no parliamentary vote and largely by-passes effective parliamentary control.

Custom

Adoption of the "incorporation" doctrine:

Ireland

In the Irish context, the classical British doctrine of automatic incorporation of customary international law appears to have been adopted. As the writer has written elsewhere, this adoption of the so-called incorporation doctine and its "monistic" trappings, appear to have been based partly on reliance on the British common law precedent (in similar fashion to what has happened in South African courts[80]) but also partly on one particular provision of the Constitution, Article 29(3), which states:

> "Ireland accepts the generally recognised principles of international law as its rule of conduct in its relations with other States."

This has happened in Ireland despite the fact that, in the writer's opinion, this constitutional provision was seemingly never intended for such a specific purpose as requiring actual automatic incorporation of customary international law into Irish law. It was essentially a pious expression of Ireland's intent to

---

[80]Thus, they have cited British and U.S. precedents, such as the *South Atlantic Islands* case (1971) (1) S.A. 234 (C) 238, cited by R.P. Schaffer, below, n.89 at p.305, including the South African-based *locus classicus* of *West Rand Central Gold Mining*. The latter is cited by Schaffer (*ibid.* at p.284) as "clearly" re-establishing the "Blackstone [*i.e.* incorporationist] rule".

generally abide by international law in its external relations, as the phrase "relations with other States" infers.[81] As such, it is very similar in effect to the bland provision in the Interim South African Constitution (seen above), which obligated South Africa to "respect international law and treaty obligations". It cannot, therefore, be stressed too strongly that there is no direct reference in Article 29(3) to the specific matter of reception of international law into the Irish domestic system. Nonetheless, this Irish constitutional provision has been repeatedly judicially cited – as early as the *De las Morenas* case[82] in 1945 – as having an important effect on the incorporation process in Ireland; most recently, by the Supreme Court in *Government of Canada v. Burke* (1992).[83] In the latter case, a *dictum* of McCarthy J. seems to make exclusive reference to this provision as controlling the incorporation position in Ireland; so the Irish judiciary may now be taking "a more independent line" rather than relying on the "common law/Irish case law perspective".[84]

The unfortunate effect of Irish judicial reliance to such a degree on Article 29(3) has been that every word and phrase of this has been scrutinised in the past in a seeming attempt to narrow down the effect of automatic incorporation in Ireland; to the extent that the writer has recently stated that "the whole section has become a forensic lottery as to just what it means in the Irish domestic context".[85] This has led not only to inconsistent or semantic interpretations of the phrase "as a rule of conduct" (in Irish "*ina dtreoir*", which translates literally "as a guide") therein, but even in several recent cases to a complete omission of mention of same.[86] Indeed, even the conservatively-minded Constitution Review Group in Ireland has concluded in their recent report that the "parameters of [the] emerging [incorporationist] doctrine are not yet clear".[87] There have been implicit admissions recently of a similar sentiment by the Irish judiciary; for example, McCarthy J. in the *Burke* case stated that he "reserved for another day the true construction of section 3" of Article 29.[88]

South Africa

Prior to the 1996 Constitution, it has been said that the relationship between South African "municipal law and public international law [was] largely de-

---

[81] See *Review Report*, above, n.24 at p.580; and for more detailed discussion of the forced judicial interpretations resulting, *ibid.* at p.581.

[82] *Saorstat and Continental Steamship Co. v. De las Morenas* [1945] I.R. 291.

[83] [1992] 2 I.R. 484, 491.

[84] See Symmons, "The Incorporation of Customary International Law into Irish Law: Recent Developments and Suggestions", (1996) XXXI Irish Jurist, 163, 167

[85] See *Review Report*, above, n.24 at p.582.

[86] Symmons, *ibid.* at p.582.

[87] See above, n.24 at p.105.

[88] See above, n.67 at p.491.

termined by common law rules inherited from the United Kingdom" since there were "no constitutional provisions dealing with this question",[89] although "prior to 1970 there was no positive judicial statement on the relationship".[90] As a result, rules of customary international law were judicially regarded as "part of South African common law"[91] or, more accurately, Roman-Dutch law,[92] most explicitly in the early *ex parte Schumann* case in 1940.[93]

Professor Devine has pointed out that the Interim South African Constitution gave a clear "status" to international customary law, whatever type it may be[94] in South Africa and that it adopted the "incorporation theory",[95] though the "practical result is probably the same as that previously prevailing under the *Nduli* doctrine"; further, that section 231(4) was a "great improvement from a point of view of clarity"[96]; and of course, that the rule on incorporation no longer depends on Roman Dutch law.[97]

Section 231(4) of the Interim Constitution stated:

> "The rules of customary international law binding on the Republic, shall, unless inconsistent with this Constitution or an Act of Parliament, *form part of the law of the Republic*." (emphasis added)

Now, in slightly changed wording – which is "substantially similar"[98] – the same-numbered new subsection of the 1996 Constitution states:

> "Customary international law is law in the Republic unless it is inconsistent with the Constitution or an Act of Parliament."

There seems to be little difference in substantive effect between the two versions, though it is immediately noticeable that the former phrase "binding on the Republic" has now been omitted. The latter phrase was supposed to act as some limitation on a generalised "automatic incorporation" interpretation, in that this process would still depend on the South African courts deciding in

---

[89] R.P. Schaffer, "The Inter-relationship between Public International Law and the Law of South Africa: An Overview" (1983) 32 I.C.L.Q. 277, 283.
[90] *ibid.* at p.296. The caselaw is discussed by Schaffer, *ibid.* at pp.297-308.
[91] *ibid.* at p.298.
[92] See *Nduli and Another v. Minister of Justice and Others* (1978) (1) S.A. 893 (cited by Schaffer, above, n.89, at p.306).
[93] (1940) W.P.D. 251. The later cases – including *S. v. Ramotse* (1970), *Parkin v. Government of the Democratic Republic of Congo* (1971), the *South Atlantic Islands* case (1971), and the *Nduli v. Minister of Justice and Others* (1978) are cited in Schaffer, above, n.89 at pp.303-308.
[94] Devine, *e.g.* (above, n.1 at p.14) says it is not clear whether the *Nduli* case covered "*all* kinds of customary international law" (emphasis added).
[95] *ibid.* at p.12.
[96] *ibid.*
[97] *ibid.* at p.13.
[98] See Dugard, *op. cit.*, above, n.1 at p.51.

each case whether "the relevant rule is binding on the Republic and thus incorporated".[99] It was also commented[100] that there was no "no doubt" as to what the phrase "binding on the Republic" meant in this context; namely, that it meant binding "according to international law" rather than the vague notion of having the "assent of the country" as the rule was asserted in *Nduli*[101]; and possibly might involve a judicial determination as to whether the Republic had been a "persistent objector" to the alleged rule.[102] Just as in Ireland, courts in South Africa would have to determine in any particular case whether any alleged rule of customary law actually exists[103]; but Professor Dugard rightly opines that the omission of the word "binding", "with its undertones of strict consent, lends support to the proposition that widespread or general acceptance [of an alleged customary rule] as opposed to universal acceptance, is sufficient for proof of customary international law" in South Africa.[104]

Undoubtedly any constitutional provision that explicitly covers customary international law, and its domestic incorporation, is a wise measure, which, through its "constitutionalisation" gives the rule "added weight"[105]; and it has existing precedents in some, but by no means all, European constitutions.[106] Unfortunately, the existing Irish Constitution makes, as seen, no such explicit provision on this vital issue in its "vaguely worded provision"[107]; and so, as the writer has commented to the recent Irish Constitution Review Group,[108] this has led to "forced literal interpretations of phrases" therein which "were surely intended to have external effect only".[109] Hence, I have advocated that Ireland should, for the sake of clarity, change its constitutional provision in this respect on basis of the South African model.[110]

---

[99] *ibid.* at p.12.

[100] *ibid.*

[101] *ibid.* at p.14. It would seem logical that this phrase should have the same meaning *vis-à-vis* customary law as that preceding in s.231(3) relating specifically to treaty law.

[102] *ibid.* at p.12. As Professor Dugard has commented, the dropping of the word "binding" – which was considered unnecessary and tautologous – may still mean that a practice to which South Africa has "persistently objected" may simply not be a "customary rule" (Dugard, *op. cit.*, n.1 at p.54). But, it may be commented that if the South African courts demur too strongly to the "practice of the executive" in this process, this provision could meet the same fate as in Ireland of meaning all things to all judges, as will be seen below.

[103] Devine, (*ibid.* at p.13) refers in n.75 to the courts possibly examining legislative and perhaps even judicial precedents. For the unsatisfactory handling of this problem by the Irish judiciary, see Symmons, above, n.68 at p.170-171.

[104] See Dugard, *op. cit.*, n.1 at p.51.

[105] *ibid.* at p.54.

[106] See C. Dominice and F. Voeffray, "L'application du droit international general dans l'ordre juridique international" in Eismann, *op. cit.*, above, n.7 at p.52, who cite Germany, Greece, Italy, Portugal and, surprisingly Ireland, in this context.

[107] *Review Report*, above, n.24 at p.580.

[108] *ibid.*, "Suggestions for the Revision of Article 29(3)", Appendix 16 at p.580.

[109] *ibid.* at p.581.

[110] *ibid.* at pp.582-583.

Exceptions

It has been stated that the applicability of customary international law in South
Africa was, prior to the new Constitution, subject to certain qualifications
inspired by English law.[111] In Ireland, such qualifications to incorporation of
customary international law have been confirmed quite independently of any
directly applicable constitutional provision; and even the most important – the
exception relating to contrary statute – is not specifically spelt out in any such
directly applicable part of the Constitution.[112] For example, in a recent case
involving aspects of the law of the sea, *ACT Shipping (PTE) Ltd v. Minister
for the Marine*,[113] Barr J. applied the incorporation doctrine "subject to [the]
established limitations", in which he included conflict with "the Constitution
or an enactment of the legislature or a rule of common law"[114]; but even this
list has, at times, been judicially added to. As the writer has stated elsewhere,[115]
at least three, and probably five, exceptions can be read out of the existing
Irish case law, namely, conflicting statute,[116] conflicting precedent ("common
law"),[117] conflicting "private constitutional right[s]", limitations resulting from
application of the phrase *"ina dtreoir"*,[118] and (alleged) lack of *locus standi*
for a private litigant.[119] Even the (in this instance timorous) Constitution Review Group has admitted (albeit without attempting to remedy the situation)
that such aspects of the Constitution "are still unresolved and uncertainties
continue"[120]; and McCarthy J. in the *Burke* case, as seen above,[121] makes a
similar comment.

Fortunately (as seen above[122]), the Interim South African Constitution
avoided such uncertainties by including in the international law section a specific and clear provision on the now-relevant two limitations to automatic incorporation of customary international law; and these have remained unchanged
under the 1996 Constitution. They are, firstly, an inconsistent provision of the
Constitution, or, secondly, an inconsistent "Act of Parliament". As has been
stated: "both constitutional sovereignty and parliamentary sovereignty over

---

[111] As confirmed in the case of *Kaffraria Property Co. (Pty) Ltd. v. Government of Zambia*
(1980) (2) S.A. 709E by Eksteen J., who stated that international law formed part of South
African law "in so far as it [did] not conflict with [South African] legislation or common
law"; cited by Schaffer, above, n.73 at p.308.
[112] See Symmons, above, n.84 at pp.165, 177.
[113] [1995] 2 I.L.R.M. 30.
[114] *ibid.* at p.43.
[115] See above, n.68 at p.176.
[116] *ibid.* at pp.177-179.
[117] *ibid.* at p.185.
[118] See above, n.86 and accompanying text.
[119] above, n.84 at p.181.
[120] above, n.24 at p.105.
[121] above, n.88.
[122] See n.91 and accompanying text.

rules of international customary law are entrenched".[123] And, as Professor Dugard has also aptly commented,[124] now only "a provision of the Constitution or an Act of Parliament which is clearly inconsistent with customary law will trump it", as emphasised by section 233, which applies an obligation on courts to prefer any "reasonable" legislative interpretation in the statutory interpretation process that is consistent with international law.

Apart from these exceptions now finding express provision in the Constitution (and no longer in Roman-Dutch law[125]), the main change over the Roman-Dutch/common law position is that conflicting judicial precedent has now been implicitly eliminated[126] as a bar to application of customary international law in South Africa. Even in the pre-new Constitution era, there were judicial attempts in South Africa to cut down on this exception.[127] Ironically, a similar judicially-inspired process may have happened recently in Ireland to remove conflicting precedent as a bar to incorporation.[128] In the Supreme Court decision of *Burke*, O'Flaherty J. stated that "[e]ven assuming that what was [set out in a previous case] was correct for its time [*i.e.* apparently adhering to an "absolute" state immunity approach], it is now clear that the general principles of international law have so developed to depart radically from the absolute state immunity doctrine to a much more restrictive view of sovereign immunity".[129] This statement implies that international law may override contrary Irish precedent. And in the new South African context, Professor Dugard has stated forthrightly that the doctrine of *stare decisis* cannot now apply. As he says: "[t]here can be no suggestion that a new rule of customary international law must give way to South African decisions recognising an earlier rule".[130]

CONCLUSION

It can be seen from the above discussion that the 1996 South African Constitution has even stronger analogies with the Irish Constitution and practice in respect of the treaty-making process "competences" than did the interim one;

---

[123] Devine, above, n.1 at p.13.

[124] See Dugard, *op. cit.*, above, n.1 at p.52.

[125] See Devine, *ibid.* at p. 13; and Schaffer, above, n.89 at pp.310-312.

[126] See Dugard, *op. cit.*, above, n.1 at p.52.

[127] See Schaffer, above, n.89 at pp.309-310, citing *Leibowitz v. Schwartz* (1974), *Inter-Science Research and Development Services (Pty.) Ltd. v. Republica Popular de Mocambique* (1980) and the *Kaffraria* case.

[128] See Symmons, above, n.84 at p.179.

[129] See above, n.83 at p.498, a *dictum* which has "shades of Lord Denning's memorable assertion in [the *Trendtex* case] that international law knows 'no doctrine of *stare decisis*'" (Symmons, above, n.84 at p.179).

[130] See *op. cit.*, above, n.1 at p.52.

and the main textual ambiguities thrown up by the Interim Constitution have now disappeared. By way of contrast, the incorporation of international law into the domestic system is clearer and more rational than the Irish equivalent. And, on my interpretation of the new South African Constitution, a "*McGimpsey* situation", where private litigation may challenge a particular treaty itself, which is already binding on the State, because of some alleged inconsistency with one or more substantive provisions of the Constitution, is unlikely to arise, except possibly if it constitutes a "self-executing provision" under section 231(4). However, this matter still remains somewhat unclear; Professor Dugard, for one, has recently referred to the power of judicial review (under section 172 of 1996) making possible a "direct challenge [albeit, it seems, only to treaty-dependant legislation] where, for example, it is argued that the procedures for ratification and incorporation of a treaty under section 231 have not been followed",[131] *i.e.* seemingly where the challenge is post-ratification in respect of a defective procedural aspect at least.

As for the matter of incorporation of international law into both domestic systems, the South African Constitution is similar to the Irish on the matter of treaty law in having a purpose-made provision that requires parliamentary intervention for domestic application of same by way of legislation; but in respect of customary international law, it is very different in laying out not only an express section (now section 231(4) of the 1996 Constitution) on automatic incorporation, but also in the listing of the two and only possible exceptions to this – inconsistent statute or constitutional provision.

My only reservation over the latter "inconsistent" constitutional provision inclusion is that such a blanket reference to the "Constitution"[132] might import into South African case law some of the semantic interpretations of Article 29(3) by the Irish judiciary, who have made strained cross-references to notionally unrelated articles in the Irish Constitution to seemingly whittle down the impact of international law in Irish domestic law.[133] As such, if Irish case law is anything to go by, this second limitation has a potentially much greater impact in watering down the effect of an automatic incorporation doctrine in South Africa.[134]

---

[131] *ibid.* at p.62 (emphasis added). He also suggests uncontroversially, (*ibid.*) that, of course, a challenge to statute may assume an indirect nature where international law is invoked "to support an interpretation in favour of the unconstitutionality" thereof, in which context he cites *Azapo v. President of the Republic of South Africa* (1996) (4) S.A. 671.

[132] See Symmons in *Review Report*, above, n.24 at p.583 ("a blanket reference to other parts of the Constitution might re-introduce all the problems of the past").

[133] See Symmons, above, n.84 at p.177, and in *Review Report*, above, n.24 at p.581.

[134] Though it has analogies with statute, it was pointed out in *Ntenteni v. Chaiman, Ciskei Council of State* (1994) 1 B.C.L.R. 168 that a constitution is on a *different footing* from other legislation, being a mechanism under which laws are made rather than declaring what the law is.

JUDICIAL REVIEW OF ADMINISTRATIVE ACTION IN IRELAND: THE INFLUENCE OF THE IRISH CONSTITUTION ON THE RULES OF NATURAL JUSTICE

AINDRIAS Ó CAOIMH[*]

Judicial review in the context of this paper refers to the supervisory jurisdiction of the High Court, and, on appeal therefrom, the Supreme Court in Ireland, over inferior courts and tribunals. The jurisdiction in question is in the field of public law and involves a variety of relief in the forms of orders of certiorari, mandamus and prohibition, together with the ancillary relief in the form of orders granting declarations and injunctions.

HISTORICAL BACKGROUND

This jurisdiction was previously in the form of prerogative writs, which were granted in the name of the Crown and resulted in the jurisdiction being referred to as "Crown Side", as it was exercised on:

— judge of the High Court of Ireland

— the Crown side of the Kings Bench Division of the High Court of Justice, previously the Court of King's Bench.

The Court of King's Bench (or where a Queen was on the throne, the Court of Queen's Bench), which was originally a committee of the *Curia Regis* (the King's Council) derived its title from the fact that the sovereign formerly sat in the Court himself. The king rarely sat in the Court himself but there remained the fiction that all proceedings in the Court were before the king in person.

The Court kept all inferior jurisdictions within the bounds of their authority and could either remove their proceedings to be determined before it or prohibit their progress below. The Court superintended all civil proceedings in the kingdom. The Court commanded magistrates and others to do what their duty required in every case in which there was no other specific remedy.

---

* Judge of the High Court of Ireland.

It protected the liberty of the subject by speedy and summary interposition. The court took cognisance of both criminal and civil cases – the former on what was called the Crown Side, or Crown Office, the latter on the Plea Side of the Court. The jurisdiction on the Plea Side of the Court merged in the general jurisdiction of the High Court, but its jurisdiction on the Crown Side was preserved intact and allocated to the King's Bench Division.

The jurisdiction on the Crown Side was divided into two classes: the strictly criminal jurisdiction, and the general superintending jurisdiction.

From the fiction of the sovereign's presence in Court some of the incidents of the prerogative of the Crown attached themselves to the Court itself.

After the Judicature Acts,[1] Rules of Court made under the Acts had statutory force and *effect,* subject to the Acts themselves.

Rules of Court made in the 1880s and 1906 governed this jurisdiction in the High Court and consequent upon Irish independence being achieved in 1922, the earlier jurisdiction was continued in force under the Constitution of the Irish Free State. What was referred to previously as Crown Side proceedings were thereafter referred to as State Side proceedings.

The Constitution of Ireland was adopted by the people in 1937 and provided for new courts to be established under the Constitution to replace those then in existence. The new courts were established in 1961 and fresh Rules of Court were adopted in 1962. The changes were largely cosmetic and the term "State Side" continued until fresh Rules of Court were adopted in 1986 when the term "State Side" disappeared. Until 1986 all such proceedings were entitled either *The King at the prosecution of A. B. [the applicant] v. X.Y. [the respondent]* or, since Irish independence, *The State at the prosecution of A.B. [the applicant] v. X.Y. [the respondent].*

Until 1986 the procedure involved an *ex parte* application to the High Court, which could issue a "conditional order' directed to the respondent to "show cause" why the conditional order should not be made absolute.

JUDICIAL REVIEW TODAY

The procedure before the High Court today is regulated by the Rules of the Superior Courts[2] and involves an initial *ex parte* application to the High Court for leave to institute proceedings by way of judicial review for one or more of the categories of relief previously referred to. In the event of leave being granted by the High Court, the matter proceeds on notice to the respondent and any

---

[1] In Ireland the change was effected by the Supreme Court of Judicature (Ireland) Act 1877 (40 & 41 Vict. c. 57). In England the change was effected by the Judicature Art 1873 (36 & 37 Vict. c. 66) and the Judicature Act 1875 (38 & 39 Vict. c. 77).
[2] Ord. 84 of the Rules of the Superior Courts. (S.I. No. 15 of 1986).

other party who may be affected by the making of the order sought. The procedure is essentially written and generally these matters proceed on the basis of sworn affidavits, with the Court being in the position to give liberty for a deponent to be cross-examined if necessary.

While the procedure has been referred to as "speedy and summary",[3] its popularity today is such that the historical speed is compromised by the multitude of such actions being brought before the High Court. This is so notwithstanding the fact that a party seeking leave to institute proceedings for judicial review is obliged to act promptly, and in any event within strict time limits and where the pleadings etc. are directed by the Court to be lodged within time limits specified by the Court itself.

Certiorari is an order issuing from the High Court to quash a decision of an inferior court or tribunal. The Court examines into the legality of the proceedings of the inferior court or tribunal or other jurisdiction in the field of public law. It will issue where the respondent acts in excess or in want of jurisdiction. A court or other body will not have jurisdiction to act in disregard of the interests of justice; accordingly, even where a court or other body is formally vested with jurisdiction, it may lose jurisdiction if it disregards the essentials of justice, including the principles of natural and constitutional justice.

In exercising this jurisdiction the High Court is directed essentially to the decision-making process and not the merits of a decision, as that is properly the subject matter of procedure by way of appeal. Only in the context of a decision-maker being shown to have acted irrationally or unreasonably in the sense that the impugned decision "plainly and unambiguously flies in the face of fundamental reason and common sense". If so, the decision-maker will be considered to have acted *ultra vires, i.e.* without jurisdiction.

Mandamus is an order directed to the respondent to whom it is addressed to perform some public or quasi-public legal duty, which he has refused to perform, and the performance of which cannot be enforced by any other adequate legal remedy. It was formerly defined as a high prerogative writ issuing from the Crown side of the King's Bench Division of the High Court.

Prohibition is an order of the High Court directed to an inferior court for the purpose of preventing the inferior court from usurping a jurisdiction with which it is not legally vested, or in other words to compel courts entrusted with judicial duties to keep within the limits of their jurisdiction. In contrast to certiorari, an order of prohibition is a preventive rather than a corrective remedy and is only used to prevent the commission of a future act and not to do an act already performed.

---

[3] See Short and Mellor's *The Practice of the Crown Office* (1908).

An injunction is distinguished from prohibition as it is directed to a particular party while prohibition is directed to the court itself. An injunction usually recognises the jurisdiction of the court in which the proceedings are pending but a prohibition strikes at one at its jurisdiction.

Natural Justice

The two fundamental rules of natural justice are expressed in Latin maxims:

(a) *audi alteram partem* (hear the other side), and

(b) *nemo iudex in causa sua* (no one shall be a judge in his own cause) indicating, firstly, the principle that a person who may be adversely affected by a decision should have the right to be heard and secondly, that the decision maker should not be biased or be perceived to be biased.

Natural justice is generally recognised as subsisting by virtue of man's nature as a being endowed with reason and capable of ascertaining objective moral values. It is registered as man's protection against the use of arbitrary power.

In Ireland reliance is placed not only on the principles of natural justice but also on what is termed constitutional justice.

It has been said that in 1965 natural justice was reincarnated as constitutional justice.[4] What was said by the Supreme Court as the time was that "in the context of the constitution, natural justice might be more appropriately termed constitutional justice and must be understood to import more that the two well-established principles, that no man should be a judge in his own cause and *audi alteram partem*" (involving the right to a fair hearing).[5]

In essence what was being stated at the time was that by reason of the recognition given in the Irish Constitution to fundamental rights, the well-established principals of natural justice, together with other principles of justice, having the protection of the Constitution, might best be described as constitutional justice. In this regard it is important to note that the constitutional tradition in Ireland has been to consider fundamental rights not to be conferred by the Constitution but rather to be given special recognition and protection by the Constitution. Article 40.3 of the Constitution provides:

> "3.1° The State guarantees in its laws to respect and, as far as practicable, by its laws to defend and vindicate the personal rights of the citizen."

What additional factors are incorporated in the concept of constitutional jus-

---

[4] Hogan and Morgan, *Administrative Law in Ireland* (3rd ed., Round Hall Sweet and Maxwell).
[5] *McDonald v. Bord na gCon* [1965] I.R. 217 at 242.

tice is difficult to divine. However, by reference to subsequent cases, other principles of justice have been declared by the courts, which appear to fall within the rubric of constitutional justice, including, the right:

(a) that tribunals should generally sit in public;[6]

(b) that one is entitled to a reasonably prompt decision;[7]

(c) that one be given reasons for a decisions;[8]

(d) in certain cases, to some form of administrative appeal against a decision;[9]

(e) of indigent parties to free legal aid for certain types of administrative decisions;[10]

(f) of an accused in a criminal trial to confront one's accusers.[11]

The High Court has held that: "Constitutional justice imposes a constitutional duty on a decision making authority to apply fair procedures in the exercise of its powers and functions."[12]

Accordingly it will be seen that the scope of constitutional justice, albeit somewhat lacking definition, is broader that that of natural justice and it acts as a guide to statutory interpretation. In England, for example, a statute can exclude the application of natural justice; but in Ireland, having regard to the Constitution, such an approach may render a statute void as being unconstitutional. Furthermore, in Ireland provisions of pre-Constitution statutes have been held not to survive the Constitution, and the courts have refused to apply them.

The Supreme Court in Ireland has indicated that the presumption of constitutionality carries with it not only the presumption that the constitutional construction is the one intended by Parliament, but also that Parliament intended that proceedings, procedures, discretions and adjudications which are permitted, provided for, or prescribed by an Act of Parliament are to be conducted in accordance with the principles of constitutional justice.

The Supreme Court has held that where precise statutory time limits would work an injustice the courts should not apply them. This was recently illustrated in a decision of the Supreme Court, delivered in August 2000, upholding as constitutional the provisions of the Illegal Immigrants (Trafficking) Act

---

[6] *Barry v. Medical Council* [1998] 3 I.R. 368.
[7] *Bosphorus Hava v. Minister for Transport (No 2)* unreported, High Court, January 22, 1996.
[8] See *e.g. Creedon v. Criminal Compensation Tribunal* [1988] I.R. 51.
[9] *Carroll v. Minister for Agriculture & Food* [1991] I.R. 230 at 235.
[10] *Kirwan v. Minister for Justice* [1994] 1 I.L.R.M.333.
[11] See *e.g. White v. Ireland* unreported, High Court, December 21, 1993.
[12] *McCormack v. Garda Síochána Complaints Board* [1997] 2 I.R. 489.

2000, which was referred to the Supreme Court by the President of Ireland under the provisions of Article 26 of the Irish Constitution to test its conformity with the Constitution before being signed into law.

With regard to bias, the number of successful claims under this heading is limited. Cases have involved either actual bias or what is referred to as objective or perceived bias. Where a reasonable person in the position of the plaintiff would consider that there was a real likelihood of prejudice (as opposed to on the basis of a suspicion which might dwell in the mind of a person who is ill informed and did not seek to direct his mind properly to the facts), the court will set aside a decision even if in such a case it is established as a matter of fact that bias was not operative.

Tribunals and administrative agencies are, of course, not required to follow the same strict rules of evidence and procedure as a court of law, provided the rules adopted are fair in themselves. Tribunals exercising quasi-judicial functions are frequently allowed to act informally, even to receive unsworn evidence, to act on hearsay and to depart from the rules of evidence. However, they must not act in a manner calculated to imperil a fair hearing. The courts have expressed reluctance to get involved in the affairs of private associations, such as sporting clubs and trade unions, save in clear cases the prevent or remedy a manifest injustice. Notwithstanding this, there has been a growing tendency to apply to the courts in cases involving sporting associations. The courts approach these cases by ascertaining and examining the procedures appropriate to the type of organisation or association in question.

LIMITATION OF RIGHT TO JUDICIAL REVIEW·

Private bodies

It must be stated that to be amenable to judicial review, a body whose decision it is sought to quash must be discharging a function of a public nature affecting private rights, and must be under a duty to act fairly in arriving at its decision. Questions that must be asked are whether the relationship of the applicant and the respondent derives merely from contract and whether the duty held is a public duty. If the decision being impugned is of a nature which might ordinarily be seen as coming within the public domain, that decision can only be excluded from the reach of jurisdiction in judicial review if it can be shown that it is solely and exclusively derived from a individual contract made in private law.

Types of decisions attaching natural and constitutional justice include:

(a) public and private employment;

(b) membership of trade unions, provisional bodies and clubs;

(c) licensing and commercial regulation;

(d) discipline;

(e) property and planning;

(f) deportation and treatment of aliens.

Recently the Supreme Court indicated that the courts should be slow to interfere with decisions of expert administrative tribunals. The court indicated that where conclusions are based upon an identifiable error of law or an unsustainable finding of fact by a tribunal, such conclusions must be corrected. Otherwise it should be recognised that tribunals that have been given statutory tasks to perform and that exercise their functions (as in now usually the case) with a high degree of expertise and provide coherent and balanced judgments on the evidence and arguments heard by them, it should not be necessary for the courts to review their decisions by way of appeal or judicial review.[13]

---

[13] *Henry Denny and Sons. (Ireland) Ltd. v. Minister for Social Welfare* [1998] 1 I.R. 34.

IRELAND'S OMBUDSMAN

DAVID GWYNN MORGAN*

INTRODUCTION

My first job out of university was teaching law in the National Institution of Public Administration in Lusaka. One of the many things I learned in Zambia was that the Barotse People in Western Zambia have a proverb which translates as: "You do not ask a monkey to decide an affair of the forest". The reason for this is that the monkey might know some of the parties involved, and consequently there would be a risk that he would be biased. Presumably, the proverb suggests, one would be wiser to ask a poodle or a goldfish to act as arbiter. This colourful rule is, of course, the Barotse equivalent of the rule known in other common law jurisdictions, as the first rule of natural justice.

My subject today is another field in which we have essentially the same institution – the Ombudsman – in respect of the detailed operation of which we may have something to learn from each other. The South African Ombudsman is known, I believe, as the Public Protector and with him in mind, I want to tell you a success story – and also one or two worries that I have – about the Irish Ombudsman – to see whether he can be a helpful example.

Next, a definition. The Ombudsman is a State official whose duty is to secure redress when a person suffers harm or loss, with an act of governmental maladministration. It is worth emphasising that phrase "suffers harm", because the basis of the Ombudsman's jurisdiction is that someone has suffered loss. I mention this because I understand that in quite a few of his cases the Public Protector has been investigating improper conduct by a Minister, for example telling lies, where there is no obvious and immediate victim. (To go back to the comparison with your Public Protector: the closest we come in Ireland is the newly established Ethics Commission; but this office is not combined with that of the Ombudsman). The significance of this is that it means that the Ombudsman figure is cast in a somewhat antagonistic role. By contrast, the Irish Ombudsman goes out of his way not to censure anyone. Partly because he needs the co-operation of public servants, he does not dwell on how or why the damage was caused; rather his approach is to see whether the victim has suffered injustice and, if so, how can he be compensated for the

---

* Professor of Law at University College, Cork, Ireland

wrong he has suffered. In this, as in other ways, the Ombudsman is a rather typical example of "alternative dispute resolution".

If one compares the Ombudsman and judicial review as mechanisms for ensuring a fair system of public administration, one feature that jumps out is that the Ombudsman requires only one set of persons, the investigators, whereas judicial review requires three sets: the court and lawyers on each side. In Ireland we have about 6,000 lawyers for a population of just under four million. In South Africa, I believe the comparable figures are 10,000 lawyers and a population of 40 million. I do not say that, because of this, things are six times as good in Ireland as in South Africa! What I do say is that in a relatively poor country, a public official with a simple procedure, who can deliver justice, without the need for a legal advisor, is a great asset to the community. The Irish (Gaelic) version of Ombudsman is "*Fear a Phobal*", which translates back into English as "Man of the People". This emphasises the fact that most of his complaints concern social welfare benefits and public housing, matters which are of special concern to the poorer sections of the community.

Tenure

Also relevant to independence is the question of the period of tenure. Judges in the common law world, at any rate, have life tenure. In the case of Ombudsmen, the tenure seems to be more like three to seven years. In Ireland it is six years, with eligibility for any number of subsequent terms. In South Africa the Public Protector can only have one term. There are some advantages to this way of doing things. One writer has remarked, "The spectre of a powerful and popular ombudsman with first-hand knowledge of the intimate workings of government and thus capable of forming a focus for political opposition may well be unacceptable to government. On the other hand, the personal prestige of an ombudsman is most important to the success of the organisation and this can only be developed over a long period". [1] The first sentence may seem unduly cynical. The conventional advantage of a one-period Ombudsman is that he has no temptation to look over his shoulder in the hope of another term. In any case, what does emerge is the need for compromise between acceptability to the Government and the potency of the office, including its independence.

A significant episode involving tenure and independence arose in Ireland in 1989. The background to this was that it seems probable that the Prime Minister of the day (Mr Haughey) did not want the incumbent of the Office (Mr Mills), who had been approached by a previous administration, to remain in the post. However, because Mr Haughey was head of a coalition government with a minority party, who supported Mr Mills, he was unable openly to

---

[1] Hatchard, "The Institution of the Ombudsman in Africa" (1986) I.C.L.Q. 255, 269.

disavow Mr Mills. Instead, he sought to take advantage of the fact that Mr Mills was 62 years of age at the time of the ending of his first term of office so that he would become 67 before the second term ended. Accordingly, if Mr Mills's term of office had come to an end and there had been a gap between the completion of his first term and his appointment for a subsequent term, the Prime Minister could have said: "Oh dear me, what a pity he is not eligible". However, so long as he was actually at the time of re-appointment the incumbent, the constituent statute allowed him to be re-appointed and to hold office until retiring age.[2]

Funding

Funding is a hugely important factor in the context of independence for any institution. Here another case study may be instructive. One of the main factors governing the Ombudsman's efficacy and public image is the provision of sufficient staff to investigate complaints adequately and promptly, and the size and grading of his staff are determined by the Minister for Finance. As King Lear remarked, "nothing comes from nothing". Now in April 1987, the new government's budget reduced the Ombudsman's vote by IR£250,000, or 13 per cent of the previous year's budget, a reduction in staff of four investigators. In July it was announced that the vote for 1988 would show a further reduction of IR£250,000. Before the reduction the Ombudsman had 20 investigators; but this reduction necessitated that in 1988 there had to be a total reduction of seven investigators, whilst the Minister for Finance also refused to allow the replacement of the Director and one of the four senior investigators upon the resignation of the existing incumbents.

These reductions were explained by reference to the crisis in public expenditure and to cuts elsewhere in the public service; it was noticeable, however, that the cuts in other sections of the public service did not amputate nearly a half of the establishment. These reductions attracted a good deal of protest in the media, the Dáil and the Senate.[3] The Ombudsman himself took to informing complainants that there was likely to be considerable delay in

---

[2] The argument being considered here is that had there been a gap of even a few days between the end of Mr Mills's first appointment and his re-appointment, it could have been argued that he would not have been eligible on the basis of s. 2(7), which states: " A person shall be not more than 61 years of age upon first being appointed ..." It might have been contended that the policy underlying the concession in the words "upon *first* being appointed" (which might have been something upon which the government was relying) is such that they would only have been relied upon to benefit a person who was actually an incumbent at the time of re-appointment rather than someone who came in from outside. See *Dáil Debates* Cols. 1675 and 1816, December 14 and 15, 1989.

[3] See *The Irish Times*, January 4, 1988, February 11, 1988, June 4 and 7, 1988, May 13, 1988; *Sunday Independent*, June 12, 1988, ("The Ombudsman and Hypocrisy"); *Cork Examiner*, November 6, 1988 ("Watchdog with No Teeth"); *Dáil Debates*, Vol. 380, col. 1423, May 12, 1988.

dealing with their complaints, and in November 1987, he made a special report on the matter – the only special report to issue so far – to the Houses of
the Oireachtas. This report[4] commences: "It is necessary under the provisions
of the Ombudsman Act to report that the Office of Ombudsman is unable, due
to staff cutbacks, to fulfil the functions assigned to it by the Oireachtas". In
response, in mid-1988, the Department of Finance carried out a review of the
Ombudsman's staffing needs. The recommendations of this review led to the
Ombudsman being able to take on three investigators and to replace the senior
investigator who had resigned. In addition, some staff were loaned to the office until the back-log of complaints – running at 2,000 cases at the end of
1988 – had been reduced to manageable proportions.

This episode seems to me to be a graphic reminder of the fact that the
effective operation of the Ombudsman – which will not always be in the Government's interest – depends on the Ombudsman being adequately funded and
that this depends, ultimately, on the Government.

TYPES OF DEFECTS

Section 4(2)(b) of the 1980 Act gives a list[5] of defects that may constitute
maladministration. Significantly, the list or indeed anything else much in the
way of reference to his statute is seldom referred to by the Ombudsman, so
there is no point in focussing on them. It is better to list some of the Ombudsman's most telling cases under the sort of catchy headings he uses in his annual reports.

Fairness, merits and policy

It is clear, from his annual reports, that the Ombudsman is more prepared than
a court would be to review questions of merits or judgement. Intertwined with
this is the fact, that he is prepared to appraise questions that reach beyond
administration to low-level policy. He has been prepared – to quote a characteristic phrase used by the first incumbent, in various public talks – "to push
the boat out".

---

[4] Published as an Appendix to his 1987 Report (Pl. 5258).
[5] ". . . the Ombudsman may investigate any action . . . where . . . it appears to the Ombudsman
. . .
(b) that the action was or may have been:
    (i)   taken without proper authority;
    (ii) taken on irrelevant grounds;
    (iii) the result of negligence or carelessness;
    (iv) based on erroneous or incomplete information;
    (v) improperly discriminatory;
    (vi) based on an undesirable administrative practice; or
    (vii) otherwise contrary to sound or fair administration."

The first illustration arises from the fact that under the rubric of "fairness", the Ombudsman was prepared to intervene when a mother complained that the Department of Education bus route for taking children to school was so drawn that her five-year-old child had to walk one and a half miles to the bus, whilst certain older children were being picked up much closer to their homes. The Ombudsman put forward a proposal which, without extra overall cost, enabled the bus to collect the five-year-old closer to his home whilst requiring some older children to walk somewhat further. The Department of Social Welfare accepted his proposal.[6]

Further examples include recommendations that a health board allow the complainant access to the medical records of his infant son[7]; that a health board permit a relation of the mother (other than her husband) to be present at the birth of her child[8]; that the Department of Foreign Affairs allow a joint passport be issued for a one-year period only at a fee of IR£3 to an elderly couple (the one-year passport being a concession formerly confined to individuals)[9]; that anomalies be removed in the rent scheme for local authority dwellings, since they seemed to allow for the payment of two different levels of rent in respect of the same household income.[10]

Often the decisions in issue involve a wide administrative scheme or circular by a public body (frequently the Department of Social Welfare or a local authority) in the exercise of a statutory authority (other than legislation). Plainly, this is an area in which the Ombudsman rightly feels that he should tread warily: on the one hand, there may be an injustice affecting not only the complainant but also several others; on the other hand, what amounts to an injustice or anomaly may really involve a policy question and section 4(1) of the Ombudsman Act 1980 confines the Ombudsman to investigation of "any action taken in the performance of administrative functions". The resolution of these divergent factors is often couched in this form "Arising from my discussions with the Department, I understand that they are reviewing the entire question."[11]

Many policy differences, of course, come down in the end to money, especially so in this era of limited public resources. The Ombudsman has naturally

---

[6] 1984 Report, p. 37. For other school transport complaints which are a fairly regular source of complaint, see 1990 Report, pp.74-75; 1992 Report, pp.94-95; 1993 Report, p 90; 1994 Report, pp:17-19.
[7] 1986 Report, p. 65.
[8] 1987 Report, p. 91.
[9] 1986 Report, p. 50. The Ombudsman's concern not to trench too far on policy matters is shown by his approach here: "I asked the Department if, at the time of initiating the concession it was their clear intention to exclude holders of a joint passport from availing of the concession. The Department considered the matter and decided that it would be the Minister's wish to interpret the rule in the most favourable way for those entitled to the concession."
[10] 1994 Report, pp.39-40.
[11] 1992 Report, p.27

been prepared to accept this as a factor justifying a public authority's action. For example, in one case concerning allegedly inadequate refuse collection arrangements, he found that "the Council's justification for those arrangements was reasonable in light of their financial constraints and I consider that it outweighed the inconvenience experienced by the complainant as a result of these arrangements."[12]

At any rate, as regards policy, the Irish position would appear to be slightly different from that in the United Kingdom. Take, for example, *R. v. Local Commissioner, ex p. Eastleigh B.C.*,[13] a case arising from a British Ombudsman's investigation of a local authority's inspection of the construction of a sewer. It was common cause among the judges of the Court of Appeal that the decision to inspect at only the four most important stages of the construction was a matter of policy and so outside the Ombudsman's jurisdiction, leaving him only to examine the execution of the inspections. One of the three judges, Taylor L.J., however, went further and held that even the question of whether an inspection required a "gradient test" to be made of every drain and sewer was also a matter of policy. It seems likely from his treatment of the complaints mentioned earlier that the Irish Ombudsman would, like his British cousin, have thought that he did have jurisdiction to appraise these "policy issues".

New facts

A less conceptually difficult area, which has involved a large number of cases, involves investigation – some of it very resourceful and imaginative – by members of the Ombudsman's staff that leads to the discovery of new facts or information, or casts a fresh light on the existing information, leading to a change of heart in the responsible authority. For example, in one case the Department of Social Welfare had decided that the complainant was not available for employment except as an actor and that this constituted "unreasonable limitations on his availability for work", which was a statutory ground for terminating his unemployment benefit. The Ombudsman suggested various new factors to the appeals officer – including the fact that the complainant has previously worked as a car-park attendant, and that this showed that he was willing to take any kind of work. Accordingly, the appeals officer reversed the original decision.[14] In another instructive case, the information given by an

---

[12] 1989 Report, p.91. See also, 1987 Report, p.32 and 1992 Report, p.35-36.

[13] [1988] Q.B. 855. The division between the majority and the dissentient judge was not primarily about the demarcation line between policy and administration, but rather about whether, as a matter of fact, the Ombudsman had crossed the line.

[14] 1984 Report, pp. 49-50; 1992 Report, pp.15-17. In an occupational injuries benefit decision, the Ombudsman discovered that a widow's late husband had been exposed to one of eight prescribed diseases in his second last employment. Consequently she was entitled to occupa-

applicant for unemployment benefit, as a result of which his claim had been refused, was wrong – it had been supplied by the applicant only because he had misunderstood the form.[15] In another case, involving an application for a contributory widow's pension, it was discovered that the complainant had paid the appropriate number of social insurance contributions but (and this feature is common to a number of cases) under her maiden name. The complainant was awarded IR£13,000 back-payment plus IR£6,000 for loss of purchasing power.[16]

Procedure

A great number of complaints to the Ombudsman fall into a category which might broadly be called "procedure". Defects naturally include breaches of natural justice or of particular procedural regulations. An example of the latter, which has come up on a number of occasions, concerns the closure of pedestrian rights of way in residential areas in violation of the statutory procedure that requires advertising in the press and, where there is an objection, an oral hearing. One notable feature of these cases is that there will often be strong public sentiment in favour of closure. This feature does not often impact upon the Ombudsman's jurisdiction: usually he is concerned with a straightforward individual-versus-State situation. He has not yet developed a coherent philosophy in a triangular case of this type.

Other aspects of procedure are, to take a rather common example, delay,[17] and bureaucratic bad manners shading into "the insolence of office". As an example of this latter category, speaking generally about the performance of the tax authorities, the Ombudsman has made the following observation:

"Coping with the harsh economic realities is a traumatic experience, particularly for widows and pensioners. Both are extremely vulnerable and dependent. When sharp cryptic demands for payments are issued from the computer system no account is taken of the age or circumstances of the recipient. The elderly are easily frightened and upset by authoritative demands for payment. It may be that such categories are difficult to identify but some thought should be given as to how the problem might be overcome in order to avoid unnecessary distress to the weak and elderly in our community."[18]

---

tional injuries benefit, which had been refused by an Appeals Officer who had considered her husband's most recent employment alone. See also 1992 Report, pp.102-103, 106 and 107.
[15] 1988 Report, p. 55.
[16] *ibid.*, p. 63.
[17] In 1984, 10 per cent. of all complaints to the Ombudsman involved delay.
[18] 1984 Report, p. 18. See also, 1987 Report, p. 25 and 1992 Report, p.48 (on the proper procedure for removing a child from foster parents).

Information

The Ombudsman in Ireland,[19] Britain,[20] and France,[21] has treated it as axiomatic that a complainant who has been given incorrect advice – whether as to the facts of the situation or the law or administrative practice – should be given a remedy. This approach has also been followed in a case where the advice was correct when given and circumstances later changed, rendering the advice bad.[22]

In a number of complaints the Ombudsman appears to have gone further and drawn upon a broad though unspecified principle that the State is under a positive duty to supply the citizen with relevant information about his rights, whether this involves legal advice or facts about his own personal situation.[23] Even if a complainant has not asked the right question, welfare agencies have been censored for failing to mention to the complainant benefits or allowances that might have applied to him. One finds, too, in the reports, strictures against the use of "language which, although technically accurate is not capable of being understood by members of the public".[24]

At a specific level, there have been a number of cases in which welfare agencies have been censored for failing to mention to the complainant benefits that might have applied to him.[25] In such circumstances, the agency has granted the benefit or allowance with retrospective effect. In addition, as a result of the Ombudsman's prompting, the Department of Social Welfare now gives farmers details of its assessment of their means where this assessment has led to a reduction in their social welfare payments.[26] Notice, likewise, the following strong statement in respect of a different area of administration:

> "[T]here are basic deficiencies in the information available about the existence and operation of the Treatment Abroad Scheme. This lack of information is evident not only among patients and members of their families, who might need to avail of the scheme but also, unfortunately, among medical and administrative personnel in the health boards. I am concerned also that the operation of the scheme is not sufficiently transparent, that practices differ between health boards and that staff, including medical staff, are not sufficiently familiar with schemes in order to advise or direct the patients at the appropriate time to the relevant administrative scheme."[27]

---

[19] 1991 Report, p.12.
[20] Mowbray, "A Right to Official Advice" [1986] Public Law 68.
[21] Clark, "The Conseil d'Etat versus Ombudsman Debate Revisited" (1984) 62 Pub. Admin. 161
[22] 1993 Report, pp.54-55.
[23] See, for example, 1990 Report, pp.42-44, 1992 Report, pp. 30-31.
[24] 1986 Report, p.15.
[25] 1985 Report, p. 23.
[26] 1985 Report, p.23.
[27] 1993 Report, p.35.

One should add here that there is naturally an obligation on the complainant to have behaved in a reasonably sensible and straightforward way. He must, for instance, have disclosed all the relevant facts to the Ombudsman. And, if it comes to a dispute as to something written or said by a public agency, the British Parliamentary Commissioner has said that the Ombudsman "could function as a kind of jury, reading the alleged attending document with a critical but neutral eye and deciding whether the misapprehension alleged was a reasonable one or a perverted reading aimed at personal advantage".[28]

A significant point is that in this area especially, the Ombudsman has gone further than would a court. As just noted, he has been uninterested in the distinction, beloved of the law of torts, between the positive and the negative duty. Again, he has held that if a public agency gives a commitment, this must be honoured. There has been no interest in the traditional notion that a public agency may not fetter the exercise of a discretionary power, which notion has been a substantial counterweight to the court's development of the legitimate expectation doctrine.[29] Finally, the Ombudsman shows no sympathy whatsoever with the well-established legal principle, which was actually put to him unavailingly on one occasion by the Department of Social Welfare,[30] that "ignorance of the law is no defence".

In recent reports, the Ombudsman has waxed even stronger on the need for better communication between public bodies and their "clients". He said: "few or perhaps none of these would have ended up in my Office had the bodies concerned be more attentive to the need for good communication with their clients."[31] As the writer E.M. Forster remarked, "only connect!"

APPRAISAL

In the first place, one should note that the Irish Ombudsman has been a "success". One could substantiate this judgment by reference to various tests and evidence. First, the office has so much established a public personae as a sage and independent arbiter that he has been asked to take on other responsibilities outside his original brief: as supervisor in regard to the Freedom of Information Act 1997; the Access to Information on the Environment Regulations, 1993; and the Administrative Procedure Bill (promised by successive governments for the past decade!). A second piece of evidence is that the Ombudsman has been replicated in parts of the private sector. Thus, the insurance and the banking and financial sectors have each established an Ombudsman in

---

[28]C. Clothier, "The Value of an Ombudsman" [1986] P.L. 204, 206.
[29]For this dilemma, see Craig, *Administrative Law* (Sweet and Maxwell, 1994), pp. 672-75.
[30]1987 Report, p.68.
[31]1998 Report, p.57.

respect of their activities. The most significant evidence, however, is that of complaints made and handled successfully in the sense that the complainant has received some assistance. In assessing the following figures, one should bear in mind that during the period for which we have had an Ombudsman, Ireland has had a steady population of four million. The most important statistic, perhaps, is that there have been well over 3,000 complaints each year. And, of the complaints upheld in the 1990s, an average of 17 per cent were resolved in favour of the complainant. Significantly, an additional 29 per cent were "assisted" in one way or another.[32] The category of "complainants assisted" covers cases in which, for instance, a complainant is told that he is not eligible for the benefit claimed but he may be eligible for another benefit – possibly benefit administered by one public agency, when a benefit administered by a different public agency was actually claimed. Where the assistance given by the Ombudsman does take the form of "information provided", this confirms one of the Ombudsman's major themes – the point, discussed earlier, that the public service should supply citizens with better-quality information. As regards the majority of complainants, who are unsuccessful, these have at least the consolation of knowing that their grievance has received a thorough investigation by an independent agency[33] – the poor man's equivalent of the "day in court". In addition, such investigations enhance confidence in the public service by giving it an independent imprimatur.

What factors have made the Ombudsman successful? Two ranges of factors may be distinguished. The first of these – the "external" factors, as it were – are those that involve not the office of the Ombudsman itself, but rather aspects of the polity over which he has jurisdiction, which favour the office. To take an Irish example: politicians and the political system are moderately unpopular (partly because of Ireland's turbulent history as a colony of conquest and partly for contemporary reasons). Thus, complaining against public bodies is regarded, by many of the population, as an act that is both pleasurable and estimable. This attitude naturally leads to the Ombudsman being popular with the public. Given that the character of South Africa and its polity are beyond our control or suggestion, I shall say no more about this range of factors. Instead, I shall concentrate on the second range of factors, namely the factors stemming from the essence and designs of the office itself and will hope that there will be an opportunity to discuss with colleagues the extent to which these factors are having an equivalent effect in Hong Kong. The following four factors appear to be relevant.

[32] The breakdown of these figures is as follows: 1990: 14 per cent (complaints upheld); and 25 per cent (assistance provided); 1991: 18 per cent and 31 per cent; 1992: 16 per cent and 38 per cent; 1993: 21 per cent and 27 per cent and 1994: 18 per cent and 25 per cent. The equivalent figures for the 1984-1988 period are 23 per cent and 27 per cent respectively.
[33] *e.g.* "When I have pointed out to pensioners the difference between the "maximum" and "minimum" rates and how it is arrived at, they have generally been satisfied that they have not been unfairly treated." (1991 Report, p.24).

Sanction

In the final analysis, the only sanction that may be exercised by the Irish Ombudsman[34] or indeed, most Ombudsmen is a formal report to the legislature. In Ireland, while there has been the occasional baring of the teeth by public servants, all of his recommendations have been followed without a report being necessary. (In the case of the British Local Government Ombudsman, it has now been provided, by an amending statute, that any local authority that defies an Ombudsman's ruling is legally obliged to publicise this fact in a local newspaper.[35]) The fact that the Ombudsman's only sanction is that of publicity is both a good and a bad thing. It is good in that it reduces the possibility of a confrontation (in contrast with the judiciary, a point which will be examined when comparing the Ombudsman with courts). It may be bad in that it may not be a sufficiently strong sanction – whether it is or not depends upon whether the Ombudsman can fairly quickly establish a strong reputation with the public, at any rate with the well-informed member of the public. This indeed is the critical feature of the Office.

It should be stressed that the advent of the Ombudsman has been deliberately designed to effect as little change as possible in existing constitutional or legal relationships. There has, for instance, been no alteration in the relationship between the individual public servant, the State and a member of the public affected by an official action. And the Ombudsman legislation is not designed to pillory or even identify the "guilty" servant and to assume (as will often not be the case) that there is a single culprit. And, in practice, the Ombudsman's attitude has manifestly been based upon the assumption that disciplining the responsible public servant is not his function and that any straying in such a direction would mean a risk of losing the co-operation of the public service upon which he depends.

Ombudsman's *modus operandi*

According to Professor Bradley, writing about the British Ombudsman,[36] "I am in no doubt that the Ombudsman's methods enable him to get closer to reconstructing the administrative history of a citizen's case than does High Court procedure". The reasons for this assessment include the fact that the Ombudsman follows an inquisitorial, flexible and private process of inquiry, with unrestricted access to departmental files, that this usually occurs in a non-confrontational milieu, and that the investigators are almost all themselves former public servants. Again, the system for devising a remedy – the interplay of recommendation from the Ombudsman and response from the public

---

[34] 1980 Act, 5.6(5), (7).
[35] See Craig, *Administrative Law* (3rd ed.) pp. 135–138.
[36] "Role of Ombudsman in Relation to Citizens' Rights" [1980] C.L.J. 304, 322.

body – is more likely to yield a result satisfactory to all parties than would the polarised concepts administered in a court. Indeed, the Ombudsman has a very conciliatory manner ("the iron hand in the velvet glove"). For example:

> "I sought the views of the Department on the circumstances of this case. Initially, they were not well disposed toward the case but they agreed to consider it if the local authority processed the application in the normal way and submitted a full report on the matter to them. The local authority did this and I am glad to report that the Department paid the IR£5,000 grant to the complainants."[37]

It should be emphasised that, although the Ombudsman entertains complaints from businesses, he plainly sees himself as the tribune of the people. During the 1990s, many of the complaints to his office have come from people who have encountered difficulty in obtaining benefits from the State's welfare systems.[38] These have been running at 800 or more annually, from an annual total of over 3,000.

The office of Ombudsman has been deliberately designed and utilised to promote maximum usage. He projects a high public profile, with substantial media publicity. A particular feature of his *modus operandi* is regional visits. He publishes attractively presented reports, with catchy headlines, within six months of the year to which they relate. It happens that in the great majority of cases described in the reports some advantage is achieved for the complainant (although this is not true of overall complaints to the Ombudsman, as can be seen below). This no doubt helps to attract other complainants.

Ombudsman compared with the courts

The subject matter of the Ombudsman and of the courts, in fact, has a great deal in common. As will be demonstrated in succeeding paragraphs, it would be mere playing with words to assert that the Ombudsman and the courts are involved in different types of regulation in that the Ombudsman is concerned with "maladministration" whereas the courts deal with judicial review or causes of action. This can be demonstrated by reference to legitimate expectations[39]; the liability of public authorities[40]; the *audi alteram partem* rule[41]; and the

---

[37] 1988 Report, p. 78. See also, for example, 1986 Report, p. 50.

[38] 1988 Report, p.4.

[39] See 1985 Report, pp. 55; 1987 Report, p. 13, 17, 75, 80, 81, 88 and 96; 1988 Report, pp. 39, 70,

[40] See 1989 Report, p. 93 – a recipient of a grant complained that renovations which a council engineer certified, for the purposes of the grant, to have been completed, were unsatisfactory. ("Council decided, while not accepting any liability in the case, to pay IR£1,000 to cover any possible defects in the work".) See also, pp. 301-302.

[41] See 1989 Report, p. 41.

duty to give reasons for decisions[42] – each of which has been the subject of both Ombudsman and court decisions. A remarkably large proportion – as many as 20-30 per cent of cases reported (although these are not typical of the entire case load) – require the Ombudsman to take a view on legal issues. This often involves the interpretation of legislative or administrative schemes that have scarcely been considered by the courts: for example, the interpretation of the Higher Education Grant Scheme as to whether certain moneys should be treated as capital or income or whether a step-parent's means were to be counted as the means of a "guardian".[43]

Furthermore, the Ombudsman does not seem concerned to observe any border line between public and private law. Complaints referring to actions by public bodies which sound in the private law field have been investigated without the issue of whether a public body is entitled to a private life even being raised. One instance arose when Bord Telecom quoted a price for a replacement telephone to the complainant, but then charged more than the quoted price.[44] Another example concerned the interpretation of the terms of an agreement for (non-compulsory) transfer of land to a local authority (whether the local authority was obliged to build a restraining wall).[45]

In Britain, overlap between the Ombudsman and the courts has been re-garded as undesirable in principle, and section 5(2)(b) of the Parliamentary Commissioner Act 1967 provides that the Ombudsman shall not investigate administrative action "in respect of which the person aggrieved has or had a remedy by way of proceedings in any court of law". However, in Ireland there is no equivalent to this English statutory provision. Nevertheless, given the respective natures and responsibilities of the courts and the Ombudsman, it remains worthy of discussion whether the Ombudsman should decide legal questions that arise in the course of considering complaints that come before him. In discussing this question, we can identify three categories of situation. The first and most common category occurs when (possibly after both the Ombudsman and the public body have taken legal advice) it is agreed that there is no dispute as to the content of the legal rule. Thus, the Ombudsman is simply following the law. Most of the Irish complaints do, in the end, fall within this class. Secondly, it is acceptable that the Ombudsman should take a view on the law where little in the way of, say, money or effect upon adminis-trative organisation is involved. More difficult is the third category, in which something substantial is at stake and the law or its application is uncertain (as

---

[42] See 1988 Report, p. 88 and 1985 Report, p. 23.
[43] See 1987 Report, p. 71; 1989 Report, p. 85; 1985 Report, p. 28, respectively. On interpreta-tion of this Scheme, see also: 1991 Report, p. 58-62; 1992 Report, pp. 93-94; 1994 Report, p. 23.
[44] 1992 Report, p.124.
[45] 1992 Report, pp.116-117.

is quite common, given the rate of change of public law). To this category, we shall return in a moment.

A more acute form of this difficulty arises, of course, where the Ombudsman decides an issue differently from the courts. Take, as an example, those statutory immunities from tort action of which section 64(1) of the Postal and Telecommunications Act 1983 is an example. This provision gives An Post immunity from all liability in respect of any loss suffered in the use of a postal service. One complaint to the Ombudsman concerned a wedding dress which had been misplaced – though subsequently found – in the post.[46] The Ombudsman took the matter up as a case of "administrative bungling" and secured the payment of IR£80 to the bride to compensate her for expenses incurred in looking for the dress in Dublin; but no mention whatever was made of the difficulty that inevitably arises where there are two jurisdictions which resolve a situation in different ways. The legislature has exercised its prerogative to determine (for policy reasons, be they good or bad, arising from the operation of the postal service) that a person who suffers loss through negligence in the postal service cannot recover against An Post. It would appear to be inconsistent to set up this statutory immunity against one person who sues for negligence before the courts, yet to allow it to be circumvented by another person who complains of "bungling" to the Ombudsman.

A rather similar, though more spectacular, episode arose out of the British Minister for Trade and Industry's failure properly to use his supervisory power over a firm of financial brokers (Barlow Clowes) with the result that persons who had invested with these brokers, were fraudulently deprived of an aggregate amount of £30 million. The British (Central Government) Ombudsman recommended that the British Government reimburse this money to the investors, and the Government – after some grumbling – did so.[47] Contrast this episode with the Privy Council case of *Yuen Kun Yeu v. A.G. of Hong Kong*.[48] Here, in comparable circumstances to those in the Barlow Clowes complaint, the Court held that a public regulatory agency owed no duty of care in negligence to the victims of a fraud.

To return to the question left hanging earlier: is it best if questions involving points of law are determined by the courts or the Ombudsman. On a conventional rule of law view the answer would plainly be the courts. They are the ultimate arbiters of the law and for centuries it has been their duty to keep administrative agencies within the law. In the long term, it seems that this expansion would lead to difficulties. The government might bite back, either by way of a court order (if the Ombudsman seemed to be exceeding his jurisdiction) or, more likely, through some bureaucratic device, for instance,

---

[46] 1984 Report, p. 39; see also 1987 Report, p. 26.
[47] [1994] Public Law 192 and 408.
[48] [1989] A.C. 53.

financial control. As mentioned already, a good deal depends on the extent of the public esteem which the Ombudsman enjoys. And this in turn depends upon how many cases he continues to receive and how successful he is in dealing with them. This is of course a circular argument: nothing succeeds like success.

Trouble-shooter

As well as his basic duty in respect of individual grievances, there is another related and, in the long run, perhaps even more important role that he can play, namely as a trouble-shooter over the entire range of government administration.[49] The Irish Ombudsman has listed 16 legislative or policy changes which have come about, partly or entirely, as a result of recommendations of the Ombudsman. For example, social welfare legislation has been amended to reduce discrimination against husbands and widowers; the Department of Social Welfare has agreed to change its practice to admit claims for unemployment from those on holiday outside the state.[50] In addition, the Ombudsman has encouraged public bodies to develop and publicise their own internal complaints procedure.[51] It will be noted that, as with the individual cases, many of these changes will be of most benefit to the poorer sections of the community. This is appropriate since other, better-off groups are often better equipped to make their own representations felt by the administrative machine, for example accountants' organisations lobbying the Revenue Commissioners for extra-statutory concessions.

In this role, the Ombudsman can counter a frequent failure of communication at the interface at which the citizen meets his government. Thus, the Ombudsman has described his duty as "giving the citizen a role in government administration".[52] On an optimistic scenario, the Ombudsman's most significant service will, in the long term, be to stimulate improvements that raise the level of public administration (for example, quicker decisions, more flexibility, better explanations, good manners). The difficulty here lies in the fact that

---

[49] See, *e.g.* 1994 Report, pp. 1-5.

[50] In at least one of the complaints of this type, the case was exacerbated by the fact that the holiday was in Northern Ireland. The Ombudsman commented, in his 1987 Report, p. 21: "It would seem reasonable in view of our often expressed attitude towards Northern Ireland that a person visiting Northern Ireland should not be regarded as "absent from the State" for the purposes of social welfare payments."

[51] 1985 Report, p. 30; 1987 Report, p. 34. See also 1994 Report, p. 42, where in the context of telephone charges, the Ombudsman notes that Telecom Éireann has agreed "to the appointment of a Premium Rate Service Regulator: this appointment is to be organised by the Director of Consumer Affairs."

[52] See, *e.g. Senate Debates*, Vol. 94; col. 1593, July 2, 1980. For debates on 1984 Annual Report, see *Dáil Debates*, Vol. 364, cols. 483 et seq., February 26, 1986; *Senate Debates*, Vol. 109, cols. 478 *et seq.* October 17 and November 7, 1985.

this function threatens to draw the Ombudsman over the borderline between policy (or even legislation) and administration. Whether he can continue to assert a role in this far-flung territory depends critically on whether he is able to maintain his high profile with the public.

CONCLUSION

What, then, does all this add up to? There are basically two points. First, the Ombudsman has been useful in Ireland and I should expect that he could be even more useful here because his procedure is so much simpler than that of a court: in essence it depends on a single respected state authority, rather than on a judge and two sets of lawyers. The other point is that there are substantial conceptual difficulties in fitting the Ombudsman into the vocabulary of our conventional legal concepts. The British Pensions Ombudsman complained recently about the number of times he had been brought before the High Court on review proceedings. He felt that in some cases the High Court had been rather inflexible in its treatment of the novel concept of the Ombudsman. He remarked: "sometimes I feel like a modern missionary in foreign territory whose inhabitants are seeking to subvert him to their ancient beliefs and traditional ways."[53]

Some of the ways in which the Ombudsman's jurisdiction and processes sit uneasily with the traditional public law system have been mentioned here, especially in the appraisal of Public Law. On the traditional view, as Dicey said, there should be no special legal regimes, even for the State: the same law applies to the State as to an ordinary private citizen. But this approach will not accommodate such developments as the Ombudsman, which represents the view that just because the State is the commonwealth of all citizens, it has to meet higher standards than private citizens. Here, there is work for the academic lawyer to do, to construct a new theory that reconciles the Ombudsman with the traditional framework of public law.

---

[53]*The Times*, August 22, 2000.

AN OVERVIEW OF THE TRANSFORMATION OF LOCAL GOVERNMENT

JAAP DE VISSER[*]

Local government in South Africa is undergoing drastic changes to its institutional framework. This paper seeks to highlight some of the most important aspects of the transformation leading up to the 2000 local government elections. Emphasis will be placed on the new electoral system.

INSTITUTIONAL FRAMEWORK

The Local Government Transition Act

The transition of local government from the pre-1994 system to a new system, which will gain momentum on the day of the forthcoming elections, has been facilitated by the Local Government Transition Act 209 of 1993 (LGT A). The LGT A provided for three phases in which the transformation of local government was to take place. In each of these three phases, different methods of appointing and electing councillors were applied.

The pre-interim phase

In the first phase, the "pre-interim phase", representative local forums made nominations for the appointment of temporary municipal councils. These councils were based on a 50/50 division between "statutory" organisations (existing town councillors from white local authorities) and "non-statutory" organisations (community representatives from black communities that were previously not represented). These locally negotiated structures governed local authorities from 1994 until the 1995-96 local elections in which, for the very first time, all South Africans received the right to vote for local representatives.

The interim phase

These elections ushered in the second phase, the "interim phase", with demo-

---

* LLB (Utrecht). LLM (UWC).

cratically elected councils based on the amalgamation of previously white and black areas. The use of ward and proportional representation attempted to accommodate black majority and white minority interests. However, because the electoral system was premised on boundaries that were based on apartheid geography, representation was still skewed. This "interim phase" ended on December 5, 2000 when the local government elections were held.

In the interim phase, critical pieces of legislation designed to implement the new local government dispensation and envisaged by Chapter 7 of the Constitution were passed by Parliament, and certain far-reaching transfonnation processes were put in place. One of the most important of those was the passing of the Local Government: Municipal Demarcation Act 27 of 1998. This Act, pursuant to section 155(1)(3)(b) of the Constitution, provided for the establishment of the Municipal Demarcation Board.

The Municipal Demarcation Board was tasked with dividing the country up into three categories of municipalities (Category A: metropolitan municipalities; Category B: local municipalities; Category C: district municipalities). The demarcation process has resulted in six metropolitan municipal councils, 47 district councils and 231 local municipal councils. In these municipalities, commonly called "unicities", there will be a single-tiered system of metropolitan local governance – one metropolitan council for the entire unicity area. This will mean that the current two-tiered system comprising an overarching metropolitan council with metropolitan substructures will be abandoned. Every square metre outside the six unicities will in future be part of a district municipality . Together with the unicities, this is an implementation of the principle of "wall-to-wall" local government, envisaged in Chapter 7 of the Constitution. Each district municipalities will include a number of local municipalities. Thus, the district municipality covers the same area as the local municipalities within its district: a number of local municipalities together make up a district municipality , subject to the existence in the district area of any "district management areas".

In some parts of the country (for example, the Kruger National Park and parts of the Karoo), huge areas of land are very sparsely populated and maintaining a local municipality would simply not be cost-effective because there are too few taxpayers to sustain a local municipal administration. The Municipal Demarcation Board declared those areas as district management areas (DMAs). There will be 26 DMAs in South Africa. A DMA is governed only by the district council: there is no local municipality.

The overall aim of the demarcation process was to replace racially based local government boundaries with a system of local governance based on rational boundaries that creates financially viable municipalities. This will enable redistribution between richer and poorer parts of the same functional area.

Further, the Board had to demarcate internal boundaries: ward boundaries within those municipalities that will have a system of ward representation.

The Board also fulfils a critical role in the overall transformation of local government and may make recommendations to national and provincial government on certain other matters.

The second key piece of legislation is the Local Government: Municipal Structures Act 117 of 1998 (commonly known as the Structures Act). The Structures Act provides for the establishment of a new generation of municipalities in the areas, demarcated by the Demarcation Board. It allows provincial government to choose the "type" of municipality to be established and introduces the contentious post of "executive mayor", an indirectly elected major with executive powers. It deals with the internal structures of municipalities (municipal council, speaker and so on) and introduces a novel system of citizen participation in the form a ward committee: a committee with advisory powers, comprising the ward councillor and members of the ward community. The division of powers and functions in the two-tiered system of local governance (in those areas where there are both district and local municipalities), is also regulated in the Structures Act. Finally, the Act establishes an electoral system for local government.

The third "pillar" for the new local government dispensation is the Local Government: Municipal Systems Bill. This Bill is to be passed by Parliament and it establishes basic principles and mechanisms to give effect to the vision of a developmentally orientated local government. It deals with issues such as integrated development planning, community participation, service delivery systems, performance management, public reporting and accountability.

The final phase

In the so-called "final phase", the aforementioned legislation will form the bedrock of the new local government system and local government's legislative powers will be squarely based on the Constitution. As far as the electoral system is concerned, true non-racialism in the representation of citizens in local government will be achieved by the new electoral system, which regulates the forthcoming municipal elections (and elections thereafter). The electoral scheme is designed to ensure a high degree of representivity and of accountability.

The local government electoral system

As alluded to above, the whole of South Africa has been divided into three categories of municipalities. In the forthcoming municipal elections, voters will elect councillors for these three different categories of municipalities.

Metropolitan municipalities

The six metropolitan municipalities are: Johannesburg, Cape Town, Durban, Port Elizabeth, East Rand and Pretoria. Their councils will consist of:

- 50 per cent ward councillors (independent or nominated by a political party);

- 50 per cent councillors who proportionally represent the political parties that participated in that municipality (PR councillors).

Local municipalities

What a council in a local municipality consists of is dependent on whether the municipality has wards or not. In general, local municipalities have wards. However, local municipalities that have fewer than seven councillors do not have wards.

In local municipalities with wards, the municipal council will consist of:

- 50 per cent ward councillors (independent or nominated by a political party);

- 50 per cent councillors who proportionally represent the parties that participated in that municipality (PR councillors).

In local municipalities without wards, the council will consist of PR councillors only.

District municipalities

A district municipality covers the same area as the local municipalities within its district. In other words, a number of local municipalities (plus any DMAs in the district) together make up a district municipality. The function of a district municipality is to co-ordinate the activities of all the local municipalities in its area and to ensure development and services for the district as a whole (including any DMAs within its district). A district municipality must also exercise the functions of a local municipality that does not have the capacity to perform those functions. Because the activities of the district municipality directly affect all the residents of the entire district, every person living in the area of the district municipality is also entitled to vote for the council of the district municipality.

A DMA is governed by the district council only: there is no local municipality. People living in a DMA have the right to vote for a party that represents the DMA on the district council. They therefore have two votes, directly to the district council.

District councils will consist of:

- 40 per cent PR councillors (elected by all the voters in the district area, including voters in a DMA);

- 60 per cent consisting of PR councillors elected by voters in DMAs within the district to represent that DMA in the district council and councillors appointed by the local municipalities in the district to represent their local municipality in the district council.

Number of votes per voter

In sum, what the voter votes for and the number of votes he or she has depends on where the voter lives.

1. Metropolitan municipalities (that is, Cape Town, Johannesburg, Durban, Pretoria, East Rand and Port Elizabeth) – two votes:

- one vote to elect a ward councillor to the metropolitan council;
- one vote to elect a party to the metropolitan council from the list of parties that participated in the election for that metropolitan council.

2. Local municipality with wards – three votes:

- one vote to elect a ward councillor to the local council;
- one vote to elect a party to the local council from the list of parties that participated in the election for that local municipality;
- one vote to elect a party to the district council from the list of parties that participated in the election for that district municipality.

3. Local municipality without wards – two votes:

- one vote to elect a party to the local council from the list of parties that participated in the election for that local municipality;
- one vote to elect a party to the district council from the list of parties that participated in the election for that district municipality.

4. District management area – two votes:

- one vote to elect a party to the district council from the list of parties that participated in the election for that district municipality;
- one vote to elect a party to the district council from the list of parties that participated in the election for that district management area.

Calculation of seats

The electoral system for local government represents a choice for a combination of constituency representation and proportional representation, as mandated by section 157 of the Constitution. However, the combination does not end with simply having both a party and a ward vote. The most interesting and progressive element in the electoral system is the integration of votes cast for party lists and votes cast for party-aligned ward candidates in the calculation of seats. This applies to elections in those municipalities that have wards, namely the metropolitan municipalities, as well as local municipalities with seven or more councillors. In those municipalities, the calculation of seats for parties that participated in the PR elections (to fill the 50 per cent of PR seats in the council) deviates from the classical PR system in that it takes into account votes cast for party-aligned ward candidates. The winner of a ward election is determined according to a "first-past-the-post" system: whoever gets the most votes, wins the ward seat.

1. Quota of votes for a PR seat

The quota of votes for a seat in a municipality with wards is calculated as follows:

the *total* number of votes cast for all parties
(that is, in both the PR ballot and in the ward ballot).   plus 1
number of seats in the council – *number of elected*
independent ward councillors

2. Allocating seats

Subsequently, seats are allocated to parties by applying the following formula:

votes cast for the party in the PR ballot plus votes cast for the party in the ward ballot

Quota

Any seats that cannot be allocated after applying the formula are allocated, in sequence, to the party with the highest fraction of seats.

3. Deducting number of elected ward councillors that represent parties

When a party wins a ward seat and its ward candidate is elected, it would benefit twice from the votes cast for that ward candidate. The votes cast for that party-aligned ward candidate are also used to boost the PR seats of that party. To restore the balance, the number of elected party-aligned ward councillors is deducted from the number of PR seats that the party is entitled to.

Conclusion

There are a number of new and interesting aspects to the electoral system. Importantly, the direct vote to the council of the district municipality is a novelty in South Africa. The 40 per cent of directly elected district councillors will have to provide for counterweight against the representatives from local municipalities and DMAs, who will primarily serve their respective constituencies. A strong district municipality that will not only co-ordinate and integrate services, but also directly provide them, is a key feature of the new dispensation. Taking this into consideration, the direct vote to the district council has potential for enhancing local democracy, depending on the kind of relationship the district municipality develops with its citizens.

At local municipality level, the electoral system represents a clever way of seeking to mitigate the distortions normally caused by constituency elections. The integration of party votes of both PR and ward elections prevents any party vote from being wasted and will undoubtedly render the end result more proportionally representative than it would have been without the integration of party votes. At the same time, the advantages of the ward system, namely accountability and accessibility of ward councillors, are retained.

A flaw in the electoral scheme is the fact that representation of DMAs to the district council takes place on a party list system. DMAs are necessarily sparsely populated and will therefore have very few representatives on the district council. In fact, most DMAs will only be entitled to one seat on the district council. This effectively disables the system of proportionally representation for contesting parties and results in an odd system of "first party past the post" (the party with the largest number of votes gets that one seat).

Broadly speaking, the biggest problem with the system seems to be its complexity. Most voters will be faced with a situation where they have to cast three votes, one of which is for a completely new structure in local government, namely the district municipality. A complex electoral system seems to be unavoidable, given the new structure of local government with its different categories and two-tiered system of governance outside metropolitan areas. The importance of voter education is evident if we expect voters to cast their votes in an informed manner.

ELECTORAL LAW, REFERENDA AND THE COURTS "TREADING DELICATELY"

DECLAN BUDD*

Introduction

A consideration of the role of the Irish courts in both the electoral process and the process for amending the Constitution provides a good illustration of how the separation of powers doctrine operates under the Irish Constitution.

In its purest form, this doctrine envisages three types of governmental function, legislative, executive and judicial, to be performed by three separate organs of government, the legislature, the executive and the judiciary, each of which is independent within its own sphere of competence. Under the Irish constitution, however, this "pure" doctrine is modified somewhat by a system of checks and balances, which gives each of the organs of government a limited power to control the functioning of the others.[2]

One of the most important aspects of this system of checks and balances is the judicial power to review the constitutionality of legislative and executive action. In the course of this paper, the scope of this power is considered in the specific context of judicial intervention in the process of the conduct of parliamentary elections and constitutional referenda. It will emerge that while in general the courts are reticent in intervening in these politically charged areas, they will do so in cases where their role under the Constitution is invoked and a clear disregard for the principles laid down in the Constitution is established.

Judicial Intervention in the Electoral Process

System for devising Constituency Boundaries

Two of the earliest instances of judicial intervention into the domain of electoral law concerned the system for revising constituency boundaries.[3]

---

* Member of the High Court. I am grateful to Brid Moriarty and Rachel Casey for diligent, enthusiastic and cheerful research. Any errors remain my responsibility.
[2] See further David Gwynn Morgan, *The Separation of Powers in the Irish Constitution* (1997, Round Hall Sweet and Maxwell).
[3] *O'Donovan v. Attorney General* [1961] I.R. 114; *Re Article 26 of the Constitution and the Electoral Amendment Bill, 1961* [1961] I.R. 169.

The task of revising constituency boundaries is constitutionally vested in Parliament (the Oireachtas),[4] as is the task of fixing the total number of members of Dáil Éireann.[5] In performing these tasks, Parliament must observe certain principles, which are laid down in the Constitution. Firstly, the total number of members of Dáil Éireann must not be fixed at less than one member for each thirty thousand of the population, nor at more than one member for each twenty thousand of the population.[6] Secondly, the ratio between the number of members to be elected at any time for each constituency and the population of each constituency as ascertained in the last preceding census, must "so far as it is practicable" be the same throughout the country.[7] Thirdly, Parliament must revise the constituencies at least once every twelve years with due regard to changes in distribution of the population.[8] Finally, the number of members to be returned for each constituency must not be less than three.[9]

In *O'Donovan v. Attorney General,*[10] the plaintiff invoked two of these principles to challenge the constitutionality of certain provisions of the Electoral Act 1959. His arguments were essentially twofold. Firstly, he submitted that the ratio between the number of members to be elected for each constituency and the population of each constituency, as ascertained in the last preceding census was not so far as practicable the same throughout the country. Secondly, he contended that the Oireachtas, in enacting the legislation, did not have due regard to changes in the distribution of population as required by Article 16.2.4. In particular, he submitted that Parliament did not pay due regard to the increase in population in County Dublin nor to the decrease in population along the western seaboard.

In the High Court, Budd J. upheld these arguments. Regarding Parliament's role in revising constituencies, he stated that although "reasonable latitude" should be accorded to Parliament in the performance of its constitutional duty of defining the constituencies and allocating members to them, a departure from the principles of Article 16, if clearly established, was unconstitutional.[11]

On the evidence presented to the Court, the plaintiff had succeeded in showing that the 1959 Act led to disparities in the ratio of members to population in different constituencies. The State had sought to justify these disparities on the basis of alleged difficulties in the working of the parliamentary system. In this regard it submitted that among the duties of members of the Dáil was the duty to keep in continual contact with their constituents in order to be able properly

---

[4] Article 16.2.1°.
[5] Article 16.2.2°.
[6] *ibid.*
[7] Article 16.2.3°.
[8] Article 16.2.4°.
[9] Article 16.2.6°.
[10] [1961] I.R. 114.
[11] *ibid.* at 127.

to represent their views in Parliament and to assist them in their everyday problems. In large sparsely populated areas, such as along the western seaboard, difficulties of communication made it hard for deputies to serve their constituents properly and deputies had to spend more time travelling to and from Dublin where the Dáil sits. Accordingly, the State submitted that there was a necessity for a greater number of T.D.s in such constituencies in order to ensure that they could perform their functions properly.

The High Court however, rejected this argument. In Budd J.'s view, the dominant principle in Article 16.2.3° was to achieve equality of ratio and representation.[12] This was qualified only by the lesser consideration of practicability. Regarding the phrase "as far as is practicable" in Article 16.2.3°, Budd J. held that this qualification only allowed Parliament to have regard to difficulties of "an administrative and statistical nature". It did not refer to problems of the type suggested by the State, such as geographical difficulties, sparsely populated areas, travelling and greater demand by constituents.

In the aftermath of this decision, the Electoral Amendment Bill 1961 was introduced. After it was passed by both Houses of Parliament, the President referred it to the Supreme Court for a decision on its constitutionality.[13]

In the course of upholding the constitutionality of the Bill, the Supreme Court set out clear limits to judicial intervention in this area. Regarding the phrase "as far as is practicable", the Court stated that the extent of the parity that was practicable was a matter for Parliament, which should not be reviewed by the courts unless there had been a manifest infringement of the provisions of the Article 16.2.3. The Court would not lay down a figure above or below which a deviation from the national average would not be permitted, but would interfere only in the case where the divergences from the national average were such as to make it clear that the requirement of the Constitution had not been carried out.

This last statement is significant in so far as it indicates a reluctance on the part of the courts to interfere with the constitutionally assigned functions of Parliament, unless there has been a clear breach of constitutional requirements. This is in line with the statement of Budd J. in *O'Donovan v. Attorney General*,[14] where he recognised that "reasonable latitude" should be accorded to Parliament in the performance of its constitutional duties, subject to the pro-

---

[12] *ibid.* at 137. The judge stated further at 156:

"I was informed during the hearing by both sides that the loser would take this case immediately to the Supreme Court. The onus on a single Judge of deciding a case of this magnitude is great, and for my own part, I was relieved to know that my decision would be reviewed by the highest tribunal."

There was no appeal but there was a referendum to allow a tolerance for greater representation for more sparsely populated constituencies. Despite government promotion, this proposition was rejected by the people.

[13] *Re Article 26 of the Constitution and the Electoral Amendment Bill* 1961 [1961] I.R. 169.

[14] [1961] I.R. 114.

viso that a departure from the principles in Article 16, if established, would be unconstitutional.

Preserving the Secrecy of the Ballot

Less than a decade after the decision in *O'Donovan v. Attorney General*,[15] the courts' role was invoked in another foray into the electoral domain in the case of *McMahon v. The Attorney General*.[16] The case involved a challenge to the constitutionality of certain provisions of the Electoral Acts 1923 and 1963. The relevant provisions created a system for the tracing of votes in the event that this became necessary in order to prosecute for an offence in relation to ballot papers or in the event of a challenge to the results of an election. By marking both the counterfoil and the ballot paper with the same serial number and noting on the counterfoil the voter's number on the electoral register, it was possible to ascertain how a person voted.

The plaintiff argued that this violated the constitutional requirement that voting shall be by secret ballot.[17] In the High Court, Pringle J. agreed, stating that secret ballot meant a secret ballot in which there is complete and inviolable secrecy.[18] This view was upheld on appeal to the Supreme Court. In O'Dalaigh C.J.'s view, the system devised by the legislation offended against both the spirit and substance of the declaration that voting shall be by a secret ballot.[19]

Extension of the Franchise in Dáil elections

A further decade passed before the Supreme Court made its next intervention into the electoral domain, this time at the request of the President. In *Re Article 26 and the Electoral Amendment Bill, 1983*[20] the Court had to consider whether the Bill, which purported to extend the franchise in Dáil elections to British citizens, who were ordinarily resident in Dáil constituencies, came within the terms of the Constitution.

In holding that it did not, the Supreme Court, *per* O'Higgins C.J., stated that Article 16 of the Constitution provided a comprehensive code for the holding of Dáil elections. Taken in its entirety, Article 16 did not contemplate the extension of the franchise to non-citizens.[21]

---

[15] *ibid.*
[16] [1972] I.R. 69.
[17] See Article 16.1.4.
[18] [1972] I.R. 69, 92.
[19] *ibid.* at 111.
[20] [1984] I.R. 268.
[21] In the wake of this case, a referendum was held, which led to the insertion of a new provision into the Constitution. This permits Parliament to extend the franchise to non-citizens.

The courts have ruled recently on the right of a member of the prison population to vote in national and European elections. In *Breathnach v. Ireland*[22] the applicant was serving a term of imprisonment pursuant to a conviction in the Special Criminal Court. Although he was registered to vote, the applicant was prevented from exercising his right to vote in local, national or general elections by virtue of his imprisonment. The applicant claimed that the exercise of his constitutional rights, recognised by statute, had been unlawfully prohibited by the respondents and that the failure to provide him with the necessary machinery to enable him to exercise his right unfairly discriminated against him and failed to vindicate his rights under Article 40.1 of the Constitution[23] and article 14 of the European Convention on Human Rights. The respondents submitted that the exercise of the right to vote could be lawfully limited by virtue of a person's detention upon conviction of an offence and that section 11 of the Electoral Act 1991[24] only recognised the right to vote when on temporary release from lawful detention. The respondents further contended that the failure to provide facilities to vote was not in itself an interference with a citizen's right to vote.

The High Court (Quirke J.) granted the relief sought. He held that the provisions of the Constitution, and Article 16.1[25] in particular, provided that citizens over the age of eighteen years had the right to vote provided they were "not disqualified by law" and that they complied with the provisions of the law relating to elections. While it was envisaged in Article 16.1 that the Oireachtas could enact legislation disqualifying persons from voting, no such legislation had been enacted. Therefore, citizens lawfully detained within the prison population enjoyed a constitutional right to vote which was unfettered by legislation:

"[C]itizens who are lawfully detained within the prison population enjoy

---

[22][2000] 3 I.R. 467 (High Court).
[23]Article 40.1 of the Constitution provides:
   All citizens shall, as human persons, be held equal before the law. This shall not be held to mean that the State shall not in its enactments have due regard to differences of capacity, physical and moral and of social function."
[24]S. 11(5) of the Electoral Act 1992 provides, *inter alia,* that:
   "Where on the qualifying date, a person is detained in any premises in legal custody, he shall be deemed for the purpose of this section to be ordinarily resident in the place where he would have been residing but for his having been so detained in legal custody."
[25]Article 16.1 of the Constitution provides that:
   "1. All citizens, and 2. such other persons in the State as may be determined by law, without distinction of sex who have reached the age of eighteen years who are not disqualified by law and comply with the provisions of the law relating to the election of members of Dáil Éireann, shall have the right to vote at an election for members of Dáil Éireann.
   3. No law shall be enacted placing any citizen under disability or incapacity for membership of Dáil Éireann on the ground of sex or disqualifying any citizen or other person from voting at an election for members of Dáil Éireann on that ground."

a right which has been conferred upon them by the Constitution to vote at elections for membership of Dáil Éireann and no legislation enacted by the legislature is currently in force which purports to remove that right or to limit it in any way."[26]

The Court held that section 11 of the Act of 1992 constituted a statutory recognition of prisoners' constitutional rights to vote, since it provided specifically for persons in custody by deeming such persons to be ordinarily resident in the place where they would have been residing but for their lawful detention. The applicant, as a prisoner, retained his constitutional right to vote in Dáil elections and his legal right to vote in presidential, European and local elections, as the restriction of that right was not at the time of his conviction a sanction prescribed or permitted by law in respect of the offences for which the applicant was convicted. Thus, the Court[27] held that:

"It follows from the foregoing that if the applicant's right to vote in national elections is a 'constitutionally protected right' then it may be exercised by the applicant provided that (a) it does not depend on the continuance of his personal liberty and (b) it does not impose unreasonable demands on the place where the applicant is imprisoned, which is Wheatfield prison."

The applicant could vote by means of postal vote[28] and therefore could exercise his right independent of his personal liberty. Quirke J. also considered that the requirement on the prison authorities to make the postal vote available to prisoners would not impose undue or unreasonable administrative demands on the State.[29] Hence, the Court granted a declaration[30] that the failure on the part

---

[26][2000] 3 I.R. 467, 471 *(per* Quirke J.).

[27]This finding was based on the judgment of Finlay C.J. in *Murray v. Ireland* [1991] I.L.R.M. 465 where the Supreme Court upheld the finding of the High Court that it would place unreasonable demands on the prison service to require prison authorities to make facilities available within the confines of the prison to enable all prisoners who fell within the appropriate category to exercise their right to beget children.

[28]28 [2000] 3 I.R. 467, 473-474. Quirke J. examined the provisions of the Act of 1992 (in particular ss. 14 and 17) and the Electoral Act 1997 and concluded:
"Part XIII of the Electoral Act, 1992 makes detailed and express provision for various categories of citizens ... to vote by post in local and national elections and in referendums. Accordingly, it has been possible for the State to accommodate the special requirements of a substantial number of citizens ... to vote ... and it has been acknowledged by and on behalf of the respondents that this accommodation has been achieved by the State without great administrative difficulty."

[29]*Breathnach v. Ireland* [2000] 3 I.R. 467, 474:
"Accordingly, it would appear *prima facie* that the exercise by the applicant of his right to vote in local and national elections and in referenda may be possible without the imposition upon the respondents of unreasonable demands." This finding was reversed on appeal to the Supreme Court.

of the State to provide for the applicant, as a citizen of the State in the prison population, the necessary machinery to enable him to exercise his franchise to vote comprised a failure on the part of the State to vindicate a right conferred upon the applicant by Article 40.1 of the Constitution to be held equal before the law.[31]

The Supreme Court[32] allowed the appeal from the decision of the High Court and dismissed the applicant's claim. The Supreme Court noted that, despite the deprivation of the applicant's liberty as a necessary result of his imprisonment, the applicant remained entitled to vote and could exercise that right if polling day in a particular election or referendum happened to coincide with a period of temporary release. What was in issue in this particular case was whether the fact that he was unable to exercise that right, in the absence of the appropriate machinery, at other times was a violation of his constitutional right to vote.

The Court cited with approval the decision in *Draper v. Attorney General*[33] and noted that the fact that some voters were unable to comply with the provisions of the electoral law then in force did not in itself oblige the State to tailor that law to suit their special needs.[34] Keane C.J. remarked:

> "Indeed, given that their [prisoners'] incapacity to vote is a result of their own voluntary actions, it has to be said that the restriction thus imposed on their right to ... vote is at least as reasonable as the restriction on the disabled which existed until the enactment of the 1986 Act."[35]

The Court[36] also quoted from the judgment of McCarthy J. in *Murray v. Ire-*

---

[30]The declaration granted by the High Court (Quirke J.) read:
"The court doth declare and adjudge that the failure on the part of the State to provide for the applicant as a citizen of the State amongst the prison population the necessary machinery to enable him to exercise his franchise to vote comprises a failure which unfairly discriminates against him and fails to vindicate the right confessed [*sic*] upon him by Article 40.1 of the Constitution of Ireland to be held equal before the law."

[31][2000] I.R. 467, 476:
"The State has, by its laws, vindicated the same limited but constitutionally protected rights of other categories *of* its citizens who for one reason or another are unable to attend at polling stations in order to vote in national and other elections."

[32]unreported, Supreme Court, July 11, 2001.

[33][1984] I.R. 277.

[34]*Breathnach v. Ireland* unreported, Supreme Court, July 11, 2001. Denham J., at p. 9 of the transcript of her judgment, summarised the finding in that case thus:
"Disability to go to a polling booth does not give rise automatically to a postal vote. In *Draper* the Supreme Court held that failure to provide facilities to enable the plaintiff (who was physically disabled and unable to go to a polling booth to cast her vote) did not amount to an interference by the State in the exercise of the right to vote declared in Article 16.1.2° of the Constitution. Nor did that failure constitute a breach by the State of the provisions of Article 40.1 of the Constitution relating to the equality of citizens before the law."

[35]*ibid.* at p. 13 of the transcript of the judgment of Keane C.J.

[36]Keane C.J. quoted this passage at p. 15 of the transcript of his judgment, while Denham J. cited

land[37] where he stated that many of the constitutional rights enjoyed by citizens must, upon their lawful detention, be suspended or placed in abeyance:

> "The suspension or abeyance of the right does not depend upon practical considerations but because of the nature of a constitutional right. If a person is deprived of liberty in accordance with law, then that person loses, for instance, the express right to vote (Article 16); the person loses the non-expressed or unenumerated right to travel, to earn a livelihood, the right to be let alone, to give some examples."

Thus, the Court held that the right to vote was suspended during the lawful detention of a citizen and that, as such, the State was under no constitutional obligation to provide machinery to ensure the exercise of this right by the applicant.[38]

With regard to the applicant's claim of discrimination contrary to Article 40.1 of the Constitution, the Court stressed that this provision permits the State to have regard to differences of capacity, physical and moral and of social function. Thus, the Court held that if there was discrimination between the applicant and other citizens, such discrimination was valid under the Constitution on the basis of the differences between the two groups which the State could take into consideration. Denham J. stated the conclusion of the Supreme Court thus:

> "The applicant is in a special category of person – he is in lawful custody. His rights are consequently affected. The applicant is in the same situation as all prisoners: there is no provision enabling any prisoners to vote. Consequently there is no inequality as between prisoners. The inequality as between a free person and a person lawfully in prison arises as a matter of law. It is a consequence of lawful custody that certain rights of the prisoner are curtailed, lawfully. Many constitutional rights are suspended as a result of the lawful deprivation of liberty. It is a consequence of a lawful order not an arbitrary decision."[39]

---

this passage at pages 8-9 of the transcript of her judgment, further stating:
"The Supreme Court has therefore already stated clearly that it is an inevitable consequence of lawful imprisonment that a great many constitutional rights of a prisoner are suspended for the duration of the imprisonment. The applicant is in a social category of persons whose rights under Article 40.1 are temporarily affected by lawful imprisonment."

[37] [1991] I.L.R.M. 465, 477.

[38] *Breathnach v. Ireland* unreported, Supreme Court, July 11, 2001, Denham J. stated at p. 12 of the transcript of her judgment:
"The applicant has no absolute right to vote under the Constitution. As a consequence of lawful custody many of his constitutional rights are suspended. The lack of facilities to enable the applicant vote is not an arbitrary or unreasonable situation. The absence of such provisions does not amount to a breach by the State of the applicant's right to equality."

[39] *ibid.*

The right of prisoners to vote has also been litigated in Europe; without success. In *Holland v. Ireland*[40] the applicant applied for leave to institute judicial review proceedings in relation to the refusal of the prison authorities to grant him a postal vote. The High Court refused leave to seek an order of mandamus on the basis that there was no statutory provision permitting postal votes for prisoners.[41] The applicant appealed this decision to the Supreme Court.[42] In 1994 the applicant applied for an injunction to suspend the European Parliament elections in order to allow him to pursue his constitutional proceedings. This was refused first by the High Court[43] and subsequently by the Supreme Court on the basis that the election had already taken place at that stage.[44] The applicant did not proceed further with the plenary proceedings but initiated proceedings before the European Commission of Human Rights.

Before the Commission, the Government argued that it was not obliged under the Convention to provide either temporary release to prisoners to vote,[45] ballot boxes in the prison[46] or the right to a postal vote.[47] The Commission held that the matter fell to be considered under Article 3 of the First Protocol to the Convention, which provides:

> "The High Contracting parties undertake to hold free elections at reasonable intervals by secret ballot, under conditions which will ensure the free expression of the opinion of the people in the choice of the legislature."

It held that the *de* facto deprivation of the right to vote imposed on a prisoner did not affect the expression of the people in the choice of a legislature. The right of universal suffrage (including the right to vote in elections for the legislature) was neither absolute nor without limitations but subject to such restrictions as are not arbitrary and do not affect the expression of the choice of the people. It concluded:

> "[T]he Commission does not consider that the suspension of the right of the applicant to vote while in prison affected the expression of the opinion of the people in the choice of legislature – the fact that all of the

---

[40]unreported, European Commission of Human Rights, April 14, 1998.
[41]unreported, High Court, November 18, 1993.
[42]unreported, Supreme Court, January 28, 1994.
[43]unreported, High Court, May 20, 1994.
[44]unreported, Supreme Court, July 29, 1994.
[45]Release of all the prisoners to vote would be far too high a security risk and would put an unfair burden on the prison system, which held 2,300 inmates at any one time.
[46]As a result of the many different areas in which prisoners would be registered to vote, hundreds of ballot boxes would be required in each prison to allow all prisoners to vote.
[47]Postal voting was not a right guaranteed by the Irish Constitution or by the Convention.

convicted prisoner population cannot vote does not affect the free expression of the opinion of the people in the choice of legislature."

In light of the above finding, the Commission held that Irish law was not arbitrary in so far as it failed to permit prison inmates to vote.

Provisions for Prisoner Voting in the Future?

The Supreme Court recognised the right of the Oireachtas in the future to legislate to provide a system to allow prisoners to vote while in lawful custody. Denham J. stated:

> "If a person is lawfully deprived of their liberty and is in prison then that person loses certain constitutional rights including the right to vote. That does not exclude the legislature from deciding in future to legislate for a scheme whereby prisoners could vote."[48]

However, the Court was pessimistic with regard to the practical difficulties involved in establishing such a system of voting. In this regard, Keane C.J. stated that:

> "[T]he applicant cannot be heard to complain that the State have failed to provide the legislative machinery necessary to enable him to vote either by post or within the precincts of the prison. His complaint must be that, in the absence of such legislative machinery, the State are obliged to make other arrangements for him to vote."[49]

The Chief Justice gave an example of such "other arrangements" as escorting the applicant to the relevant polling station in the constituency where he is registered as an elector. Such provision would then have to be made for every prisoner and this, the Court held, would impose unreasonable demands on the administration.[50] The Court stated that the provision of a postal voting service to the prison population "would not be wholly impractical"[51] but would require legislation.

It remains to be seen whether the Oireachtas will grasp this nettle and sur-

---

[48] *Breathnach v. Ireland* unreported, Supreme Court, July 11, 2001 at p. 13 of the transcript of the judgment of Denham J.

[49] *ibid.* at p. 10 of the transcript of the judgment.

[50] "The implications in terms of security, cost and inconvenience of such a procedure need no elaboration." *ibid.* at page 10 of the transcript of the judgment of Keane C.J.

[51] *ibid.* at p. 16 of the transcript of the judgment of Keane C.J. He continued:
"[H]owever, there is no obligation on the State to provide the machinery, since the right remains in suspension or abeyance during the period of the applicants' imprisonment."

mount the identified administrative difficulties. In this context, it is interesting to note what Quirke J. in the High Court had said:[52]

> "Part XIII of the Electoral Act, 1992 makes detailed and express provision for various categories of citizens who are prescribed in the manner just outlined to vote by post in local and national elections and in referendums. Accordingly, it has been possible for the State to accommodate the special requirements of a substantial number of citizens [including certain categories of citizens who, for one reason or another, are unable to attend personally] to vote in local and national elections and in referendums *and it has been acknowledged by and on behalf of the respondents that this accommodation has been achieved by the State without great administrative difficulty. It has not been argued on behalf of the respondents that the extension of a system for postal voting to citizens who are lawfully detained within the prison population would impose undue administrative demands upon the State.*
>
>   *Accordingly, it would appear prima facie that the exercise by the applicant of his right to vote in local and national elections and in referenda may be possible without the imposition upon the respondents of unreasonable demands."*

I have emphasised the pertinent passage indicating the attitude adopted by the State in the High Court.

The deposit requirement in national and European elections

The High Court (Herbert J.) has recently ruled that the requirement for candidates to provide a deposit before being accepted on to the ballot paper for national or European elections is repugnant to the Constitution. In *Redmond v. Minister for the Environment*[53] the applicant, an unemployed citizen of limited means, challenged the constitutionality of section 47 of the Electoral Act 1992 and section 13 of the European Parliament Elections Act 1997.[54] Both these sections require a deposit (of £300[55] and £1,000 respectively) before an applicant, whose nomination has been accepted, can enter his or her name on the ballot paper. Neither Act grants any power to the returning officer to waive or

---

[52] *Breathnach v. Ireland* [2000] 3 I.R. 467, 474.

[53] unreported, High Court, Herbert J., July 31, 2001.

[54] Herbert J. was satisfied that the applicant had the *locus standi* to bring this claim based on: *East Donegal Co-operative Livestock Mart Ltd. v. Attorney General* [1970] I.R. 317; *Cahill v. Sutton* [1980] I.R. 269; and *Norris v. Attorney General* [1984] I.R. 36.

[55] S. 47 of the Electoral Act 1992 increases the amount of the deposit required to be made by applicants at Dáil elections from £100, as previously required under s. 20(1) of the Electoral Act 1923, to £300.

reduce the deposit required. The applicant in this case had twice applied to be
registered as a candidate for the elections to the Dáil in 1992 and in 1997 and
the elections for the European Assembly in 1994, but each time the returning
officer refused to include him on the ballot paper by reason of his failure to pay
the requisite deposit. The Court accepted that the applicant could not, without
suffering undue hardship, provide these deposits, and that, as he was otherwise
eligible, would be unable to have his name inserted on the ballot paper "solely
by reason of this inability".[56]

Article 16 of the Constitution provides the "total code for the holding of
elections to Dáil Éireann, setting out the matters which would appear to be
necessary other than minor regulatory provisions,"[57] the latter being governed
by Article 16.7 which provides that such matters shall be "regulated in accordance with law". Thus, it would appear that the Oireachtas is free to legislate
regarding minor electoral issues such as "the fixing of the date of a general
election subject to a restriction as to the maximum period after the dissolution
of the Dáil".[58] The High Court held that the limited right of citizens to be
electable to membership of Dáil Éireann is identified as deriving from - and
constituting an essential feature of -this Article 16 code and not from any regulatory laws authorised by Article 16.7. In this regard the trial judge stated that:

> "The right of all adult citizens to stand for election to the national legisla-
> ture is an essential feature of a democratic State. The power therefore
> granted to the Oireachtas by the Constitution to place citizens under dis-
> ability or incapacity for eligibility for membership of Dáil Éireann must
> be limited in its application."

Thus, the Court held that Article 16.7 does nothing more than confer a right to
regulate elections. The Oireachtas is empowered under this provision to establish by law procedural and administrative rules and measures for the proper
and orderly conduct of elections. However, the Court held that the requirement
of a deposit is not just a matter of rules and procedures. In the opinion of the
trial judge, such a requirement involves the imposition of an impediment to
participation in the election and is not the mere ordering of such participation
as *per* Article 16.7. Based on this finding, Herbert J. held that the provisions of
section 47 of the Electoral Act 1992 were *ultra vires* the powers of the Oireachtas
and were, therefore, unconstitutional.

While the trial judge decided that the requirement of a deposit did not comprise the regulation of elections under Article 16.7, but constituted an impediment to eligibility contrary to the Article 16 code, it is arguable that the

---

[56]*Redmond v. Minister for the Environment* unreported, High Court, Herbert J., July 31, 2001 at p.
14 of the transcript of his judgment.
[57]*Re Article 26 and the Electoral (Amendment) Bill*, 1983 [1984] I.R. 268, 274.
[58]*ibid.* at 275, *per* O'Higgins C.J.

requirement to pay a deposit does not, *as a matter of law,* render a person of limited means *incapable* of being eligible for membership of the Dáil, but rather it renders such membership impractical. Thus, the requirement might be more properly categorised as a regulation of elections as permitted under Article 16.7 of the Constitution.

One of the bases for Herbert J.'s conclusion that the requirement of a deposit did not fall within Article 16.7[59] was the fact that the power to render citizens ineligible for election to Dáil Éireann is expressly conferred upon the Oireachtas by Article 16.1.1[60] of the Constitution so that it was therefore "totally unlikely that the framers of the Constitution intended to confer the selfsame powers by Article 16.7".[61] One might have reservations about this finding by the trial judge. The words of Article 16.1.1 indicate that the disability or incapacity placed on a person's eligibility for membership of Dáil Éireann may take place by law or *"by this Constitution"*. Thus, Article 16.1.1 can be interpreted to include the provisions of Article 16.7 of the Constitution, which itself is stated to be "subject to the foregoing provisions of this Article". On this understanding of these provisions, the Oireachtas is free to legislate, not only to regulate elections but to place persons under disabilities with regard to their eligibility for membership of the Dáil, provided such disability is in accordance with other provisions of the Constitution such as Article 40.1.

The applicant also asserted that the relevant statutory provisions were contrary to Article 40.1 of the Constitution which provides that:

> "All citizens shall, as human persons, be held equal before the law.
>
> This shall not be held to mean that the State shall not in its enactments have due regard to differences of capacity, physical and moral, and of social function."

The Court acknowledged that the provisions of the impugned statutory schemes applied to all citizens electable to membership of Dáil Éireann or the European Parliament without distinction or qualification, but asserted that they would impact upon such persons differently according to their means. The trial judge found on the evidence that:

---

[59] Article 16.7 of the Constitution provides:
  "Subject to the foregoing provisions of this Article, elections for membership of Dáil Éireann, including the filling of casual vacancies, shall be regulated in accordance with law."

[60] Article 16.1.1 of the Constitution provides:
  "Every citizen without distinction of sex who has reached the age of twenty-one years, and who is not placed under disability or incapacity by this Constitution or by law, shall be eligible for membership of Dáil Éireann."

[61] *Redmond v. Minister for the Environment* unreported, High Court, Herbert J., July 31, 2001 at p. 21 of the transcript of the judgment.

> "[A] considerable percentage of the adult population of the State who
> would otherwise be eligible to stand for election ... would be prevented
> by these requirements [of deposit] from putting themselves forward for
> election."[62]

The High Court concluded that the statutory schemes offended the equality
guarantee since, in the opinion of the trial judge, any law which had the effect,
even if totally unintended, of discriminating between human persons on the
basis of money was an attack on the dignity of those persons, as human beings,
who had limited means.[63] Thus, it remained to be ascertained whether such
laws were justified under the second sentence in Article 40.1 which allows the
Oireachtas to have regard to differences in capacity. Having heard expert evidence on the matter,[64] the learned judge concluded:

> "In my judgment none of the matters advanced by the defendants as stated
> to be necessary to prevent abuse of the electoral system are sufficient to
> justify such discrimination and unfairness."[65]

Thus the Court concluded that section 47 and section 48 of the Electoral Act
1992, and section 13 and Rules 8 and 9 in the Second Schedule of the European Parliament Elections Act 1997 were repugnant to the provisions of Article 40.1 of the Constitution and, as a result of this finding, should be severed
from the rest of the Acts.

It may be suggested that the facts in issue admit of a different result. The
question was whether the requirement of deposits, as a condition precedent to
acceptance on to the ballot, constituted a discrimination as a matter of law
between those citizens with sufficient disposable income and those with limited means. Herbert J. stated in relation to Article 40.1 that:

> "It is essential to note, as has time and again been emphasised by the
> courts that what is guaranteed by Article 40 section 1 to every citizen is a
> right to be treated equally by the laws of the State as human persons."[66]

---

[62] *ibid.* at p. 21 of the transcript of the judgment.

[63] Herbert J. commented at p. 24 of the transcript of his judgment that:
"In my judgment, this is exactly the type of discrimination for which the framers of the first
sentence of Article 40.1 of the Constitution were providing."

[64] *ibid.* at p. 36 of the transcript of the judgment:
"It was urged upon the Court by the defendants that these deposit provisions are necessary and
justified as protection to the electoral system from abuse, that is, from misuse by the outland-
ish, the eccentric, the frivolous, the obsessive, the anti-democratic, and, those wishing to ex-
ploit the system for commercial gain. It has not been demonstrated by evidence that these
deposits have provided or would provide a deterrent of this nature."

[65] *Redmond v. Minister for the Environment* unreported, High Court, Herbert J., July 31, 2001 at p.
34 of the transcript of the judgment.

[66] *ibid.* at p. 22 of the transcript of the judgment.

The requirement of a deposit is applied, by law, to every citizen without distinction. What is in issue here is a difference in *fact* or practical impact in the application of the requirement, rather than, as envisaged by Article 40.1, a difference in law. The laws in question cannot be said to constitute a failure to observe equality between citizens with regard to "the characteristics inherent in the idea of human personality".[67] The attempt to link the characteristic of human dignity with the inability to pay the requisite deposit and, accordingly, to find the relevant law unconstitutional might seem a rather strained interpretation of the Constitution and not one which was envisaged at the time of enactment.

Both of the impugned statutes enjoy a presumption of constitutionality, that is, the applicant bears the onus of proving that the statutory provision is unconstitutional and it is presumed that the Oireachtas intended to exercise its powers under these sections in accordance with its constitutional obligations. The applicant in this case had the onus of proving the unconstitutionality of the impugned statutory provisions at issue. No doubt, the Court gave careful consideration to the doctrine of the separation of powers and the respect due from one organ of government to another.[68] Nevertheless, the High Court declared the sections to be unconstitutional and, accordingly, severed them from the body of the Acts.

Parliament's Duty is to Provide a Reasonable Regulation of Elections

A case on the other side of the line on whether the court is obliged to intervene is *Draper v. Attorney General*.[69] The case involved a challenge to the constitutionality of certain provisions of the electoral Acts, which required all electors, other than the police and members of the defence forces, to cast their votes at polling stations. The plaintiff, who was disabled and unable to attend a polling station, argued that, pursuant to Article 16.1.2, the State had a duty to provide such facilities as would enable her to cast her vote. In particular, she argued that as the facility of postal voting in local government elections had been given to the physically disabled, it must be practicable to give it also in Dáil elections.

Her claims were rejected by both the High Court and the Supreme Court. In the High Court, McMahon J. stated that the courts could not strike down legis-

---

[67] *Quinn's Supermarket Ltd. v. Attorney General* [1972] I.R. 1, 31 *per* Kenny J.
[68] *Goodman International v. Hamilton (No. 1)* [1992] 2 I.R. 542, 586 *per* Finlay C.J.:
"It seems to me inescapable that having regard to the fact that the presumption of constitutional validity which attaches to both statutes and bills derives, as the authorities clearly establish, from the respect shown by one organ of State to another, and by the necessary comity between the different organs of State, then it must apply in precisely the same way to a resolution of both Houses of the Oireachtas, even though it does not constitute legislation."
[69] [1984] I.R. 277.

lation as unconstitutional on the basis that it omitted appropriate provisions to enable a constitutional right to be exercised unless it was manifest that the omission was one that could not be justified. Postal voting necessarily involved some risk of abuse and it was for the legislature to strike the balance between the right of persons with physical disabilities to vote and the risks of abuse.[70]

In a similar vein, the Supreme Court concluded that the existing statute law provided a "reasonable regulation of Dáil elections", having regard to the obligations of secrecy, the need to prevent abuses and other requirements of the common good. The fact that some voters were unable to comply with its provisions did not of itself oblige the State to tailor that law to suit their special needs. The State might well regard the cost and risk involved in providing special facilities for particular groups as not justified, having regard to the numbers involved, their wide dispersal throughout the country and the risk of electoral abuses.[71]

This view that Parliament's constitutional duty is merely to provide a "reasonable regulation of Dáil elections" was reiterated in *O'Reilly v. Minister for the Environment*[72] which involved a challenge to the electoral procedure set out in the Electoral Act 1963. The plaintiff argued that the procedure for the alphabetical listing of candidates' names offended Article 40 in that it gave those whose names appeared at the top of the ballot paper an unfair advantage over those whose names appeared further down the paper. In rejecting this submission, the High Court (Murphy J.), held that the alphabetical system of listing candidates constituted a reasonable regulation of elections to Dáil Éireann. While it had over the years resulted in a significant over-representation of candidates whose surnames began with letters at the start of the alphabet, Murphy J. considered that such a bias disclosed more an indifference on the part of the electorate than a defect in the system itself. He also pointed out that it was the function and duty of the Oireachtas under Article 16.7 of the Constitution and not primarily of the courts to evaluate the merits of competing voting systems.

Revision of Constituency Boundaries

A point which has arisen, but which has not yet been determined definitively, is whether Parliament has an obligation to carry out a revision of constituencies once a census discloses major changes in the distribution of population. In *O'Malley v. An Taoiseach*[73] Hamilton P. in the High Court stated *obiter* that the constitutional obligation placed on Parliament to revise constituencies at least once every twelve years with due regard to changes in distribution of popula-

---

[70]*ibid.* at 284-285.
[71]*ibid.* at 290-291.
[72][1986] I.R. 143. In Australia the phenomenon of a marked preference for candidates whose names appear higher up on the ballot paper is known as the "donkey vote".
[73][1990] I.L.R.M. 461.

tion was not discharged by revising the constituencies once every twelve years. In his view, where a census discloses major changes in the distribution of the population, there was a constitutional obligation on Parliament to revise the constituencies.[74]

Constitutional Requirements regarding the holding of by-elections

Another point, which had yet to be determined definitively, is whether there exists a constitutional obligation to hold a by-election within a reasonable time of a vacancy occurring. In *Dudley v. An Taoiseach*[75] the matter arose in the context of an application for leave to apply for judicial review. The applicant contended that the opposition of the Government to the holding of a by-election to fill a vacancy in Dublin South-Central, which had arisen fourteen months previously, was unlawful. In the High Court, Geoghegan J. held that, having regard to Article 16 of the Constitution and in particular, Article 16.7 which envisages that casual vacancies will be filled and that the filling of them shall be regulated in accordance with law, there was at least an arguable case that there was a constitutional obligation to hold a by-election within a reasonable time of a vacancy occurring and this period had elapsed.

As to whether the court could grant leave to apply for judicial review in the context of the failure to hold a by-election within a reasonable time, Geoghegan J. held that on the facts of the case before him, it was arguable that the Government could be judicially reviewed. In this context Geoghegan J. observed that pursuant to the Electoral Act 1992, a by-election could not be held until a writ had been issued to the returning officer for the constituency. The writ to the returning officer had to be issued by the clerk of the Dáil once the Dáil so directed and the Dáil could only give a direction if the majority of its members voted for the motion. While the court could not grant an order of *mandamus* compelling the members of the Dáil to vote in a particular way, there was an arguable case that the Government was constitutionally obliged to set down and support motions for the issue of a writ for the holding of a by-election after a reasonable time has elapsed except in the context of substituting its own motion.

Judicial Intervention in the Referendum Process

The courts have been wary of being ensnared in an interference in the Referendum process.

---

[74]These comments were *obiter* since the actual form of relief sought by the plaintiff (an injunction restraining the Taoiseach from advising the President to dissolve the Dáil) could not be granted by the court.
[75][1994] 2 I.L.R.M. 321.

The Eighth Amendment to the Constitution, 1983 (concerning the right to life of the unborn) was challenged in two cases: *Roche v. Ireland*[76] and *Finn v. Attorney General.*[77] In *Roche,* Carroll J., in the High Court dismissed the claim, holding that the wording of the proposed amendment could not be subject to judicial scrutiny at the stage when wording, as passed by the Oireachtas, had to be submitted to the People for their decision. In *Finn,* the plaintiff was seeking a declaration that the terms of the proposal were repugnant to the Constitution. Both the High Court and the Supreme Court held that the matter was not justiciable. The Supreme Court stated that the judicial power to review legislation on the ground of constitutionality is confined to enacted laws, except for references by the President under Article 26.

Notwithstanding the emphatic nature of these decisions, a further attempt was made to obstruct a referendum in *Slattery v. An Taoiseach.*[78] The plaintiff sought an injunction to prevent the holding of a referendum on the Eleventh Amendment to the Constitution Bill, 1992 arguing that the Government had failed to supply the public with adequate information regarding the impact of the Treaty on European Union. In line with the decisions in the *Roche* and *Finn* cases, the Supreme Court held that it had no jurisdiction to prevent the operation of the legislative and constitutional procedures which were in train. In this regard, McCarthy J. stated:

"The plaintiffs sought the intervention of the courts, the judicial organ of Government, to arrest this constitutional procedure, involving both the legislative and executive organs of government, and, further, involving the source of all powers of government, the People. It may be that circumstances could arise in which the judicial organ of government would properly intervene in this process; such is not the case here. In my judgment, the application made by the plaintiffs has no foundation whatever; to grant an order such as sought would be a wholly unwarranted and unwarrantable intervention by the judiciary in clearly a legislative and popular domain – see *Finn v. Attorney General and others* [1983] I.R. 154. As the courts are jealous of their constitutional role and will repel any attempt by the legislature or executive to interfere in the judicial domain, so must the courts be jealous of what lies wholly within the domain of the legislature, the executive and the People – jealous to ensure that the courts do not intervene in the constitutional process I have outlined."[79]

---

[76] *Roche v. Ireland* unreported, High Court, Carroll J., June 17, 1983.
[77] [1983] I.R. 154.
[78] [1993] 1 I.R. 286.
[79] *ibid.* at 301.

A similar view was taken in *McKenna v. An Taoiseach (No. 1).*[80] The plaintiff objected to the Government's advertising campaign using public funds in favour of a "yes" vote in a forthcoming referendum.[81] The High Court (Costello J.) held that the matter was not one for resolution by the courts. In his view, the matter was essentially a political rather than a justiciable issue.

However, Patricia McKenna met with success in her second challenge to the Government's use of public funds to promote an affirmative vote in the referendum to allow the introduction of divorce (being the Fifteenth Amendment to the Constitution Bill, 1995) in *McKenna v. An Taoiseach (No.2).*[82]

In the High Court, Keane J., in dismissing the plaintiff's claim, said clearly and succinctly:

> "The extent to which, and the manner in which, the revenue and borrowing powers of the State are exercised and the purposes for which funds are spent are the perennial subject of political debate and controversy, but the paramount role of those two organs of state, the Government and the Dáil, in this area is beyond question. For the courts to review decisions by Government or Dáil Éireann would be for them to assume a role which is exclusively entrusted to those organs of state, and one which the courts are conspicuously ill-equipped to undertake. While the expenditure by the Government of £500,000 in this case has given rise to debate and controversy, it is not the function of the courts under the Constitution to enter into, still less, to purport to resolve such disputes."[83]

Despite this line of strong authority and the reluctance of the courts to review decisions of the executive and the legislature in respect of the allocation of funds, on appeal, a majority of the Supreme Court held that the court had jurisdiction to consider the matter. In this regard, Hamilton C.J., having considered the scope of the doctrine of separation of powers in light of certain dicta in the judgments of the Supreme Court in *Boland v. An Taoiseach*[84] and *Crotty v. An Taoiseach*[85] concluded that these clearly established that, while generally the courts had no jurisdiction, express or implied, to interfere with the exercise of Government functions, nevertheless the courts are entitled and obliged to intervene if it is shown that the Government has acted otherwise than in accordance with the Constitution and in clear disregard thereof.[86]

---

[80][1995] 2 I.R. 1.
[81]The amendment in question involved the ratification of the Treaty on European Union, known as the Maastricht Treaty.
[82][1995] 2 I.R. 10; [1996] 1 I.L.R.M. 81.
[83]*ibid.* at 18.
[84][1974] I.R. 338.
[85][1987] I.R. 713.
[86]*McKenna (No. 2) op. cit.* at 31 *et seq.*

He held that the Government was entitled to give factual information regarding the proposed amendment, to express its views regarding the proposal and to urge the acceptance of its views. However, the use of public funds to finance a campaign designed to influence the voters in favour of a "Yes" vote was an interference with the democratic process and the constitutional process for the amendment of the Constitution and had infringed the concept of equality, which is fundamental to the democratic nature of the State.[87]

In a similar vein, O'Flaherty J. stated that, while the Government was entitled to campaign in favour of the proposed amendment:

> "[T]he Government must stop short of spending public money in favour of one side which has the consequence of being to the detriment of those opposed to the constitutional amendment.

> To spend money in this way breaches the equality rights of the citizen enshrined in the Constitution as well as having the effect of putting the voting rights of one class of citizen (those in favour of the change) above those of another class of citizen (those against)."[88]

The only dissenting judgment was delivered by Egan J. who held that in the absence of an express constitutional or statutory provision on such spending, the Government's decision was not for the scrutiny of the courts.

Challenge to the Validity of a Referendum

Section 43 of the Referendum Act 1994 sets out a number of grounds upon which the result of a referendum may be challenged by means of a referendum petition. These include a situation where there has been an interference with or an irregularity in the conduct of the referendum.

The scope of these provisions was considered in *Hanafin v. Minister for the Environment.*[89]

The petitioner challenged the result of the divorce referendum, *inter alia,* on the basis that the Government's advertising campaign, which was held to be unconstitutional by the Supreme Court in *McKenna v. An Taoiseach (No. 2),*[90] had amounted to an interference with the conduct of the referendum, which materially affected the result of the referendum as a whole.

In support of this argument, the plaintiff adduced expert evidence with regard to opinion polls, the factors that affected voting patterns and the intentions of the electorate.

---

[87] *ibid.* at 42.
[88] *ibid.* at 43. Similar views were expressed by Blayney J. and Denham J.
[89] [1996] 2 I.L.R.M. 161.
[90] [1995] 2 I.R. 1.

In the High Court, his petition was dismissed. While the Court was divided on the question of whether or not section 43 was broad enough to encompass unconstitutional conduct, the Court unanimously held that the petitioner had not discharged the onus of proving that the Government's campaign had materially affected the result of the referendum.

On appeal to the Supreme Court, this decision was upheld. Regarding the scope of section 43, the Supreme Court held that, when interpreted in the light of the presumption of constitutionality, the phrase "conduct of the referendum" in section 43 was not to be interpreted narrowly so as to be limited to administrative procedures or the practical and physical aspects of taking a poll. It also covered unlawful and unconstitutional conduct in the referendum campaign, which materially affected the result.

However, in determining whether this conduct had materially affected the result, there was a presumption that the People knew what they wanted and had understood the proposed amendment and all its implication. In the Court's view, there was no basis upon which it could interfere with the High Court's finding of fact that the advertising campaign had not materially affected the result.

The plaintiff in *Riordan v. An Taoiseach (No. 1)*[91] also challenged the divorce referendum, albeit indirectly, by, *inter alia,* challenging the constitutionality of the Fifteenth Amendment of the Constitution Act, 1995, on the basis that it infringed Article 41.3.2 of the Constitution.[92] The High Court (Costello P.) dismissed the plaintiff's claims holding that, having regard to the difference provided for in the Constitution between the power to make laws for the State (Article 15) and the power to amend the Constitution (Article 46), the "laws" referred to in Article 15.2.1° and Article 15.4.1° of the Constitution did not include laws to amend the Constitution. He stated that:

> "It is clear, therefore, that the Oireachtas has no power to enact laws which amend the Constitution, its power is merely to submit constitutional amendments for the approval of the people. It follows, therefore, that the "laws" referred to in Article 15.2.1° and which the Article empowers the Oireachtas to make, do not include laws which amend the Constitution. Furthermore the prohibition against the enactment of "laws"

---

[91] [1999] 4 I.R. 321.

[92] The plaintiff's claim was ingenious. At the time of his claim, the amendment to the Constitution already formed part of the Constitution itself and, therefore, could not be attacked in the light of the Constitution itself. The plaintiff claimed that Article 46.5 of the Constitution provides that if a bill containing a proposal for the amendment of the Constitution had been duly approved by the people in accordance with Article 47.1, the bill "shall be duly promulgated by the President as law". Thus, he submitted that the Fifteenth Amendment to the Constitution Act 1995, was a "law" passed by the Oireachtas with the approval of the people and was therefore governed by Article 15.4 of the Constitution which provides that the Oireachtas shall not enact any law which is in any respect repugnant to the Constitution and that any such law shall be invalid.

repugnant to the Constitution contained in Article 15.4.1 must be a reference to "laws" other than laws to amend the Constitution itself."[93]

Accordingly, Article 34.3.2° of the Constitution did not permit the High Court to consider the constitutionality of a "law" which contained an amendment to the Constitution, since a judge's duty was to uphold the Constitution as enacted and amended and since decisions relating to the amendment of the Constitution involved decisions of national policy which were, in the final appeal, to be decided by the people pursuant to Article 6 of the Constitution. Thus, the High Court declared that the courts were precluded from reviewing such a decision which had been taken by the people.

The Supreme Court upheld the decision of the High Court. It held that a bill which contained an amendment to the Constitution and which had been passed by the people in a referendum could not be unconstitutional because it had been passed by the people who, under Article 6 of the Constitution, had the right to decide all questions of national policy in the final appeal. Unlike ordinary legislation passed by the Oireachtas pursuant to Article 15 of the Constitution, the courts and the President had no function in relation to the content of legislation which proposed to amend the Constitution as this was a matter exclusively for the people. In a judgment that highlighted the boundaries of the separation of powers, Barrington J. stated:

> "[The referendum] is a procedure in which parliament proposes and the people dispose. The people either approve of the proposal and it is carried, or disapprove of the proposal, in which event it is defeated. The role of the President and the courts is simply to ensure that the proposal is properly placed before the people in accordance with the procedures set out in Article 46 and that the referendum is properly conducted as provided by law. They have no function in relation to the content of the proposed referendum. That is a matter for the people.[94]

The same applicant challenged the constitutionality of the nineteenth amendment to the Constitution, which provided for the amendment of Articles 2 and 3 of the Constitution, as part of the Northern Ireland Peace Process. In *Riordan v. An Taoiseach (No. 2)*[95] the applicant sought to prohibit the holding of the referendum since he claimed that Article 46 of the Constitution had been violated in the procedure which had been adopted by the respondents. The applicant objected to the fact that the Constitution was only to be amended once certain other events had taken place to the satisfaction of the Government,

---

[93][1999] 4 I.R. 321, 325 (per Costello P.).
[94][1999] 4 I.R. 321, 335 (per Barrington J.).
[95][1999] 4 I.R. 343.

since he contended that the Constitution had to be amended once any referendum was passed by the people. The High Court (Kelly J.) refused the reliefs sought and held that the appropriate procedures under Article 46 of the Constitution had been complied with in full. The Supreme Court agreed and held that, as the sovereign right to grant or withhold an amendment to the Constitution belonged to the people, there was no reason why they should not give their approval to an amendment to the Constitution subject to a condition. The Court reiterated that, provided the proper procedures were complied with, there were no circumstances in which the court could purport to review the authentic expression of the people's will or an amendment of the Constitution made in accordance with the provision of Article 46.

> "This Court has repeatedly stated that under our constitutional system the people are sovereign. Provided the appropriate procedures are complied with there are no circumstances in which this Court could purport to sit in judgment on an authentic expression of the people's will or an amendment to the Constitution made in accordance with the provisions of Article 46."[96]

CONCLUSION

It is clear that when judges have been called upon to decide whether statutes governing electoral matters are repugnant to the Constitution, then the judges "tread delicately" and take cognisance of the need to respect the terrain of the other great organs of State. In particular the courts have been slow to interfere in the conduct of the process for referenda. On the other hand when legislation is clearly established to be repugnant to the provisions of the Constitution, then statutes, even when concerned with electoral law at the heartland of the legislature, have been declared to be invalid, often with far-reaching consequences. Acceptance of such decisions is a healthy sign for the acceptance of the rule of law in a democracy.

---

[96] *ibid.* at 358-359.

ACCESS TO INFORMATION, PUBLIC PARTICIPATION AND ACCESS TO JUSTICE IN ENVIRONMENTAL MATTERS IN IRELAND

YVONNE SCANNELL[*]

SUMMARY

Most countries recognise that there are problems enforcing environmental laws. One approach adopted in the EU and Ireland to remedying the enforcement deficit is to require the publication of much more environmental information of all kinds, as well as providing for public participation in environmental decision-making and for, greater access to the courts by individuals and non-governmental organisations (NGOs) enforcing environmental legislation. EU legislation requires all Member States to provide public access to environmental legislation and EU draft legislation will require measures to ensure greater access to the courts for those enforcing environmental legislation. The Aarhus Convention on Access to Information, Public Participation and Access to Justice in Environmental Matters has now been signed by all EU Member States.

This paper addresses the extent to which Ireland meets the aspirations of Article 9 of the Aarhus Convention. Ireland signed this Convention on June 25, 1998. Even though the Convention does not stipulate any definition of access to justice, Article 9 speaks of "access to a review procedure before a court of law and/or another independent and impartial body established by law, to challenge the substantive and procedural legality of any decision, act or omission" relating to decisions on specific activities.

Irish environmental law is particularly generous in the granting of standing to individuals, NGOs and incorporated and unincorporated associations challenging administrative decisions by public authorities in the courts. This applies irrespective of the identity of the authority, and no special doctrinal distinctions have developed granting a special status to decisions made by ministers or central government departments.

---

* M.A., LL.M (Cantab.), Ph.D., LL.D. (*h.c.*). F.T.C.D.: Barrister. Professor Scannell lectures in environmental law in the Law School, Trinity College, Dublin and also practices as a consultant in environmental law to Arthur Cox, Solicitors, the leading Dublin environmental law firm. She is a founding member and was first Chairperson of the Irish Environmental Law Association. She is also on the boards of several legal journals and public companies. She has written five books and many articles on environmental law.

Decisions may be challenged for failure to comply with procedures, for violation of the rule of law, on constitutional grounds, or on their merits. All courts are extremely deferential to the decisions of specialist public bodies when the merits of decisions are challenged. They will only be overturned in limited and rare cases. Extensive and generous provision is made for access to information, the right to participate in decision-making, and the right to appeal against initial decisions on environmental authorisations, but only when these decisions are made by local authorities and appellate administrative tribunals. Decisions made by ministers are never subjected to an administrative appellate process. They can only be challenged by judicial review or, in rare cases, by statutory appeal to the courts. The right to make a statutory appeal is governed by the relevant legislation and is generally limited to prescribed persons, such as the applicants for authorisations or persons aggrieved. The courts almost invariably regard persons genuinely pursuing environmental protection interests as persons aggrieved. No discrimination has ever been made by a court or an administrative body on the grounds of nationality, status or domicile of a person challenging any decision in an environmental case.

The position with respect to access to information and rights to participate in policy-making, programmes and action plans or in the legislative process is much less favourable. Although there are rights to information in these instances, public bodies do not encourage public participation (except when obliged to do so by statute) and are reluctant to involve the public in scrutinising their policy-making, activities and their performance. The basis for much decision-making on priorities addressed by regulatory authorities is obscure, and information on the performance of public authorities in carrying out their environmental protection functions is scarce. Indeed, there is a tremendous absence of information, other than statistical information, on how legislation works in practice or on the enforcement policies and achievements of public bodies. There is practically no encouragement of persons interested in legislative reform. The lack of transparency in environmental policy-making and in legislation generally is exacerbated by lack of co-ordination of sectoral policies and public sector activities and by the multiplicity and unnecessary complexity of environmental laws and practices. In particular, the fact that most environmental legislation consists of regulations that sometimes amend primary legislation and are not usually subject to parliamentary scrutiny or public debate militates against effective public access to information and participation.

ACCESS TO JUSTICE IN ENVIRONMENTAL MATTERS

Introduction

The main sources of Irish environmental law include the Constitution, common law, primary legislation, delegated legislation, European Union law, international law and the jurisprudence of the Irish courts and of the European Courts of Justice. Judgments of other courts are also influential, including those of the European Court of Human Rights and the English, U.S. and Commonwealth courts. Most environmental law is now statute-based, and reflects the obligation on Ireland as a Member State of the European Union to implement Community environmental law.

Much statutory environmental law has now been codified in a series of framework statutes, although increasing pressures on the environment and the obligations of membership of the E.U. have undermined efforts to consolidate these in an accessible form. Framework legislation dealing with the environmental management and pollution of the various environmental media (air, water and land) consists of the Air Pollution Act 1987, the Local Government (Water Pollution) Acts 1977-90 and the Waste Management Act 1996, all of which are administered by local authorities, although the Environmental Protection Agency also administers aspects of the Waste Management Act 1996. In addition, the Environmental Protection Agency Act 1992 established a system of integrated pollution control over specified activities particularly liable to cause environmental problems and conferred many research, supervisory, enforcement and administrative functions relating to environmental protection on the Environmental Protection Agency. This is an independent, centralised authority. Land-use law is contained in no less than nine statutes, the Local Government (Planning and Development) Acts 1963-99, which are currently being revised and consolidated into one Act. Local authorities administer this legislation. Nature conservation is largely the responsibility of the Department of Arts, Culture, the Gaeltacht and the Islands under the Wildlife Acts 1976-99, and the European Communities (Habitats) Regulations 1997-98. Much E.U. environmental legislation consists of subordinate legislation made under the abovementioned framework statutes or the European Communities Acts 1972-73, one of the purposes of which is to ensure expeditious implementation of E.U. Directives. International environmental law, which has not been incorporated into E.U. policy and legislation, is largely implemented by legislation administered by central government departments.

Administration of environmental laws

Local authorities administer most environmental legislation dealing with the management of the environmental media, pollution control and land-use. A distinction tends to be made in some environmental legislation between public-sector and private-sector activities, the former being subjected to different, and often less stringent and transparent, controls. Generally, local authorities carrying out development in their own areas are not subject to external administrative controls except when E.U. law requires this, for example in cases where environmental impact statements are involved. Central government departments acting for their ministers administer most nature conservation legislation, and many statutes implementing international conventions, especially conventions concerning marine pollution. Sometimes other public authorities implement specific legislation, which is not generally applicable. Thus, for example, harbour authorities implement some marine law and the Radiological Protection Institute deals with nuclear and radiation protection matters.

An independent appellate administrative body, An Bord Pleanála (the Planning Appeals Board), determines appeals and deals with other matters relating to local authority decisions on planning applications to develop land and applications for air and water emission licences. The Environmental Protection Agency (EPA) administers integrated pollution control (IPC) legislation, legislation on genetically modified organisms, and much legislation on waste disposal under the Environmental Protection Agency Act 1992 and the Waste Management Act 1996 respectively. It also exercises important functions relating to environmental management, including advising government ministers and local authorities on the environment, supervising local authorities in carrying out their environmental management functions, and licensing most waste disposal activities carried out by local authorities and others.

GENERAL PRINCIPLES

The constitutional context

Ireland has a written Constitution, which was adopted in 1937 and which can only be amended by general referenda. The rule of law and the separation of powers are basic principles of Irish law under the Constitution. These concepts underlie the structure of Irish government and provide the basis for a vigorous and much activated system of judicial review of administrative actions, especially in the environmental area. All administrative actions affecting citizen's rights, interests or legitimate expectations must be justified by reference to a specific rule in a statute or the common law; otherwise they may be declared *ultra vires* by the courts.[1] In addition, the superior courts exercising their judicial review functions enforce what are termed the principles of natural or constitutional justice and ensure respect for other constitutional rights, including the right to bodily integrity and property rights. In applying the rule of law, the courts may also review administrative decisions to ensure that discretionary powers are exercised reasonably and for their proper purposes. Under the Constitution, the sovereign is the people of Ireland and everyone, includ-

---

[1] *Director of Public Prosecutions v. Fagan* [1994] I.R. 265 at 228.

ing the government and its servants and agents is subject to the rule of law.[2]

Article 34 of the Constitution provides that justice must be administered in courts established by law but restricts jurisdiction to deal with matters relating to the constitutionality of any laws to the High Court or the Supreme Court. Article 37, however, permits Parliament to enact legislation permitting a person or body to exercise limited functions and powers of a judicial nature in non-criminal matters, thus enabling, *inter alia*, regulatory authorities, including ministers, local authorities, the EPA, and the Planning Appeals Board, to administer environmental legislation. The Constitution provides that judges are to be independent in the exercise of their functions[3] and the jurisprudence of the courts has established that the State itself is bound by statute unless the statue provides otherwise.[4] Access to the courts to challenge actions by the State or public authorities cannot be restricted by the executive arm of government.[5] Justice must be administered in public unless the law expressly provides for exceptions, and the law itself must be ascertainable and its operation predictable.[6]

The separation of powers is provided for, somewhat imperfectly, in the Constitution.[7] Article 15.2 provides that the sole and exclusive power to make laws for the State vests in the Oireachtas (Parliament) but also provides for the creation or recognition of subordinate legislatures. The Oireachtas may empower ministers and other persons and bodies to make delegated legislation subject to judicial controls, which may be invoked to ensure that it is Constitutional and *intra vires*. The Constitution was amended in 1972 when Ireland became a member of the European Communities to ensure the constitutionality of laws, acts done and measures adopted by the State necessitated by the obligations of membership of the Communities and the applicability of European Union law in Ireland.[8] Legislation to incorporate the European Convention of Human Rights into Irish law is imminent, although many rights in this Convention mirror those in the Constitution.

Unlike in the Republic of South Africa, the Irish Constitution does not expressly confer a constitutional right to a healthy environment, although an implicit constitutional right to bodily integrity was recognised in *Ryan v. Attorney General*.[9] Conduct violating this right may be challenged.[10]

---

[2] *McCauley v. Minister for Posts and Telegraphs* [1966] I.R. 345; *Byrne v. Ireland* [1972] I.R. 241; *Howard v. Commissioners of Public Works* [1994] 1 I.R. 101.
[3] Article 34.
[4] *Howard v. Commissioners of Public Works* [1994] 1 I.R. 101.
[5] *Macauley v. Minister for Posts and Telegraphs* [1966] I.R. 345.
[6] Article 34.1. See Hogan and Morgan, *Administrative Law in Ireland* (3rd ed., Round Hall Sweet and Maxwell, 1998),pp. 9-10.
[7] Articles 6, 15, 28, 34.
[8] Article 29.4.3.
[9] [1965] I.R. 294.
[10]The conduct may be by the State or its emanations, or even by the private sector, although the

PUBLIC PARTICIPATION IN ADMINISTRATIVE ENVIRONMENTAL DECISION-MAKING

Transparency of environmental decision-making

Historically, Irish public authorities were reluctant to make information on environmental decision-making available to the public. So, for example, for many years, the Planning Appeals Board refused to make its internal reports on appeals available to the appellants or members of the public, and only did so when compelled by statute. In recent years, the Government has pursued a policy of greater openness and transparency on decision-making, particularly where decisions are made on applications for environmental authorisations of various kinds. Most environmental legislation requires pubic authorities to record specified information (including information on authorisations and enforcement actions taken) in registers, which must be made available to the public;[11] but the nature and extent of this obligation is somewhat limited. There is much less transparency in the manner in which legislation and policy decisions are made.

For many years periodic reports on the general state of the environment were published by An Foras Forbartha.[12] These are now published by the EPA[13] and summaries are available on the Internet.[14] These reports deal not only with the state of the environmental but also with environmental quality and the pressures on the environment.[15] The EPA has a statutory obligation to publish periodic reports on drinking water quality, on compliance by sanitary authorities with sewage disposal obligations, and on the management and operation of local authority landfill sites.[16] Reports on compliance with certain E.U. Directives are now available to the public under access to information legislation, and all government departments and many local authorities publish progress reports of varying quality on the implementation of their legislative responsibilities. The Department of the Environment (DOE) also publishes an annual report, which is laid before Parliament, and it publishes a free Environmental Bulletin periodically. A free Environmental Information Service is provided to members of the public by ENFO, an agency established by the DOE. This well-resourced and user-friendly service is most useful and widely appreciated, not least by the academic community.

Supreme Court held in *Hanrahan v. Merck Sharpe & Dohme* [1988] I.L.R.M. 629 that constitutional remedies will only be available if the common law or statute do not provide an adequate remedy.
[11] See, for example, Local Government (Planning and Development) Act 1963, ss. 5-6; Local Government (Planning and Development) Regulations 1994, arts. 36, 37, 51, 59, 64, 121, 133, 160; Local Government (Planning and Development) (No.2) Regulations 1995.
[12] This was a state-sponsored body which specialised in environmental research.
[13] The EPA has published two reports on the state of the environment.
[14] www.epa.ie
[15] See *Ireland's Environment – A Millennium Report* (EPA 2000).
[16] Environmental Protection Agency Act 1992, ss. 58, 59, 62.

The public right of access to environmental information improved considerably when Council Directive 90/313 on freedom of access to information on the environment was implemented in 1993. The manner of implementation was subsequently improved by the European Communities (Access to Information on the Environment) Regulations 1998[17] which substantially, though not generously, implement the Directive.

In addition to rights under the European Communities (Access to Information on the Environment) Regulations 1998, a general (and sometimes more generous) right to information held by public authorities, including ministries, local and regional authorities, the Planning Appeals Board and the EPA, is available under the Freedom of Information Act 1997 (FOI Act). However, section 46(2) of the Act provides that the Act does not apply to information available to members of the public for inspection, removal or purchase under other legislative provisions. The Department of the Environment and the EPA interpret this section to mean that the FOI Act does not apply in respect of information on the environment covered by the European Communities (Access to Information on the Environment) Regulations 1998. Ryall has commented that this "means that information on the environment is subjected to a less favourable access regime than other categories of official information".[18] In particular, the appeals mechanism to the Information Commissioner does not apply to the excluded information; refusals by public bodies to supply information under specific legislative provisions can only be challenged by way of judicial review, or if they are under the jurisdiction of the Ombudsman, by complaint to the Ombudsman. The Planning Appeals Board and the EPA are not subject to the Ombudsman's jurisdiction.

Participation in the legislative process

Public participation rights in the legislative process are extremely limited, even when environmental standards with widespread implications are made. There are no statutory requirements for public consultation in draft primary legislation, although recent Ministers for the Environment have taken informal initiatives to broaden the consultative processes for environmental legislation. Neither is there usually any statutory requirement for public participation when subordinate legislation is made by ministers and certain other public authorities under most environmental statutes. For example, there is no provision for public consultation when orders declaring or recognising nature reserves and refuges are made under the Wildlife Act 1976 nor is there a public right to participate in these decisions. Notable exceptions to this include section 21 of

---

[17]See Ryall. "Access to Information on the Environment". 5 *Irish Planning and Environmental Law Journal* 48-51.
[18]*ibid.*, p. 48.

the Local Government (Water Pollution) (Amendment) Act 1990, under which local authority bye-laws to prevent or eliminate the entry of polluting matter to waters can be appealed by "aggrieved" persons to the Minister for the Environment; section 11 of the Fisheries (Consolidation) Act 1959, providing that the High Court can confirm or annul a bye-law made by the Minister for Fisheries; and section 54(7) of the Fisheries Act 1980, which provides that "any person aggrieved" may appeal to the High Court against a Ministerial order designating areas for aquaculture uses.[19] Persons promoting environmental interests are normally considered persons aggrieved in these contexts. So, for example, in *Dunne v. Minister for Fisheries*,[20] environmentally-motivated persons successfully appealed to the High Court against a ministerial bye-law revoking certain restrictions on drift-net fishing, and in *Courtney v. Minister for the Marine*[21] standing to challenge an aquaculture designation was granted to local residents objecting on environmental grounds.

Participation in procedures for granting environmental authorisations[22]

The Local Government (Planning and Development) Acts 1963-99 make the most comprehensive provision for public participation in procedures for obtaining permissions to develop land (town and country planning). These procedures also apply, with minor variations, when other environmental authorisations are required from local authorities and the EPA. So, for example, the pubic participation procedures for considering applications for air, water, waste and IPC licences are closely modelled on those in planning legislation.

Almost all environmental statutes provide that applicants for environmental authorisations of various kinds publish notice of intention to apply for the authorisation. All information submitted by applicants, and all internal reports made on these by authorising authorities, must be made available for public inspection. Any person may make representations to the authorising authority concerning the application made. Most legislation also provides that specific notice of receipt of applications for authorisations be given to prescribed bodies, including environmental protection authorities (most of which are state-sponsored) and prescribed NGOs. For example, in some planning and IPC cases, notice and copies of environmental impact statements may be given to over 20 different bodies including An Taisce (the National Trust), the Heritage Council and Bord Fáilte (the National Tourist Authority). Many public

---

[19] In *Courtney v. Minister for the Marine* [1989] I.R. 605, local residents objecting to an aquaculture designation on environmental grounds were held to be persons aggrieved.
[20] [1984] I.R. 230.
[21] [1989] I.R. 605
[22] See generally Scannell, *Environmental and Planning Law* (Round Hall Sweet and Maxwell, 1995).

bodies and An Taisce comment on applications that impact on their responsibilities. Local authorities, the Planning Appeals Board and the EPA tend to give particular weight to inputs by prescribed bodies. Their comments may result in refusals of authorisations or in the attachment of conditions to authorisations designed to meet their concerns. Decisions made must be published in a specified manner and notified to persons who have made representations. Some important applications (for example, applications involving Environmental Impact Assessments (EISs), IPC and waste licence applications) and some decisions must be also published in appropriate newspapers.

Public participation rights in nature conservation legislation and in legislation regulating development on the foreshore are less extensive, probably because they are administered at central government level. (Nature conservation legislation is largely administered by the Minister for Arts, Culture, Gaeltacht and the Islands.[23]) Foreshore legislation is administered by the Minister for the Marine under the Foreshore Acts 1933–1992. Consents for plans or projects that could have a significant adverse effect on European sites regulated by the European Communities (Natural Habitats) Regulations 1997[24] must be obtained from the Minister for Arts, if they are not subject to other statutory authorisation procedures. Only persons on whom the Minister has served notices restricting activities[25] may appeal against these notices. The opinion of the general public on an application for consent to carry on an activity in a European site must only be obtained where when the Minister considers this "appropriate". There is no administrative appeal against the Minister's decision or against the decision of any other Minister implementing any environmental protection legislation.

Participation in making environmental management plans

Public participation rights in strategic environmental management plans[26] are extensive, particularly when local authorities make these. Unfortunately, these rights are not extensively used, except perhaps by persons protecting proprietary interests or endeavouring to forestall "not in my backyard" concerns or what are perceived to be "bad neighbour" developments, such as waste disposal facilities, pubic and social housing and roads. All local authorities must make development plans or review existing plans for their areas every five

---

[23] The objectives of specific nature conservation legislation are also integrated into other environmental legislation, notably planning and pollution control legislation.
[24] For a critical analysis of these Regulations, which allegedly implement Directives 79/409 and 92/43, see Scannell, Cannon, Clarke and Doyle, *The Habitats Directive in Ireland* (Centre for Environmental Law and Policy, Law School, Trinity College, Dublin, 1999).
[25] These are the owners, occupiers or users of the land affected.
[26] Environmental management plans include development plans, which all local authorities must make for their areas, water and air quality management plans, and waste plans.

years. Most local authorities do not meet this deadline. Development plans detail local authority objectives for their areas and deal with matters such as zoning, protection of the cultural and archaeological heritage, the provision infrastructure (roads, sewage and water facilities, public housing, amenities, etc.), the provision of amenities, protection of the natural environment, flora and fauna, implementation of Directives 79/409 and 92/43 (the Birds and Habitats Directives), etc. As a rule, all development, including public sector development, must comply with objectives in development plans, although provision is made for exceptions to this rule. Draft development plans and draft variations to development plans must be notified to the public and put on public display for at least three months. Background studies may be available on request, or as a right under the Freedom of Access to Environmental Information Regulations 1998 or the Freedom of Information Act 1997. Specific notice of the making of the plans must be published in newspapers and given to specified persons whose proprietary interests may be affected. Copies of the draft plans must be given to numerous specified public authorities and An Taisce. Any person may make representations with respect to them. Any rate-payer[27] currently has a right to an oral hearing of his or her case by request. Material amendments to draft plans made after compliance with public consultation procedures must be re-advertised and subjected to a shorter consultation process. Similar procedures must be observed when waste management and hazardous waste management plans are made under the Waste Management Act 1996, or if air or water quality management plans are made, except that ratepayers have no right to a public hearing of their cases in these instances.

Only those with an interest in land may object when the Minister for Arts, Heritage, the Gaeltacht and the Islands proposes areas for designation as Special Protection Areas or Special Areas of Conservation when implementing Directives 79/409 and 92/43.

ADMINISTRATIVE APPEALS AGAINST DECISIONS

Appeals to administrative tribunals

Most legislation requiring authorisations for activities liable to have an environmental impact provide that decisions by regulatory authorities may be challenged by any member of the public by way of an administrative appeal to an independent appellate tribunal such as the Planning Appeals Board, the Environmental Protection Agency, the Aquaculture Licensing Board, or, less frequently, to a Minister. Environmental interests are represented on all of the aforementioned bodies.

---

[27] A ratepayer is a person subject to local authority property taxes.

All local authority decisions on applications to develop land and on licences to discharge effluents to waters or emissions to the air may be appealed
to the Planning Appeals Board. Appeals against decisions on IPC licences
may be made to the EPA. Any person or NGO may make these appeals, whether
or not they have a personal or proprietary interest in the matter. However,
appeals against licences to discharge to sewers may only be made by the applicant for the licence. There is no discrimination on the grounds of nationality,
domicile or residence. The Board and the EPA have powers to dismiss appeals
that are frivolous or vexatious or without substance or foundation, but these
powers are very rarely, indeed too rarely, exercised.[28] The Planning Appeals
Board; and the EPA have powers to hold a public hearing of any appeal made.
Any appellant has a right to participate in this. Persons who have made submissions or observations may be heard at the discretion of the presiding officer. In practice, this is always exercised in their favour. Appellants have a
right to be legally represented and to use expert witnesses. Decisions on appeals must be notified to participants in the appeals. The Planning Appeals
Board and the EPA publish their decisions on the Internet.

Appellants must pay their own costs in appealing, including the costs of
expert witnesses. Expert witnesses frequently volunteer their services to NGOs
and meritorious individuals in environmental cases, and costs are sometimes
raised by public appeals for funds. A fee, which does not reflect transaction
costs and which is reduced for prescribed environmental organisations (including An Taisce) and public authorities, is payable for appealing. Any person or NGO also has a right to make submissions or observations on any
appeal for a token fee. There is no provision for an administrative appeal against
the Minister's decision on applications for consents under the European Communities (Natural Habitats) Regulations 1987. Indeed, provision is rarely ever
made for administrative appeals against ministerial decisions on applications
for environmental authorisations or against subordinate legislation made under any environmental statute.[29]

Experience with public participation in administrative appeals

The Irish public has made extensive use of the above participation rights. In
1998, for example, 39 per cent of the 4,446 appeals to the Planning Appeals
Board against local authority decisions on applications to develop land were

---

[28] For example, only 32 of the 4,446 planning appeals received by the Planning Appeals Board
in 1998 were dismissed on this ground. See *Annual Report of the Planning Appeals Board
1998.*
[29] Notable exceptions are s. 11 of the Fisheries (Consolidation) Act 1959, which provides that
the High Court can confirm or annul a bye-law made by the Minister for Fisheries, and s. 54
of the Fisheries Act 1980, under which aggrieved persons may appeal to the High Court against
the making of an aquaculture order.

taken by third parties, *i.e.* persons other than the applicant for permission. Third-party[30] appeals have a high chance of influencing decisions made. So, in 1998, for example, the Planning Appeals Board granted permissions appealed by third parties with the same conditions in two per cent of cases, revised conditions in 67 per cent of appeals and refused permissions in 31 per cent of appeals.[31] The decisions of planning authorities were reversed in 22 per cent of cases, amended in 37 per cent and confirmed in 41 per cent of all appeals made. Developers, therefore, have an incentive to win the support of the public and their neighbours for their projects before lodging applications to carry them out.

Less provision is made for public participation in decision-making on local authority developments in their own jurisdictions, because this is exempt from the requirement to obtain planning permission. There is a consultation process substantially similar to that described above,[32] but appeals cannot be taken against local authority decisions to permit their own developments. However, some democratic control over local authority development is ensured by requirements that decisions to carry out local authority developments must usually be taken by the elected members of the local authority

There is very little public participation in local authority licensing of water and air emissions.[33] Although the level of participation in water and air emission licensing is slight, the same cannot be said about public involvement in IPC licensing. Participation rights under the Environmental Protection Agency Act 1992 and the Waste Management Act 1996 are substantially the same as those available under planning legislation. The main difference is that the EPA itself hears appeals (called objections) against its initial decision (called a proposed determination) on an application for an IPC licence or waste licence. The EPA made 133 determinations on applications for IPC licences in 1997. It received 693 submissions when making its initial assessment. Applicants for licences objected to 68 proposed licences and 33 third parties, members of the public and environmental organisations, also objected. In addition, 22 submissions were made on objections lodged. (Submissions are not legally formal objections because the full objection fee of £100 for individuals and £50 for prescribed bodies is not paid for them, but they may amount to the same thing.) Occasionally, submissions support applicants' proposals.

There is some anecdotal evidence of third-party abuse of rights to appeal to the Planning Appeals Board and the EPA. Opportunistic third parties have been known to use the appeal process to extract benefits from developers and

[30]This is the term given to appeals by persons other than the applicant for the authorisation or the authority which granted it.
[31]*Annual Review of An Bord Pleanála, 1998*, p. 23.
[32]Local Government (Planning and Development) Regulations 1994, Part X.
[33]The Planning Appeals Board only received six air pollution and seven water pollution appeals in 1998.

industrialists, and neighbours to proposed developments frequently avail of participation rights to ensure that stringent environmental protection standards are imposed on applicants for planning permissions and other environmental authorisations. Possibilities of resolving difficulties by mediation have not been explored. The costs of appealing to the Planning Appeals Board and the EPA can sometimes be very substantial. Many appellants are legally represented and expert witnesses are almost invariably employed. These costs may increase greatly if an oral hearing is held.[34]

The Ombudsman

The Ombudsman Act 1980 established the Office of Ombudsman, who is independent of the Government in the exercise of his functions. The Ombudsman's fundamental functions are protecting the rights of individuals in their dealings with public bodies; providing redress where necessary; promoting high standards of public administration; and acting independently in support of parliamentary control of the executive in the interests of fair and sound administration.[35] The Ombudsman has power to investigate an action where a complaint has been made to him, or on his own initiative, and where, having carried out a preliminary examination of the matter, it appears to him that an action taken in the performance of an administrative function has adversely effected the person, and that the action:

– was or may have been taken without proper authority;

– was taken on irrelevant grounds;

– is the result of negligence or carelessness;

– is based on erroneous or incomplete information;

– is improperly discriminatory;

– is based on an undesirable administrative practice; or

– is otherwise contrary to fair or sound administration.[36]

The Ombudsman may adopt any procedures considered appropriate in carrying out his investigative functions, but his power is limited to making recommendations only. His findings are not binding but if they are not followed, he may make a special report on the matter to Parliament. He may not carry out an investigation or examination where the matter is before the courts, where

---

[34]The costs of oral hearing of an appeal involving an important industrial development can easily exceed IR£20,000 a day.
[35]*Annual Report of the Ombudsman* 1998.
[36]Ombudsman Act 1980, s. 4(2)(b).

the aggrieved person has a statutory right of appeal to the courts, or where there is a right of appeal to an independent appeal body. Local authorities are subject to the jurisdiction of the Ombudsman since April 1, 1985, except when "when performing reserved functions within the meaning of the County Management Acts, 1940 to 1955, or reserved functions within the meaning of any of the Acts relating to the management of a county borough".[37] The Planning Appeals Board and the EPA are not subject to his jurisdiction because these are appellate tribunals.

In 1998, 27.4 per cent of complaints made to the Ombudsman related to maladministration by local authorities. Of these, 165 related to planning matters, of which 111 related to complaints about the enforcement of planning laws.

JUDICIAL SUPERVISION OF THE ADMINISTRATION

Judicial review is the means by which the High Court supervises the decision-making of bodies exercising public law functions. It is not a statutory appeal against an administrative decision and the courts have repeatedly emphasised that their concern when exercising this jurisdiction is not with the decision itself but with *the manner in which the decision has been taken.*

The Constitution expressly provides for judicial review of the constitutionality of all laws.[38] There is also an implied constitutional right of access to the courts,[39] which has been interpreted to include the right "to litigate claims which are justiciable"[40] and to initiate litigation in the courts.[41] The High Court's power of judicial review is an inherent jurisdiction derived from Article 34.3.1° of the Constitution, which probably cannot be abolished by Parliament. Some statutes, particularly modern environmental statutes, expressly provide for the manner in which administrative decisions may be challenged by way of judicial review. Otherwise, judicial review is largely the creature of the common law and in all cases is exercised by the courts, mainly by applying presumptions and rules of statutory interpretation. The courts are particularly influenced by the jurisprudence of the English, E.U. and U.S. courts in this

---

[37] Reserved functions are functions exercisable by the elected members of a local authority only, not by the executive. They include adopting environmental management plans and granting permissions for developments that materially contravene development plans.

[38] Article 34.3.2°. An exception to this rule is provided for in Article 34.3.3°, which immunises any Bill that the President refers to the Supreme Court to determine its constitutionality prior to its enactment.

[39] *Macauley v. Minister for Posts and Telegraphs* [1966] I.R. 345. This right is not unqualified. See Hogan and Whyte (eds.), *The Irish Constitution* (3rd ed., Butterworths, 1994).pp. 328-334.

[40] *O'Brien v. Manufacturing Engineering Ltd.* [1973] I.R. 334, 364.

[41] *State (McCormack) v. Curran* [1987] I.L.R.M. 225, 237.

regard. The courts will also review the compatibility of any law with E.U. law.

There is no specific legislation of general application regulating the exercise of administrative powers or judicial review. Consequently, most law relating to judicial review has been made by the judiciary, which has been very active and progressive, not only in ensuring that administrative bodies act properly but also in developing and extending grounds for judicial review. Not unnaturally, this leads to some lack of coherence in the jurisprudence. This paper, therefore, concentrates on judicial review as it has operated in environmental cases.

Decisions of administrative bodies may be challenged on constitutional and/or on public law grounds. As in the U.K., distinctions must be made between statutory applications and appeals to the High Court on the one hand, and an application (again to the High Court) for judicial review on the other. The rules on standing and the remedies available may differ according to which action is brought. Judicial review is confined to matters of public law. It is not available to challenge private law decisions, although there have been many decisions on the public law/private law division. Almost all decisions by public authorities administering environmental law are classifiable as public law decisions.

In 1986, Order 84 of the Rules of the Superior Courts[42] established a comprehensive new judicial review procedure enabling an aggrieved party to challenge the legality of administrative actions in the courts. This procedure is frequently used in environmental cases, particularly in planning cases. Applications for judicial review under Order 84 must be brought in the High Court. But Order 84 is not necessarily an exclusive procedure and it is arguable that public law issues can also be litigated by way of plenary proceedings when this option has not been removed by statute.[43]

Applicants under Order 84 must first seek the court's permission to start the proceedings. This is a screening process to provide against unmeritorious applications. In *G. v. Director of Public Prosecutions*[44] the Supreme Court held that leave should be granted at this preliminary stage if the applicant could demonstrate that he had an "arguable" or "stateable" case.[45] The application may be made ex parte, *i.e.* without notifying persons affected. If leave is granted, the applicant will be directed to proceed by way of notice of motion to directly affected parties, who have 14 days or such further period as the court allows[46] (typically four weeks) after service of the notice of motion to

---

[42]S.I. No. 15 of 1986.

[43] See Hogan and Morgan, *op. cit.*, pp. 788-798.

[44][1994] 1 I.R. 374.

[45]Ord.84 r.21 of the Rules of the Supreme Court. See generally Hogan and Morgan, *op. cit.*, 691-798. Contrast this with judicial reviews challenging decisions made on planning applications, waste licences and IPC licences, where statute law provides that the applicants must show that they have "substantial grounds" for impugning decisions.

[46]Ord. 84, r.22(1).

file responses. This period is frequently extended, usually for another two months. A date for the hearing is set when responses have been lodged.

Judicial review is usually conducted on affidavit evidence, and is regarded as an unsuitable forum for resolving factual disputes. Where the case involves complex issues of fact and/or law, an applicant may proceed (or be directed to proceed) by way of plenary summons. Applicants may apply for discovery or interrogatories and cross-examination may be permitted.[47] Any respondent who intends to oppose the application must file a statement or affidavit of opposition and serve this on all parties within seven days from the date the notice of motion was served or such other period as the court directs. The burden of proof is on the applicant, the standard of proof being that of the balance of probabilities.

Standing of individuals

Any person with a "sufficient interest"[48] in the matter may seek a judicial review of the constitutionality of any legislation or administrative decision on public law grounds. The leading authorities establish that in order to show a "sufficient interest", an applicant must show an injury or prejudice which he has either suffered or is in imminent danger of suffering.[49] But this is merely a rule of practice and exceptions are permitted "where the justice of the case so requires". Examples of when the justice of a case requires an exception are where an applicant, although not personally affected, speaks for others who are not in a position to bring the proceedings,[50] where access to the courts would be denied to *bona fide* individuals,[51] where the impugned act is of such a nature as to affect all citizens equally,[52] or where the application of strict rules on standing would result in a failure of an Irish court to ensure that relevant principles of European Law are applied to the State.[53]

The experience with environmental cases to date has been that the courts will deal with each case on its own facts but that they are assiduous in finding reasons why applicants for judicial review have a "sufficient interest" in the matter. In *ESB v. Gormley*,[54] and later in *Chambers v. An Bord Pleanála*[55] and in *Lancefort*,[56] the Supreme Court stated that judicial review is a remedy to

---

[47]Ord. 84, r.25.
[48]Order 84, r.20(4) requires that an applicant for leave to apply for judicial review must have a "sufficient interest" in the matter to which the application relates.
[49]See Hogan and Morgan, *op.cit.* pp. 741-751.
[50]*Cahill v. Sutton* [1980] I.R. 269 at 284-285.
[51]Morris J. in *Lancefort v. An Bord Pleanála*[1998] 2 I.R. 511.
[52]*Lancefort v. An Bord Pleanála* [1998] 2 I.L.R.M. 401.
[53]*ibid.*
[54][1985] I.R. 129.
[55][1992] 1 I.R. 134.
[56][1998] 2 I.L.R.M. 401.

uphold the rule of law, not to vindicate private interests. Judges appear to consider that there is an element of the *actio popularis* in environmental cases, which justifies a liberal approach to granting standing.[57] Standing is usually taken for granted and there is only one recently reported case where it was denied to an individual in an environmental case.[58] That was largely because the litigation had been secretly financed by a commercial competitor of an applicant for planning permission.

Standing of NGOs and incorporated and unincorporated associations

A special status has been granted to An Taisce (the National Trust, which is a company limited by guarantee) under planning and some other environmental legislation. Its standing to bring judicial review proceedings has never been successfully challenged. Other incorporated and unincorporated environmental associations frequently apply for judicial reviews of environmental decisions. The Supreme Court in *Lancefort* accepted, as a general proposition, that a limited company may have standing to bring judicial review proceedings even where it has no property or economic interests affected by the relevant decision, stating that:

> "Our law, however, recognises the right of persons associating together for non-profit making or charitable activities to incorporate themselves as limited companies and the fact that they have chosen so to do should not of itself deprive them in every case of locus standi."

Although some judges have expressed reservations about this,[59] in only two cases to date, *Lancefort*[60] and *Springview Management Company Ltd. v. Cavan Developments Ltd*[61] was standing denied to an incorporated association in an environmental case. (Other reasons were relied upon to support the denial in both of these cases.[62]) In *Lancefort*,[63] for example, Morris J. in the High Court, when granting leave to apply for judicial review, held that while persons claim-

---

[57] See *Haverty v. An Bord Pleanála* [1987] I.R. 485 at 490: ("Every citizen has, as a person residing in a civilised community, an interest in seeing that the Planning Acts are applied and observed"). *Village Residents Association Ltd v. An Bord Pleanála* (High Court, November 5, 1999) and Denham J.'s powerful dissenting judgment in *Lancefort* [1998] I.L.R.M. 401.

[58] *Goonery v. Lagan Cement Company Limited*, unreported, High Court, July 16, 1999.

[59] The first hint of judicial reservations about individuals incorporating to avoid personal liability for costs, was expressed *obiter* by Lynch J. in *Malahide Community Council Ltd. v. Fingal County Council* [1997] 3 I.R. 383, where he stated that, in the absence of economic interests, a limited company is not an appropriate body to litigate planning matters.

[60] [1998] 2 I.L.R.M. 401.

[61] High Court, September 29, 1999.

[62] See *Special Statutory Provisions Regulating Judicial Review* below.

[63] [1998] 2 I.L.R.M. 511.

ing standing are required to show a sufficient interest, lack of *locus standi* may be overlooked "if there are weighty countervailing circumstances to justify the departure from the rule". He held that the fact that a number of "conscientious concerned persons would be denied access to the courts" if refused standing constituted "weighty countervailing circumstances" in that case. Misgivings about the reasonableness of applicants and their tactics have been resolved, not by denying standing, but by making an order for security for costs.[64] The Supreme Court in *Lancefort* even accepted that a company will not necessarily lack standing if it is incorporated *after* the impugned decision is taken, although the majority stated that this would present it with "serious difficulties" in establishing an interest in the subject matter. Subsequently, these "serious difficulties" manifested themselves in *Springview Management Company Ltd. v. Cavan Developments Ltd*[65] when O'Higgins J. in the High Court refused leave to apply for judicial review to a company promoted by residents protecting their private interests partly because it had incorporated after the final administrative decision.

If a court finds "as a matter of probability" there was "nothing but an abuse of process" in forming a company, it will deny it standing.[66]

Requirements to exhaust administrative law remedies

In principle, it is desirable that an applicant for judicial review should first avail of any administrative appeal procedure against the challenged decision. But a failure to do this is not necessarily fatal to establishing standing.

The Supreme Court in *Lancefort*[67] stated that:

> "It is clear, as was held by this court in Chambers v. An Bord Pleanala, that the fact that a person affected by a proposed development did not participate in the appeals procedure is not of itself a reason for refusing locus standi."

Notwithstanding that a group has expressly incorporated for financial reasons (to escape liability for costs if an action is unsuccessful), the courts will entertain the case if the interests of justice require it, particularly when allegations of infringement of constitutional rights are involved. In *Eircell Limited v. Lei-*

---

[64] See *Blessington Heritage Trust Ltd. v. Wicklow County Council*, High Court, January 21, 1998.

[65] High Court, unreported, September 29, 1999. Standing was also granted to a company which had incorporated after the decision of an administrative appellate tribunal was made in *Village Residents Association Ltd v. An Bord Pleanála*, High Court, March 23, 2000.

[66] Per Geoghegan J. in *Village Residents Association Ltd. v. An Bord Pleanála*, High Court, November 5, 1999.

[67] [1998] I.L.R.M. 401.

trim County Council[68] Donovan J., distinguishing *Hughes v. An Bord Pleanála*[69] excused a failure to appeal to An Bord Pleanala because he held that " the public at large was entitled to know that the planning authority cannot ride roughshod over principles of constitutional justice and fair procedures". If the applicant had pursued an administrative appeal, this would not have come into the public domain.

In *State (Abenglen Properties Limited) v. Dublin Corporation*[70] O'Higgins C.J. in the Supreme Court stated that the existence of a right of appeal or an alternative remedy ought not to prevent a court from acting. It was a question of justice and if the decision impugned was made without jurisdiction or was in breach of natural justice,[71] then, normally, the existence of a right of appeal or of a failure to avail of such should be immaterial. Nonetheless, in all environmental cases to date where applicants for judicial review had not exhausted administrative law remedies, they were able to show that they had either participated actively in some of the procedures for objecting to the initial decision[72] or that special considerations justified granting them standing[73] or that they had a special interest in the outcome of the appeal.[74]

The courts look unfavourably on applicants who raise new matters when they, or NGOs with which they were associated, did not do so in an administrative appeal.[75] A court is entitled to take into account a failure to raise an objection when there was an opportunity to do so in the course of the administrative appeal when it exercises its discretion to grant or refuse relief by way of judicial review.[76]

---

[68] High Court, October 29, 1999, *Irish Times*, December 13, 1999.
[69] High Court, July 30, 1999.
[70] [1984] I.R. 381.
[71] The rules of natural justice are regarded as principles of constitutional law.
[72] *Chambers v. An Bord Pleanála* [1992] I.R. 134 (the applicant had been involved in an NGO which had appealed the decision); *Law v. Minister for Local Government*, High Court, May 7, 1974 (the applicant, although he had not been a formal appellant to the Minister, had actively opposed the project and had participated in the oral hearing of the administrative appeal to the Minister).
[73] *State (CIE) v. An Bord Pleanála*, Supreme Court, December 12, 1984 (the applicant was a public authority acting in an important public interest); *Brady v. Donegal County Council* [1989] I.L.R.M. 283 (the applicant was deprived of opportunity to appeal by alleged failure to publish public notice properly).
[74] *ibid*. Chambers was a resident in the area where a pharmaceutical plant was to be built and thus a person who would be affected by the decision. He had not even read the environmental impact statement he challenged when it was placed on public display in his locality.
[75] *Lancefort v. An Bord Pleanála* [1998] 2 I.L.R.M. 401.
[76] *Cunningham v. An Bord Pleanála* High Court, unreported, May 3, 1990; *Max Developments Ltd. v. An Bord Pleanála* [1994] 2 I.R. 121; *Chambers v. An Bord Pleanála* [1992] 1 I.R. 134; [1992] I.L.R.M. 296; *Lancefort v. An Bord Pleanála* [1998] 2 I.L.R.M. 401.

Grounds for judicial review

Judicial review is essentially about misuse of public powers. The grounds for judicial review in Ireland are very similar to those in the U.K., with an added constitutional law dimension and a somewhat more enthusiastic attitude to the reception and applicability of European Union law. The exercise of any discretionary power conferred by statute on an administrative body or tribunal may be challenged on a number of grounds. An attempt to define them was made by Lord Radcliffe in *Smith v. East Elloe RDC*:[77]

> "Of course it is well known that courts of law have always exercised a certain authority to restrain the abuse of statutory powers. Such powers are not conferred for the private advantage of their holders. They are given for certain limited purposes, which the holders are not entitled to depart from; and if the authority that confers them prescribes, explicitly or by implications, certain conditions as to their exercise, those conditions should be adhered to. It is, or may be, an abuse of power not to observe the conditions. It is certainly an abuse of power to exercise it when the statute does not truly confer it, and the invalidity of the act does not depend in any way on the question whether the person concerned knows or does not know that he is acting ultra vires. It is an abuse of power to exercise it for a purpose different to that for which it was entrusted to the holder, not the less because he may be acting ostensibly for that authorised purpose. Probably most of the recognised grounds for invalidity could be brought under this head: the introduction of illegitimate considerations, arbitrary or capricious conduct, the motive of personal advantage or the gratification of personal ill-will."

Irish courts have stressed the limited nature of the judicial review function, especially in the context of decisions taken by specialised administrative tribunals such as the Planning Appeals Board and the EPA. While the Irish courts enthusiastically review decisions to ensure the procedural fairness of decisions, they will only examine the substantive fairness or merits of decisions of administrative authorities when it is alleged that the decision is unreasonable, *i.e.* when it is a decision which "plainly and unambiguously flies in the face of fundamental reason or common sense".[78] In *O'Keefe v. An Bord Pleanála*[79] the Supreme Court held that a court will not interfere with planning decisions merely on the grounds that:

---

[77][1956] A.C. 736 at 767. Approved by O'Dalaigh C.J. in *Listowel UDC v. McDonagh* [1968] I.R. 312 at 317.

[78]*State (Keegan) v. Stardust Tribunal* [1984] I.R. 642; [1987] I.L.R.M. 202. The doctrine of the separation of powers inhibits the courts from pronouncing on the merits of executive decision-making.

[79][1993] 1 I.R. 39.

"(a) it is satisfied that on the facts as found, it would have raised different inferences or conclusions, or

(b) it is satisfied that the case against the decision made by the authority was much stronger than the case for it.The courts set a very high (arguably an unreasonably high) threshold of unreasonableness justifying judicial condemnation and will only examine the merits of decisions in 'limited and rare instances'."[80]

The courts have set a very high (arguably an unreasonably high) threshold of unreasonableness justifying judicial condemnation and the courts will not get involved in examining the substantive merits of a decision except in "limited and rare instances".[81] Very few environmental decisions have been overturned on grounds of unreasonableness. Many decisions have, however, been nullified for procedural impropriety (for example, failures to observe the rules of natural or constitutional justice or failures to comply with statutory requirements) or because they exceeded the statutory powers of the decision-maker.[82]

Time limits

An application for judicial review under Order 84 must be made promptly and in any event within three months or, in the case of certiorari, six months. These periods may, and often are, extended by the courts under Order 84, rule 21 when there is "good reason" to do so. These time limits may be varied by statute. Thus for example, judicial reviews under planning, waste and IPC legislation must be made within two months of the decision challenged. An argument that the two-month time period made it excessively difficult for the applicant to exercise rights under E.U. law and that it should be extended was dismissed by the Supreme Court in *McNamara v. An Bord Pleanála*.[83]

Remedies

The remedies available when a successful application is made under Order 84 are certiorari, prohibition, mandamus, declaratory orders, injunctions and damages. These remedies are interchangeable and the courts have power to make the most appropriate order in the circumstances even if the applicant does not

---

[80] [1992] I.L.R.M. 262.
[81] [1992] I.L.R.M. 237 at 262.
[82] See Scannell. *Environmental and Planning Law, op. cit.*, pp. 185-209.
[83] [2000] I.L.R.M. 313. European Court of Justice case law, particularly Case 33/76 *Rewe-Zentralfinanz v. Landwirtshafskammer fur das Saarland* [1976] 2 E.C.R. 1989 and Case 45/76 *Comet BV Produktschap voor Siergewassen* [1976] E.C.R. 2043, requires that national procedural limits should not render the exercise of Community rights virtually impossible or excessively difficult.

specifically claim that remedy. The ordinary court mechanisms to assist litigants (discovery, interrogatories, etc.) are available. Interim relief may be granted at the discretion of the court and even *quid timet* injunctions can be granted.[84] The courts have powers to require oral evidence and cross-examination of deponents on their affidavits. The above remedies are discretionary and the court is entitled at the substantive hearing to refuse relief even if it considers that the decision was unlawful. An example of the court doing this is when it decides that even if the decision had been taken lawfully, the outcome would have been the same,[85] or that the consequences of giving relief will be extreme.[86]

COSTS

Legal aid is not normally available in environmental cases. In practice, lawyers are generous in providing services at little or no cost in important cases, particularly when the prospects of success – and of ultimately being paid – are good. Costs in all cases are awarded at the discretion of the court[87] but the general rule is that the losing party must pay all the costs of the case.[88] Sometimes the courts depart from this rule, particularly where points of law of general importance are raised or where the respondent is a public authority. Or, they may make no order for costs, which in effect means that parties must bear their own costs. In practice, public authorities and profitable corporations rarely enforce orders for costs.[89]

The courts have discretion to require an applicant for judicial review to lodge security for costs, *i.e.* a sum of money in court payable to the successful party to the litigation. Orders for security for costs against a private individual challenging environmental decisions are rarely made, even in circumstances where it is obvious that he or she has no assets.[90] A common and judicially

---

[84] *Raggett v. Athy UDC* [2000] I.L.R.M. 396, where the applicant was granted an injunction restraining the adoption of an amendment to a development plan because of failure to comply with public consultation procedures.

[85] *McBride v. Galway Corporation* [1998] I.R. 485. The relevant Minister had assessed the environmental impact statement even though it had not been submitted to him under separate procedures applicable to foreshore developments.

[86] *State (CIE) v. An Bord Pleanála*, Supreme Court, December 12, 1984. An important strategy for public transport would have been compromised if the applicant had succeeded.

[87] Ord. 99, r.1(1).

[88] *ibid.*, paras (3) and (4).

[89] This writer knows of no case where costs were enforced against NGOs or unsuccessful applicants for judicial review. Developers and industrialists are deterred from enforcing costs against groups who may have attracted a good deal of public support by prospects of bad publicity and continuing vendettas.

[90] *Maher v. Phelan* [1996] I.R. 95 at 98; *Fallon v. An Bord Pleanála* [1992] 2 I.R. 380.

acknowledged[91] strategy of NGOs and residents' associations challenging decisions who cannot find an individual willing to incur the risk of being bankrupted by the high costs of Irish litigation is to select an impecunious applicant who will not be a mark for costs if the application is unsuccessful. Another strategy increasingly being adopted is incorporation specifically to provide a shield against personal liability for costs. This strategy, although well known to the courts,[92] was never seriously challenged until recently. In appropriate cases, orders for security for costs may be made under section 390 of the Companies Act 1963. This has only happened twice in environmental cases to date.[93] When an application for security for costs was made in *Blessington Heritage Trust Limited v. Roadstone (Dublin) Ltd.*[94] McGuinness J. in the High Court refused the application, stating that the scheme of planning legislation is essentially one of balance between a number of interests: the developer, the local planning authority, the Minister for the Environment, and that the courts should at all times "endeavour to maintain the balance envisaged in the legislation". While accepting that incorporating to provide a shield against costs could sometimes tip the balance too far in favour of objectors, she stated that it could also tip it in favour of large-scale and well-resourced developers. Accordingly, she held that each case should be considered on its own facts and that the balance would best be maintained by making an order for security for costs if this was necessary to maintain that balance. The applicant company was granted standing and was not required to provide security for costs, presumably because the developer was a wealthy multinational.

The position of unincorporated associations is unclear. In practice, applications by unincorporated associations are usually brought by a number of named individuals bringing a representative action. Irish law does not provide for class actions.

---

[91] In *Fallon v. An Bord Pleanála* [1992] 2 I.R. 380, the applicant was identified as someone who had been " specifically chosen from a number of people to take the action, in that he was not a mark for costs and had no special material interest in the result of the action or any very special aesthetic or general interest" He was in fact a 28-year-old telephonist who certainly could not pay the high costs of judicial reviews in Ireland. Nonetheless, the court granted him standing. In *Chambers v. An Bord Pleanála* [1992] 1 I.R. 134, the applicant was unemployed. In *McBride v. Galway Corporation* [1998] I.R. 485, the applicant was an out-of-work actor. In *Murphy v. Wicklow County Council*, Supreme Court, January 28, 2000, the applicant was an eco-warrior.

[92] See *Village Residents Association v. An Bord Pleanála* High Court, March 23, 2000 where Laffoy J. stated that "it is reasonable to infer that its immediate sole *raison d'être* was to constitute a vehicle for bringing these proceedings".

[93] *Lancefort Limited v. An Bord Pleanála* [1998] 2 I.R. 511. On July 17, 1998, the Supreme Court dismissed an appeal against a High Courts award of costs by Lancefort. Security for costs was also required in *Village Residents Association Ltd v. An Bord Pleanála*, High Court, March 23, 2000.

[94] High Court, January 21, 1998.

Ground for dismissing applications for judicial review

Order 19, rule 28 of the Rules of the Superior Courts 1986 provides that a court may order a pleading to be struck out *in limine* on the grounds that it "discloses no reasonable cause to answer" and that in any case where the action of defence is shown by the pleadings to be "frivolous or vexatious", the court may order that the action be stayed or dismissed or that judgment may be entered accordingly. This jurisdiction will only be exercised if the pleadings disclose no reasonable cause of action on their face.[95] Likewise the courts have emphasised that in order to invoke Order 19, vexatiousness or frivolity must appear from the pleadings alone.[96]

In addition to their jurisdiction under Order 19, the courts have inherent powers to dismiss claims on broadly similar grounds. But in this case, they are not limited to considering the pleadings; they are free to hear evidence on affidavit relating to the issues in the case.[97] Case law establishes that in exercising their inherent jurisdiction, the courts will resolve conflicts in favour of the plaintiff and will only dismiss a case *in limine* where there is no possibility of success.[98] So, in *Sun Fat Chan v. Osseous Ltd,* [99] McCarthy J. stated in the Supreme Court that "generally the High Court should be slow to entertain an application of this kind." In *Supermac's Ireland Ltd v. Katesan (Naas) Ltd*[100] Macken J. held in the High Court that the power to dismiss a case on the grounds that it cannot possibly succeed is a remedy which "in general ought to be applied only to circumstances where there are undisputed facts". Indeed McCarthy J. in *Sun Fat* considered that it might even be permissible to allow pleadings to be amended in ordinary judicial review cases if this would save the action. As will be clear from the next paragraph, different rules apply when judicial review is regulated by statute.

Special statutory provisions regulating judicial review

Concern about the number of applications for judicial review in planning cases and the difficulties these presented for the rapidly expanding Irish economy led to important legal changes in section 19 of the Local Government (Planning and Development) Act 1992, amending section 82(3)(A) of the Local

---

[95] *Barry v. Buckley* [1981] I.R. 306. 308; *D.K. v. King* [1994] 1 I.R. 166, 170.
[96] *McCabe v. Harding Investments Ltd.* [1984] ILRM 105.108. *Moffit v. Bank of Ireland.* Supreme Court, February 19, 1999.
[97] *Barry v. Buckley* [1981] I.R. 30, 308. *Tassan Din v. Banco Ambrosiano SPA* [1991] 1 I.R. 569.
[98] H. Delany, "Striking Out Where No Reasonable Cause of Action, Where Claim Frivolous or Vexatious or Where Clearly Unsustainable" (2000) 8 *Irish Law Times,* 127-130.
[99] [1992] I.R. 425.
[100] High Court. March 15, 1999, 20. See also *Doe v. Armour Pharmaceutical Inc..* High Court, July 31, 1997.

Government (Planning and Development) Act 1963. Section 82 now provides that a person shall not question the validity of a decision of a planning authority on an application for a planning permission or approval or a decision of the Planing Appeals Board on any appeal or any reference except by way of judicial review by motion on notice under Order 84 of the Rules of the Superior Courts. It then provides that such leave shall not be granted unless the High Court is satisfied that there are "substantial grounds for contending that the decision is invalid or ought to be quashed". This restriction does not apply where the High Court decision involves the constitutionality of any law. "Substantial" has been held to mean reasonable, arguable and weighty,[101] but it does not mean that the applicant must be likely to succeed. Section 82 further provides that the High Court decision on the matter is final and that no appeal shall lie from it to the Supreme Court save by leave of the High Court, which shall only be granted where the High Court certifies that its decision involves a point of law of exceptional public importance and that it is desirable in the public interest that an appeal should be taken to the Supreme Court. Leave to appeal to the Supreme Court was granted in *Lancefort*.

Section 82(3)(A), as interpreted by the Supreme Court in *Lancefort*,[102] means that *locus standi* in these cases involves not just showing a sufficient interest to ground the application for leave for judicial review but also establishing substantial grounds for granting leave to apply. This finding has somewhat frustrated the objectives of the procedure whereby leave must be obtained for judicial reviews, because establishing substantial grounds involves pleading the merits of the case. This sometimes involves lengthy arguments.[103]

Similar restrictions have been placed on judicial reviews of integrated pollution control licences, aquaculture licences and waste licences.

Section 82(3)(A) is a form of the English rule in *O'Reilly v. Mackman*,[104] a decision which has not been otherwise approved by the Irish judiciary. It was enacted to deal with an increasing number of what were perceived to be unmeritorious or frivolous applications where a suspected motive was a desire to delay and frustrate developers. Experience is that it has been singularly unsuccessful in its objectives. All applications for judicial review under this section must be made within two months of the date the decision was made. This short time limit is to ensure legal protection for persons who have obtained environmental authorisations against subsequent challenges.[105] Although the court has powers to prohibit implementation of the challenged authorisation, this

---

[101] *McNamara v. An Bord Pleanála* [1995] I.L.R.M. 125 at 130, approved by the Supreme Court in *Lancefort*. It will be remembered that in ordinary judicial review cases the grounds need only be arguable.

[102] [1998] I.L.R.M. 401.

[103] In *McNamara v. An Bord Pleanála* [1995] 2 I.L.R.M. 125, an application for leave to apply for judicial review lasted five days in the High Court.

[104] [1983] 2 A.C. 237.

[105] *KSK Enterprises Ltd v. An Bord Pleanála* [1994] 2 I.L.R.M. 1.

has rarely been exercised. Persons who implement authorisations in these cases do so at the risk of subsequently finding that their authorisations are invalid.

Statutory appeals to the courts

Occasionally, a right to appeal is available by way of a statutory appeal to a court.[106] The nature and scope of the court's jurisdiction in these cases is a matter of statutory construction. A statutory appeal to a court is not quite the same as a judicial review.[107] It is usually, but not always, confined to an appeal on a point of law.[108] Courts dealing with statutory appeals that are not confined to points of law usually have greater latitude to examine the merits of administrative decisions and to annul, amend or vary them than when they are dealing with judicial reviews.[109]

Decisions made by all appellate administrative bodies and lower courts are subject to judicial review, although the conditions governing this may be regulated by the applicable statute.[110]

There are no public funds available for persons involved in opposing activities that might impair the environment, but the Government has provided a truly excellent and free environmental information service for members of the public.[111] In theory, the Planning Appeals Board or the EPA may require an unsuccessful appellant to pay the expenses of other parties but they have never (to my knowledge) done this.[112]

Public participation in the enforcement of environmental laws

Space constraints prevent an adequate description of the civil remedies available to individuals and groups under planning, air and water pollution, waste and integrated pollution legislation, and only an outline is given here.[113]

Individuals may use the ordinary common law remedies of negligence,

---

[106] For example, s. 21(3) of the Local Government (Planning and Development) Act 1963, provides that any person may appeal to the Circuit Court against inclusion of a public right of way in a development plan or varied development plan.

[107] See *Dunne v. Minister for Fisheries* [1984] I.R. 230 where Costello J. in the High Court explained differences between statutory appeals and judicial reviews.

[108] See, for example, s. 42 of the Local Government (Planning and Development) Act 1976, under which the Planning Appeals Board has power to state a case on a point of law to the High Court.

[109] *Dunne v. Minister for Fisheries* [1984] I.R. 230; *Courtney v. Minister for the Marine* [1989] I.L.R.M. 605.

[110] See below.

[111] ENFO, a State-sponsored environmental awareness organisation located in 17 St. Andrew Street, Dublin 2, is an excellent resource for environmental and academic researchers.

[112] Local Government (Planning and Development) Act 1976, s. 19(1)(a) as amended by s. 19(4)(a) of the 1992 Act.

[113] See Scannell, *op. cit.*, pp. 9-12.

nuisance, *Rylands and Fletcher*, and trespass to secure environmental protection on broadly the same grounds as in the U.K. Air, water and waste legislation provides statutory remedies for pollution damage by which people may recover damages for losses to their person or property incurred as a result of persons causing or permitting discharges to the environment in contravention of licences granted.[114] These remedies are sometimes more effective than traditional common law remedies. Although in principle public laws are generally enforceable by public authorities only, Irish environmental law increasingly provides for the "privatisation" of the enforcement of environmental laws by enabling any person, irrespective of whether or not he or she has a personal or proprietary interest in the matter, to enforce most of the major environmental controls. Barrington J., when considering an application for an injunction by residents under section 27 of the Local Government (Planning and Development) Act 1976,[115] stated that "every citizen is a watchdog for the environment".[116]

Again, planning legislation provides the model, which is replicated in air, water, waste and integrated pollution control legislation. Any person, regardless of his or her interest in the matter, may enforce provisions in the Local Government (Planning and Development) Acts 1963-99, which require planning permission for all development of land unless it is expressly exempted from planning control. Any individual or group and may also bring proceedings to ensure compliance with planning permissions and conditions attached to them. Any person or NGO may also sue to ensure that appropriate licences are obtained for discharging effluents to waters or certain emissions to the air, or for waste disposal activities or certain developments on the foreshore and may also compliance with licences and conditions attached to them. In planning cases, actions must be taken in the Circuit Court or the High Court actions to enforce air, water, waste and integrated pollution controls may be brought in any court of appropriate jurisdiction, even the District Court. This reduces the costs of enforcement. The Local Government (Water Pollution) Acts 1977-90, the Air Pollution Act 1987 and the Waste Management Act 1996 expressly provide that persons who take enforcement actions may be awarded their costs in investigating, mitigating or remedying environmental damage complained of at the discretion of the courts.

CONCLUSION

The privatisation of the enforcement of many environmental laws has been

---

[114] See, for example, Local Government (Water Pollution) Act 1990, s. 21.
[115] *Stafford v. Roadstone* [1980] I.L.R.M. 1.
[116] *ibid.*

extremely effective, although it is not reflected in the numbers of judicial cases actually brought. The statistics on participation in planning and IPC appeals are indicative of a high level of public awareness of environmental rights. Relatively free access to the courts, the apparent reluctance of public authorities, developers and industrialists to enforce orders for costs, and the willingness of some lawyers to provide services *pro bono* have facilitated the exercise of these rights, but lack of funding for meritorious cases is still a problem. The experience of practitioners is that industrialists, in particular, are conscious of public rights of access to information and to enforce environmental legislation. These rights are powerful incentives for ensuring compliance with environmental laws. Much remedial action, and indeed some unnecessary litigation, has been inspired by individuals, NGOs and residents' associations invoking their enforcement powers. Factors such as greater access to environmental information, conditions in authorisations requiring developers and holders of pollution emission licences to publish Annual Environmental Reports and to consult regularly with local residents, and the availability of information on the Internet have ensured greater transparency in environmental management and public access to monitoring results and other information held by public (and sometimes private) bodies. This has facilitated members of the public using political and other measures, including litigation, to enforce environmental laws.

RECENT DEVELOPMENTS IN THE AREA OF WOMEN'S RIGHTS IN SOUTH AFRICA: FOCUSING ON DOMESTIC VIOLENCE AND FEMICIDE

WAHEEDA AMIEN*

Women's rights are human rights[1]

INTRODUCTION

Although women comprise about 52 per cent of the South African population,[2] it has been acknowledged that they constitute one of the most marginalised and vulnerable groups in this country. One of the social mechanisms that has contributed to their historical disadvantage is the gender-based violence that women suffer in various forms. Nevertheless, our constitutional dispensation has provided the vehicle for legislative and judicial intervention to deal with the prevailing violence increasingly perpetrated against women, and for the progressive empowerment of women. It has also enabled women's groups to lobby around issues for the advancement of their rights. Recent years have seen various legal developments to attempt to improve the position of women in the areas of, *inter alia*, domestic violence, sexual offences,[3] and family law.[4] In this paper, however, I have attempted to focus on some of the more distinctive developments that have affected women's rights directly or indirectly in the areas of domestic violence and femicide.

---

* B.A. LL.B. (UCT), LL.M. (UWC); Gender Convenor: Gender Unit, Legal Aid Clinic (University of the Western Cape).

[1] Article 14, Fourth World Conference on Women, Beijing Declaration, 1995.

[2] Statistics South Africa, *The People of South Africa Population Census, 1996: Census in Brief* (1998); Central Statistics *Women and Men in South Africa* (1998), p.3.

[3] See South African Law Commission, *Executive Summary and Draft Bill of Discussion Paper 85, Sexual Offences: The Substantive Law* Project 107.

[4] This refers to the family courts established in terms of Regulation No. 19458, the passing of the Maintenance Act 99 of 1998, the Natural Fathers of Children Born out of Wedlock Act 86 of 1997, and the Guardianship Act 192 of 1993 as amended.

INTERNATIONAL INSTRUMENTS

Various international instruments recognise that extensive discrimination continues to be practised against women, and that one of the most pervasive forms of discrimination against women is the endemic violence they suffer on a global scale, particularly at the hands of men.[5] These instruments also acknowledge that violence against women is a manifestation of the unequal power relations between men and women, which has forced women into a subordinate position in relation to men, and has impeded their full advancement in the social, cultural, political and economic spheres of society.

International and regional instruments[6] have furthermore recognised and entrenched a number of human rights, which are impacted on directly by the gender-specific forms of violence committed against women. These rights include the rights to life; dignity; integrity of the person; liberty and security of the person; to enjoy the best attainable state of physical and mental health; not to be subjected to any form of exploitation and degradation; and particularly prohibiting any form of torture, cruel, inhuman or degrading treatment or punishment.

SOUTH AFRICA

Within the South African context, the *Women's Charter and Aims* in 1954 claimed that:

> "The level of civilization which any society has reached can be measured by the degree of freedom that its members enjoy. The status of women is a test of civilization. Measured by that standard, South Africa must be considered low in the scale of civilized nations."

Forty years later, *The Women's Charter for Effective Equality (1994)* acknowledged that domestic violence and sexual violence are still pervasive, and that women continue to live under the threat of violence, and continue to experience violence.[7] In fact, if one were to use the "test for civilisation" espoused

---

[5] Convention on the Elimination of All Forms of Discrimination against Women, G.A. Res. 34/180 of December 18, 1979 – ratified by South Africa in 1995; Declaration on the Elimination of Violence against Women, G.A. Res. 48/104 of 1993.

[6] Articles 1, 3 and 5 of the Universal Declaration of Human Rights, G.A. Res. 217A(III) of December 10, 1948; Convention on the Elimination of All Forms of Discrimination against Women, G.A. Res. 34/180 of December 18, 1989 – ratified by South Africa in 1995; Declaration on the Elimination of Violence against Women, G.A. Res. 48/104 of 1993; Articles 3(2), 4, 5, 6 and 16(1) of the African Charter on Human and Peoples' Rights (1981) – ratified by South Africa in 1996.

[7] Article 10.

in the *Women's Charter and Aims* (1954), then recent statistics in relation to violence against women indicate that South Africa would still not be considered a civilised nation. The following information illustrates this point.

- South Africa has the highest statistics for violence against women in the world (for a country not at war).[8]

- Violence against women occurs in different instances including, *inter alia*, domestic violence, rape, other forms of sexual assault and femicide. The violence that women experience differs from the type of violence experienced by men. For example, women are susceptible to domestic violence and sexual assault in a way that men are not.[9]

- Although men are sometimes the victims of domestic violence, the large majority of victims of this socio-economic evil are women.[10]

- Compared to men, women are more likely to be victimised by men; to know their attacker; to be attacked in their own homes; and to be blamed for their victimisation.[11]

- More often than not, the violence experienced by women is at the hands of men they know.[12]

- The nexus between violence against women and poverty means that African women, who constitute the poorest sector in South Africa, are at greater risk of being subjected to violence than any other group in our society.[13]

- One in every four women in South Africa is regularly battered by her husband, partner or boyfriend. The Department of Justice also estimates that

---

[8] Masimanyane CEDAW Government Report, Working Group, *NGO Shadow Report to CEDAW: South Africa: Violence Against Women* (1998) 3.

[9] R. Emerson Dobash and Russell P. Dobash, *Women, Violence and Social Change* (1992); John H. Laub, "Patterns of Criminal Victimisation in the United States" in Arthur J. Lurigo *et al.* ed., *Victims of Crime* (1990); John Lea and Jock Young, *What is to be Done About Law and Order?* (2nd ed., 1993); J. Campbell "'If I Can't Have You, No One Can': Power and Control in Homicide of Female Partners" in J. Radford ed., *Femicide: The Politics of Woman Killing* (1992).

[10] People Opposing Women Abuse (POWA), *Women Abuse: The Basic Facts* from http// www.womensnet.org.za/pvaw/help/abusefac.htm. Here they state that 95 per cent of the time, women are the victims of violent abuse in their homes. Furthermore, about 31,000 interdicts had been issued in the Western Cape in terms of the Prevention of Family Violence Act 133 of 1993 for the period December 1993 to November 1997. Of these about 98 per cent were to women and 2 per cent to men (see note 14).

[11] Allison Morris, *Women, Crime and Criminal Justice* (1987).

[12] n.8.

[13] Noreen Callaghan *et al.*, *A Triad of Oppression: Violence, Women and Poverty* (Centre for the Study of Violence and Reconciliation; http://www.wits.ac.za/csvr/artgend.htm).

[14] Dawn Blaser, *Statistics on Violence Against Women in South Africa and Internationally* (NICRO Women's Support Centre 1998). Also available from http://www.womensnet.org.za/ pvaw/understand/nicrostats.htm#dvsa.

one out of every four women in South Africa is a survivor of domestic violence.[14]

• In about 46 per cent of domestic violence cases, children are also abused by
the batterer.[15]

• An abused woman stays in an abusive relationship for an average period of
10.5 years before leaving. She suffers being battered an average of 39 times
before eventually seeking outside assistance.[16]

• At least one woman is killed every six days by her male partner, and one in
every six women is murdered by her male intimate.[17]

• About 41 per cent of female homicides are perpetrated by the woman's spouse
or partner.[18] These figures indicate that just under half of all the women
killed in South Africa lose their lives at the hands of men whom they know,
and who supposedly love them.

• Domestic violence and other related crimes against women and children
have increased to such an extent over the past number of years that the
South African Police Service (SAPS) was forced to declare these types of
crimes a policing priority.[19]

DOMESTIC VIOLENCE

In the recent case of *S v. Baloyi*,[20] the Constitutional Court expressed the view
that domestic violence compels constitutional concern because "… it is systemic, pervasive and overwhelmingly gender-specific, … [and it] reflects and
reinforces patriarchal domination, … in a particularly brutal form".[21] The Court
gave recognition to the fact that domestic violence is distinguished by its hidden and repetitive nature, and moreover, that it cuts across race, class, culture,
and geographical location.[22] The Court, furthermore, found that the state is
under a number of direct constitutional obligations to deal with domestic violence and to protect every person's right to be free from domestic (or private)
violence.[23] This is a significant acknowledgement by the Court because it

---

[15] Jane Keene and Clare Vale, *An Investigation into the Effectiveness of Interdicts Granted in Terms of the Prevention of Family Violence Act (133) 1993* (National Institute for Crime Prevention and the Rehabilitation of Offenders, 1997) 15.
[16] n. 14.
[17] n. 8.
[18] n. 14.
[19] Institute for Security Studies Volume 2 No 4 *Crime Index* July–August 1998.
[20] 2000 (1) B.C.L.R. 86 (CC).
[21] At 93 F.
[22] At 92 E.
[23] At 93 D.

puts to rest the incorrect perception that domestic violence is simply a case of private or domestic disputes between the parties. The Court held that these obligations arise from the constitutional injunction that the state must respect, protect, promote and fulfil the rights in the Bill of Rights.[24] These rights include everyone's right to have their dignity respected and protected (section 10); everyone's right to freedom and security of the person, which includes the right to be free from all forms of violence from either public or private sources (section 12(1)(c)); the right not to be tortured in any way (section 12(1)(d)), nor to be treated or punished in a cruel, inhuman and degrading way (section 12(1)(e)); and every person's right to bodily and psychological integrity (section 12(2)). A violation of these constitutional rights would entitle a victim of domestic violence to claim constitutional damages as an alternative where other remedies have failed.[25]

The Domestic Violence Act

The Court in *S v. Baloyi*[26] found that section 12(1)(c) of the Constitution[27] provides the imperative for legislation dealing with domestic violence.[28] However, the Court realised that the mechanisms created by this type of legislation could not, by themselves, eradicate domestic violence. Rather, the legislation amounts to a preventive measure, seeking to offer protection to victims of domestic violence, to prevent future misconduct by abusers, and to ultimately promote restorative justice.[29]

This legislation has been packaged in the form of the Domestic Violence Act 116 of 1998 (hereafter referred to as 'DVA') which replaced the Prevention of Family Violence Act 133 of 1993 (hereafter referred to as "PFVA") on 15 December 1999, in recognition of the fact that the remedies offered by the PFVA were narrow and insufficient, and had clearly proved to be ineffective.[30] However, it retained the prohibition on marital rape that had been in-

---

[24] s.7(2) of The Constitution of the Republic of South Africa Act 108 of 1996 (hereafter referred to as "the Constitution"). The Bill of Rights is contained in Chapter 2 of the Constitution (at 93 D of the judgment).
[25] See *Fose v. Minister of Safety and Security* 1997 (7) B.C.L.R. 851 (CC). Furthermore, these damages could be claimed *inter partes* in light of the acknowledged horizontal application of the Bill of Rights (see *Du Plessis v. De Klerk* 1996 (5) B.C.L.R. 658 (CC)).
[26] n.19.
[27] The Constitution of the Republic of South Africa Act 108 of 1996.
[28] At 93 B-C.
[29] At 97 D-E.
[30] The NICRO (National Institute for Crime and the Reintegration of Offenders) Women's Centre conducted a research project at seven courts in the Western Cape, in which information was collected from 100 women who had applied for and been granted interdicts in terms of the Prevention of Family Violence Act. Some of the results as at October 1997 indicate that the remedies provided by the Act were ineffective. Fifty-one women were granted final interdicts, 42 temporary interdicts and seven were given notice to appear in court. In only 10 cases were

troduced into South African law for the first time by the PFVA.[31] The DVA certainly takes a more gender-sensitive approach to the problem of domestic violence. Its application is substantially broader than the PFVA. This is made possible, *inter alia*, by the widening of the definitions of "domestic violence" and "domestic relationships", and the extension of legal remedies, as well as greater police involvement in cases of domestic violence.

The content of the DVA is largely accredited to submissions made at parliamentary hearings on violence against women, which were jointly conducted in 1997 and 1998 by the Portfolio Committee on Justice and the Ad Hoc Committee on Improvement of the Quality of Life and Status of Women.[32] One of the failings of this process, however, is the fact that the DVA does not recognise domestic violence as a specific crime. Victims of domestic violence can therefore still only lodge criminal charges of assault or assault with intent to do grievous bodily harm (GBH) and/or malicious damage to property where applicable, in addition to obtaining a protection order. One of the consequences of this is that the police statistics only capture the charge as assault or assault GBH, without reflecting the gender-based nature of the conduct. Without specific data it is therefore difficult to obtain an accurate picture of the incidence of domestic violence.

Nevertheless, the DVA conveys South Africa's national,[33] regional[34] and

---

the magistrates not prepared to grant all the protection asked for in the application and six of these cases concerned eviction orders. Forty women asked for eviction orders, of which 33 were granted but only in 12 cases were these fully obeyed by the respondent. Forty six women received their final interdicts on the same day they applied, and waited an average of just over two hours for them to be processed, three women had to wait three days before they could pick their orders up, and two had to wait a week. For temporary interdicts, women generally had to wait between one and four weeks. The courts sent the interdict papers to the sheriff in only 20 cases. Seventy of the remaining 80 women said they took the interdict themselves to the sheriff for delivery, 26 women could not afford to pay for the sheriff, and a further eight had to borrow money. Only six were informed about possible financial assistance from the court. In 20 cases, the sheriff delivered the interdict within one day. In other cases it took longer. In one case it took 30 days for the sheriff to deliver the interdict. Fifty-five of the women were abused again after being granted interdicts – 31 received physical abuse, 12 sexual abuse, and practically all of them verbal and emotional abuse. Twenty-three women reported the abuse to the police. In nine cases, the police warned the respondent but did nothing further. In one case, the respondent bribed the police. Only four of the respondents were convicted. The 100 women interviewed had a total of 230 children between them, many of whom would have been affected by the violence.

[31] s.5 thereof.

[32] A total of thirty-two written submissions were received. Some of these include: Commission on Gender Equality (August 17, 1998 from http://www.womensnet.org.za/news/domvi.htm); Women and Human Rights Project (Community Law Centre University of the Western Cape); Rape Crisis Cape Town; ANC Parliamentary Women's Caucus (May 30, 1997 from http://www.womensnet.org.za/pvaw/laws/dvsum.htm); Women on Farms Project (March 20, 1998 from http://www.womensnet.org.za/pvaw/laws/farms.htm); South African Human Rights Commission March 1998; Gender Advocacy Programme (March 20, 1998); NICRO Western Cape Support for Abused Women Project (June 6, 1997).

[33] By having regard particularly to the constitutional entrenchment of the rights to equality (sec-

international[35] commitments to the elimination of domestic violence for the achievement of gender equality.[36] It notes that domestic violence is a serious crime in our society, and constitutes a grave obstacle to the achievement of gender equality.[37] The DVA improves on the PFVA in a number of ways, including the following:

Definition of "domestic relationship"

Unlike the PFVA, which offered protection only to abused parties in a marital or co-habitational relationship, the DVA extends its remedies to all victims who are or were in a "domestic relationship" with the abuser.[38] It includes parties who either are or were married to each other by custom, religion or any law; who live or lived together in a heterosexual or homosexual relationship; who share or recently shared the same residence; who are or were in a relationship of any duration, including those of an actual or perceived romantic, intimate or sexual nature (which could arguably include one-night stands); parents of a child or persons who have or had parental responsibility for that child; and family members related by consanguinity, adoption or affinity. The amendment therefore recognises that abuse does not just occur within the confines of a marriage or a similarly perceived relationship.

Definition of "domestic violence"

"Domestic violence" in the DVA is defined as physical abuse, sexual abuse, economic abuse, psychological or emotional abuse, verbal abuse, intimidation, stalking, harassment, damage to property, entry into the complainant's residence without consent (where the parties do not live together), as well as any other controlling or abusive behaviour towards the complainant.[39] This broad definition is a welcome extension to the PFVA, which was limited to physical abuse only. It gives recognition to the fact that domestic violence manifests itself in many forms.[40] The types of abuse recognised by the DVA is also wider than those reflected in the relevant international instruments.[41]

---

tion 9 of Act 108 of 1996), and to freedom and security of the person (section 12 of Act 108 of 1996).

[34] African Charter on Human and Peoples' Rights, ratified by South Africa in June 1996.

[35] Convention on the Elimination of All Forms of Discrimination against Women, G.A. Res. 34/180 (1979), ratified by South Africa in September 1995.

[36] Preamble.

[37] *ibid.*

[38] s.1(vii).

[39] s.1(viii).

[40] South African Human Rights Commission *Submission on Violence Against Women* (1998).

[41] For example, Article 2 of the Declaration on the Elimination of Violence against Women, G.A. Res. 48/104 of 1993.

Police participation

The DVA widens police participation in the prevention and handling of domestic violence. It places a positive duty on the South African Police Service (SAPS) to assist a complainant and, where necessary, to find suitable shelter and to obtain medical treatment.[42] The police must inform the victim of her or his rights, including the right to lodge a criminal complaint where applicable.[43] Police are authorised to arrest the respondent without a warrant, at the scene of domestic violence, if there is a reasonable suspicion that an offence containing an element of violence has been committed against the complainant.[44] The DVA also makes provision for the issuing of national guidelines that must be observed when dealing with incidents of domestic violence. Failure to comply with these guidelines will result in disciplinary action being taken against police officers.[45] The amendments reflect a legislative attempt to define the role of the SAPS more clearly in light of their problematic implementation of the PFVA. Nevertheless, it has been argued that these changes will be ineffective if the dismissive attitudes of police officers to domestic violence cases remain unchanged, and if they do not receive adequate training.[46]

The protection order

The DVA makes provision for a complainant to apply to court for a protection order (similar to an interdict under the PFVA).[47] An application may be brought outside of ordinary court hours, if the court is satisfied that the complainant requires urgent intervention.[48] All proceedings must be held *in camera*, to protect the interests and the identity of the victims of domestic violence.[49] The protection order is enforceable throughout the Republic.[50] This is beneficial to a complainant who moves to another jurisdiction and is followed by the respondent. Because victims of domestic violence are disempowered people, the DVA retains the provision that the application can be brought on behalf of the complainant by a third party who has a material interest in the well-being of the complainant.[51] This has been extended to include members of the SAPS

---

[42] s.2(a).
[43] ss.2(b) and (c).
[44] s.3.
[45] ss.18(2) and (4).
[46] n.40.
[47] n.4(1). In its submission to the South African Law Commission on "Domestic Violence", *Discussion Paper* No 70 (1997) 3, the Gender Unit at the Department of Justice suggested that another term be used instead of "interdict", so that it could be better understood by the community, and would be more expressive of the relief being sought.
[48] s.4(5).
[49] ss.11(1)(a) and (b), 11(2)(a).
[50] s.12(3).
[51] s.4(3).

as well.[52] Furthermore, a minor or any person on behalf of a minor may also apply for a protection order without the assistance of the parent or guardian.[53]

Interim protection order

The PFVA only allowed a court to grant a final interdict. The DVA now directs the court to grant an interim protection order, if it is satisfied that there is a prima facie case of domestic violence, even though the respondent may not have been notified of the proceedings.[54] This will prevent courts from refusing to grant interim orders on the basis that the respondent did not receive notice thereof.[55] A suspended warrant of arrest must be issued contemporaneously with the interim order, in anticipation of the respondent breaching the conditions set out therein.[56] If the warrant is lost, destroyed or already executed and cancelled, the clerk of the court must issue a further warrant of arrest.[57] Unfortunately, police officers have discretion to decide whether or not to arrest the respondent.[58] Although certain factors are outlined to guide them in their decision-making,[59] the discretion could be abused by police officers who have received insufficient training, and who are gender-insensitive to domestic violence cases.

Final protection order

The DVA makes provision for a return date whereby the respondent is afforded the opportunity to appear in court. This effectively deals with the problem encountered by the PFVA in terms of which the *audi alteram partem* principle had been violated, because provision had only been made for one interdict to be granted, without requiring the presence of the respondent at court.

The court must grant a final order on the return date specified in the interim order, if it finds, on a balance of probabilities, that the respondent is committing or has committed an act of domestic violence.[60] If the respondent fails to appear, the court must still issue a final order, provided it is satisfied that proper service has been effected on the respondent, and that prima facie evidence exists that the respondent is committing or has committed an act of

---

[52] *ibid.*
[53] s.4(4).
[54] ss.5(2)(a) and (b).
[55] NICRO Western Cape Support for Abused Women Project. *Changes Proposed by the SA Law Commission in respect of the Prevention of Family Violence Act 133 of 1993* (1997).
[56] s.8.
[57] s.8(3).
[58] s.8(4)(b).
[59] s.8(5).
[60] s.6(4).

domestic violence.[61] The court may not refuse to grant protection orders merely because there are other legal remedies available to the complainant.[62] Furthermore, the court cannot amend or set aside a protection order, unless it is satisfied that the complainant has made application freely and voluntarily.[63] This provision recognises the fact that the complainant may be manipulated by the respondent. The DVA also does not place a time limit on the duration of the final protection order. This is a welcome change, because in certain magisterial districts, such as Mitchell's Plain (Western Cape), interdicts granted under the PFVA were only valid for one year.[64]

Relief granted in terms of interim and final protection orders

Unlike the PFVA, which provided for limited relief only, the DVA grants the court wide powers in respect of both interim and final protection orders. It may prohibit the respondent from:[65]

• committing any act of domestic violence;

• enlisting the assistance of any other person to commit an act of domestic violence;

• entering a residence shared by the complainant and the respondent;

• entering a specified part of such shared residence;

• entering the complainant's residence (if they do not live together);

• entering the complainant's place of employment;

• committing any other act specified in the protection order.

The court may also order the seizure of dangerous weapons in the possession or under the control of the respondent, and that a police officer accompany the complainant to assist with the collection of personal property.[66] Significantly, to alleviate financial hardships borne by the complainant, the court may order the respondent to pay the rent or mortgage, as well as emergency monetary relief to the complainant.[67] Where a child is involved, the court may refuse the respondent any contact with that child, if the court is satisfied that this would be in the best interests of the child.[68] This provision offers protection

---

[61] s.6(1).
[62] s.7(7).
[63] s.10.
[64] n.55.
[65] s.7(1).
[66] s.7(2).
[67] s.7(3) and (4).
[68] s.7(6).

to children, and prevents respondents from gaining control over complainants through their children.

Legal representation

Applicants in certain magisterial districts are sometimes denied legal representation.[69] However, the DVA clearly provides for legal representation at all stages of the proceedings.[70] If the complainant is not legally represented, the clerk of the court must inform the victim of available relief, and of the right to lodge a criminal charge against the respondent.[71]

Breach of order

Under the DVA, it is an offence to breach the conditions of a protection order. On conviction, the respondent is liable to a fine or imprisonment not exceeding a period of five years.[72] This is a considerable increase in penal jurisdiction, because the PFVA only allowed courts to impose a period of imprisonment not exceeding 12 months.[73] It is regrettable that the recommendation that the court be directed to make an additional order for rehabilitative counselling was not included, as this could have assisted in remedying the problem of domestic violence in South Africa.[74]

FEMICIDE

Femicide occurs when women are murdered by their intimate male partners (including husbands, boyfriends or common-law partners, as well as men from whom they are estranged, separated or divorced).[75] Given the alarming statistics set out earlier in this paper, the manner in which the criminal justice system has handled the perpetrators of this heinous crime is extremely frightening.

---

[69] Women and Human Rights Project (Community Law Centre University of the Western Cape), Rape Crisis Cape Town, ANC Parliamentary Women's Caucus (1997), *Violence Against Women in Relationships: Summary of Proposals* from http://www.womensnet.org.za/pvaw/laws/dvsum.htm.

[70] s.14.

[71] s.4(2).

[72] s.17(a).

[73] s.6(b) of the PFVA.

[74] n.69.

[75] Karen Stout, "'Intimate Femicide': Effect of Legislation and Social Services" in *Femicide: The Politics of Woman Killing* 1992, J. Radford and Diana E.H. Russell eds, p.133. Lisa Vetten also uses this definition in her article entitled "Man Shoots Wife" from http://www.womensnet.org.za/pvaw/understand/manshoots.html. See also The Joint Committee on the Improvement of the Quality of Life and Status of Women, *Violence Against Women Hearings* (1998).

Below is an example of the narrow extent that the judicial system has adopted in dealing with these types of cases.

In *S v. Ramontoedi*,[76] the accused killed his wife in the maintenance office at the Johannesburg Magistrates' Court. After being charged with murder, he pleaded self-defence.[77] The Court rejected his testimony, convicted him, and sentenced him to a mere three years' correctional supervision.[78] During sentencing, the Court acknowledged that the sentence for inter-family murder would normally merit a long period of imprisonment, given the increase in South Africa of inter-family violence resulting in death.[79] However, in this matter, the Court imposed a lighter sentence, based on its deduction that the accused had been provoked over a long period of time. The Court arrived at this conclusion in light of the accused's testimony that he had suspected his wife of conducting an extra-marital affair, and that the child born during the course of the marriage was not his. I wish to submit that the Court's deduction was unsubstantiated, given that the accused had not pleaded provocation at all. In fact, the Court admitted that it was "in the dark as to what that provocation actually was and the degree of it".[80]

The Court accepted evidence that the accused had accosted the deceased en route to the maintenance office.[81] The Court even said that "[b]ecause the deceased feared the accused ... it is noteworthy, ... that [she] thought it necessary to obtain a police escort on the morning of the maintenance hearing".[82] Despite the fact that the accused had displayed violent tendencies, and that the deceased feared him, I submit that the Court did not investigate the possibility that the murder had been a culmination of violent behaviour by the accused. Instead, the Court was intent on finding some type of "plausible" justification for the actions of the accused, hence the Court's insistence that the accused had been provoked.

THE WAY FORWARD

The sentence imposed in the *Ramontoedi*[83] case clearly sent a message to abusive men that the courts will "understand" if they are provoked into killing their wives, and will give them a lighter sentence. My submission is that even if provocation is proven, it is unacceptable that courts should consider provo-

---

[76] Unreported Case No: 188 / 96 Witwatersrand Local Division. June 23, 1996.
[77] At 2 of the judgment.
[78] In terms of section 276(1)(i) of Act 51 of 1977. At 5-6 of the sentence.
[79] At 2-6 of the sentence.
[80] At 3 of the sentence.
[81] At 8 of the judgment.
[82] At 8-9 of the judgment.
[83] n.75.

cation as any type of justification for a violent outburst resulting in femicide. Furthermore, given the increasing statistics for intimate femicide, strong arguments can be advanced for the imposition of more stringent sentences as a deterrent for these types of crimes.[84]

The *Ramontoedi*[85] case constitutes a blow for the advancement of women's rights in South Africa. It particularly highlights the court's ignorance and lack of understanding of the phenomena surrounding this type of violence against women in our society, for example, the battered woman syndrome. Within the context of domestic violence and its extreme form of femicide, there is therefore a clear indication that extensive training is required with regard to the dynamics of these two areas in respect of all the relevant role-players, including clerks, police officials, prosecutors, attorneys, advocates, judicial officers, and district surgeons. In other words, to ensure the effective interpretation and application of the DVA, the role-players must receive mandatory training about the causes and effects of domestic violence and femicide. To date, there is no national initiative co-ordinating such training. Training has only been occurring on an ad hoc basis by some non-governmental organisations (NGOs)[86] and the Justice College.[87] This is problematic because NGOs should really only be playing a supplementary role in respect of training, particularly in light of the state's constitutional obligation to deal with domestic violence effectively. Furthermore, ad hoc training is insufficient. The state therefore needs to organise and implement a nationally co-ordinated programme of training that will be sustainable on an ongoing basis. NGOs could be co-opted as part of this programme.

Despite the fact that the DVA could be regarded as one of the most progressive pieces of legislation that attempt to offer victims of domestic violence the widest possible protection, the real work has only just begun. The actual interpretation and implementation of the legislation is the real test of the extent of its effectiveness. Thus, a properly co-ordinated monitoring strategy in respect of all the relevant role-players on a national level is required. Again, no such strategy exists, despite the constitutional obligation placed on the state to deal effectively with domestic violence. There is also no proper monitoring strategy in respect of femicide matters or in cases where battered women kill their intimates as a result of constant abuse. Various NGOs have undertaken the task of monitoring the implementation of the DVA in a few selected areas,[88] but it is questionable whether their findings will be a true

---

[84]Lisa Vetten quoted in *The Sunday Times*, August 2, 1998, editorial page.

[85]n.75.

[86]Such as the Law, Race and Gender Research Unit, University of Cape Town, which incorporates training on domestic violence into their broader framework of social context training for magistrates and prosecutors.

[87]This is the official training centre for magistrates and prosecutors in South Africa. It is situated in Pretoria.

[88]For example, a consortium of three NGOs in the Western Cape have raised funding to conduct

reflection of what is happening at ground level in all the regions of South Africa. At best, their findings will be specific to the areas targeted for their research.

Some of the problems that have been noted thus far on an ad hoc basis in the Western Cape include the following:

• A magistrate was reluctant to grant a protection order on the basis that the respondent's attorney raised the point that Muslim law permits chastisement of a wife by her husband (the parties had been married to each other by Muslim rites). The magistrate therefore postponed the matter to afford the parties the opportunity of bringing in experts in Muslim law to confirm or deny this point. Unfortunately, the complainant was left without any kind of protection from further abuse by her husband during the interim period.

• A magistrate was unwilling to grant an exclusionary order preventing the husband from entering the shared premises of the parties on the basis that the parties had been married to each other in community of property. This was done irrespective of the fact that the matrimonial property regime of the parties is irrelevant to the inquiry of whether the complainant is in need of protection or not, and the extent of that protection.

• It has been found that men have been abusing the system by applying for protection orders for the sole reason of evicting their partners from the common home. It seems that these applications are being granted because magistrates are not applying their minds to the circumstances of the case, nor are they alerting themselves to the fact that caution needs to be exercised when the applicant is a male (given the statistics indicating that victims of domestic violence are usually women).

• An anomaly exists in the application form for the protection order,[89] in that the form requires the applicant to include her/his residential address, yet the magistrate, upon granting the protection order, may order that the address of the complainant not be revealed to the respondent. The problem is that the DVA instructs the clerk of the court to serve a copy of the order, suspended warrant of arrest, and the application form filled in and signed by the applicant on the respondent. The respondent would therefore know where the complainant is despite the intention of the legislation to prevent the respondent from finding the complainant and continuing to inflict harm.

• Various NGOs have placed trained volunteers at some of the courts to assist

---

monitoring of the implementation of the Domestic Violence Act 116 of 1998 in Cape Town, Mitchells Plain and George. The consortium consists of the Gender Project, Community Law Centre (University of the Western Cape), Institute of Criminology (University of Cape Town) and Rape Crisis (Cape Town).

[89] Form 2 of the domestic violence regulations.

complainants in filling out application forms for protection orders. However, these volunteers do not have full knowledge of the law, including customary and religious law, and are therefore not always able to advise complainants about all the existing remedies. For example, a Muslim woman who has received a final *talaq* (Muslim pronouncement of divorce) and is seeking a protection order during her *idda* period[90] could very well also ask the court to grant a maintenance order in her favour for the duration of her *idda*. There is nothing that precludes the court from granting this type of relief in the protection order, since the DVA specifically makes provision for the granting of economic orders. However, a volunteer who is unaware of this right of a Muslim woman would not advise her to include that in the founding affidavit, with the result that the court would not be able to *mero motu* grant that particular relief as part of the final order.

Furthermore, research into the PFVA conducted in rural areas indicated that rural women (who constitute one of the most vulnerable groups to domestic violence)[91] experienced a number of problems specific to their location that were not being experienced in the urban areas.[92] I wish to submit that these problems could be similarly experienced in relation to the DVA, but definitive research needs to be undertaken to ascertain this.

CONCLUSION

It seems that for every step forward, there are usually a few steps back. The

---

[90] This is the waiting period, which commences immediately upon the pronunciation of the final and irrevocable *talaq* and ends three months thereafter. During this time, the husband is under a religious obligation to maintain (*nafqah*) the wife. The *nafqah* in its narrowest form comprises food, clothing and lodging. This right to maintenance during the *idda* period was recognised in *Ryland v. Edros* 1997 (1) B.C.L.R. 77 (CC).

[91] Women on Farms Project, *Submission on Domestic Violence, Access to Justice, Maintenance* (1998) from http://www.womensnet.org.za/pvaw/laws/farms.htm. Also, in a study conducted in the rural Southern Cape, it was found that about 80 per cent of women were victims of domestic violence – see Lillian Artz, Gender Project, Institute of Criminology University of Cape Town (1997). Referred to in Lillian Artz, *Submission by the Institute of Criminology: Gender Analysis* (Institute for Security Studies: Cape Town Crime Survey 1998), p.4.

[92] Applications for interdicts are difficult to access because often women have to go to the urban areas to obtain them. Women have to use costly and unreliable transport systems. This means that an application could take an entire day, resulting in a loss of a day's wages. Violations of orders usually involve contacting the police telephonically, but telephones are a limited resource on farms. The work and accommodation of women on farms is dependent on them having a relationship with a male labourer. They automatically lose their work, income, and accommodation if the man is arrested and loses his job. There are few support services for these women, and no safe accommodation if they have to leave their homes. See Women on Farms Project, *Submission on Domestic Violence, Access to Justice, Maintenance* (1998) from http://www.womensnet.org.za/pvaw/laws/farms.htm.

same is true of domestic violence and femicide. While attempts have been made to deal positively with the problem of domestic violence (albeit on one level only, that is, the passing of the DVA), no similar efforts are evident in relation to femicide. Femicide cannot be seen in isolation from domestic violence. The former is a result of the latter. It is illogical that while domestic violence is now being considered in a more serious manner than previously, femicide is being treated as dismissively as domestic violence once was.

These two social evils can only be effectively combatted once a holistic approach is adopted by the state, in tandem with the relevant role-players and NGOs. This approach must allow for a nationally co-ordinated programme in respect of both monitoring of the implementation of the DVA, as well as judgments and sentences handed down in femicide matters and where battered women kill their intimates. It must also include a nationally co-ordinated strategy in respect of training around the substantive and procedural issues relating to domestic violence and femicide, targeting all the relevant role-players who are instrumental for the effective implementation of the legislation. It is only through the adoption of these approaches that substantive justice can be rendered to both the victims and perpetrators of gender-based violence, and to protect and give substantive effect to the constitutional rights of victims to be free from gender-based forms of violence.

THE RIGHT TO FREEDOM FROM VIOLENCE AND THE REFORM OF SEXUAL ASSAULT LAW IN SOUTH AFRICA[1]

HELÉNE COMBRINCK[*]

*Hitherto the philosophers have interpreted the world;
the point however is to change it.*[2]

INTRODUCTION

The inclusion of the right to freedom from violence in the 1996 Constitution was generally praised as a victory for South African women.[3] It can be said that although this right is framed in general terms, its recognition is of particular significance in the area of violence against women.[4]

This paper examines one of the aspects of the constitutional entrenchment of the right to freedom from violence, namely the relationship between this right and a process of re-examining the South African law relating to sexual assault.[5] By means of introduction, the interpretation of the right to freedom from violence in the framework of both the Bill of Rights[6] and international human rights jurisprudence is described. An overview of the current status of sexual assault law in South Africa follows. The paper concludes by evaluating the role of law reform in addressing sexual assault.

[*] Senior legal researcher at the Gender Project, Community Law Centre, University of the Western Cape.
[1] This paper is based on research currently in progress at the Gender Project, Community Law Centre, University of the Western Cape. The financial assistance of the Swedish International Development Co-operation Agency and the Ford Foundation towards the completion of this research is acknowledged with gratitude.
[2] Karl Marx as cited in R. Kasrils, *Armed and Dangerous* (1993).
[3] Section 12(1)(c) of the Constitution of the Republic of South Africa 108 of 1996 [hereinafter referred to as "the Constitution"] provides that every person has the right "to be free from all forms of violence from either public or private sources".
[4] See H. Combrinck, "Positive State Duties to Protect Women from Violence: Recent South African Developments" (1998) *Human Rights Quarterly* at 667.
[5] The term "sexual assault" is employed in this paper as a collective term for the criminal offences recognised as "rape", "indecent assault" and "*crimen iniuria*" respectively. See J. Burchell and J. Milton, *Principles of Criminal Law* (2nd ed., 1997) at pp. 487–500, 501–505, 510–517 for a definition and discussion of each of these offences.
[6] Chapter 2 of the Constitution.

THE REFORM OF SEXUAL ASSAULT LAW: CONSTITUTIONAL AND INTERNATIONAL
HUMAN RIGHTS JURISPRUDENCE

The right to freedom from violence in the South African Constitution

The right to freedom from violence is enunciated in the Constitution as an
aspect of the right to freedom and security of the person.[7] The formulation of
this right is significant: the inclusion of the phrase "from either public or private sources" clearly indicates that the Constitution does not sustain any distinction between "public" and "private" violence. This distinction, the subject
of extensive feminist criticism, has traditionally operated to justify an unwillingness on the part of the state to intervene in, for example, domestic violence.[8]

Apart from its formulation, the very fact that the right to freedom from
violence has been "spelled out" in the Bill of Rights is important for purposes
of its recognition as a discrete right, and dispels any possible argument that
the right to freedom and security provides no more than a guarantee against
arbitrary arrest and detention.[9] A brief analysis of the experience in the USA
and Canada illustrates that this distinction is of more than semantic consequence. Section 7 of the Canadian Charter states that the deprivation of the
right to life, liberty and security of the person can only occur in accordance
with principles of fundamental justice. While it has been argued that this formulation allows for a dominant "due process" interpretation,[11] it is significant
that this right has been developed by judicial interpretation to clearly encompass a right to protection from "private" violence.[12]

On the other hand, in the USA the right to liberty (which forms part of the

---

[7] s.12(1) of the Constitution.
[8] See, for example, E. Schneider, "The violence of privacy" in M.A. Fineman and R. Mykitiuk
ed., *The Public Nature of Private Violence* (1994), p.40; R. Graycar and J. Morgan, *The
Hidden Gender of Law* (1990), pp.30–40. For a graphic description of police reluctance to
intervene in domestic violence matters, see Human Rights Watch Africa, *Violence Against
Women in South Africa: State Response to Domestic Violence and Rape* (1995), p.77.
[9] The combination of the rights to freedom and to security in the majority of human rights
instruments has led to some debate as to whether these are in fact separate and distinct rights.
The European Commission has held that the term "liberty and security" must be read as a
whole. "Liberty of the person" as employed in article 5(1) of the European Convention therefore means freedom from arrest and detention, and "security of the person" means no more
than the protection against arbitrary interference with this liberty. The formulation of section
12 of the South African Constitution counters any suggestion that the right to security should
only apply in the context of "due process" relating to arrest and detention. See Combrinck, *op.
cit.*, pp.682–683 and authorities cited there.
[11] See L. du Plessis and J. de Ville, "Personal Rights: Life, Freedom and Security of the Person,
Privacy and Freedom of Movement" in D. van Wyk *et al.* eds., *Rights and Constitutionalism*
(1994), p.235.
[12] See *Doe v. Board of Commissioners of Police for Municipality of Metropolitan Toronto* (1990)
1 C.R.R. (2d) 211 (O.D.C.).

"due process" clause of the Fifth and Fourteenth Amendments of the U.S. Constitution) has been interpreted in a "narrow" sense. In *DeShaney v. Winnebago County Department of Social Services*[13] it was held that the state's failure to protect an individual against private violence generally does not constitute a violation of the right to liberty as guaranteed in the Fourteenth Amendment. This is because the Amendment does not impose any duty on the state to provide members of the general public with adequate protective services.[14]

It is therefore argued here that the specific articulation of an "independent" right to freedom from violence is powerful in outlining the ambit of this right in South African law.

The effect of section 12(1)(c) is further amplified when this provision is read with section 7(2) of the Constitution, which requires the state to "*respect, protect, promote and fulfil* the rights in the Bill of Rights".[15] This section thus makes it clear that in addition to (obviously) refraining from the commission of acts of violence against individuals, the state should also take certain positive steps to ensure the realisation of the right to freedom from violence.

The right to freedom from violence and international human rights jurisprudence

The above interpretation of section 12(1)(c), which concludes that the Constitution imposes certain positive state duties to address violence against women, is strengthened by an examination of international human rights jurisprudence.

In the well-known *Velasquez Rodriguez* case,[16] the Inter-American Court of Human Rights held that an obligation to ensure the exercise of rights included a requirement that states should prevent, investigate and punish any violation of the recognised rights. The state should moreover attempt to restore the right and provide compensation for damages resulting from the violation.[17] This dictum has found resonance in the treatment of violence against women in the international human rights sphere. The Special Rapporteur on Violence Against Women (appointed by the UN Commission on Human Rights) describes state responsibility as follows in her preliminary report dealing with domestic violence:

> "In the context of norms recently established by the international community, a State that does not act against crimes of violence against women is as guilty as the perpetrators. States are under a positive duty to pre-

---

[13]489 U.S. 189 (1989).
[14]*ibid.,* 201–202.
[15]Emphasis added.
[16]*Velasquez Rodriguez Case,* Case 7920, Ser. C. No. 4, Inter-American Court of Human Rights (judgment of July 29, 1988) at Para. 166.
[17]*ibid.*

vent, investigate and punish crimes associates with violence against women."[18]

These principles are also set out in the provisions of a number of international human rights instruments. While the Convention on the Elimination of All Forms of Discrimination Against Women[19] does not explicitly refer to violence against women,[20] the Committee[21] tasked with the implementation of the Convention has provided guidelines for its interpretation in the context of violence against women.[22] In General Recommendation 19, the Committee states:

"Under general international law and specific human rights covenants, States may also be responsible for private acts of they fail to act with due diligence to prevent violations of rights or to investigate and punish acts of violence, and for providing compensation."[23]

The Committee accordingly recommends that state parties should ensure that laws against family violence and abuse, rape, sexual assault and other gender-based violence give adequate protection to all women, and respect their integrity and dignity.[24] In addition, state parties should take effective legal measures to protect women against violence, including penal sanctions, civil remedies and compensatory provisions.[25]

The Committee's recommendations are echoed in the provisions of the Declaration on the Elimination of Violence Against Women.[26] Article 4(c) determines that states should (*inter alia*) develop penal sanctions in domestic legislation to "punish and redress the wrongs caused to women who are subjected to violence".

---

[18] *Preliminary Report submitted by the Special Rapporteur on Violence Against Women, its Causes and Consequences, Ms. Radhika Coomaraswamy, Submitted in Accordance with Commission on Human Rights Resolution 1994/45*, UN ESCOR, Commission on Human Rights, 50th Session, Agenda Item 11(a), UN Doc. E/CN.4/1995/42 (1995) at p. 18.

[19] UN Doc. A/RES/34/180 (1980). The Convention was adopted for signature and ratification and accession by the UN General Assembly on December 18, 1979 and entered into force on September 3, 1981 [hereinafter referred to as "the Women's Convention"].

[20] J. Fitzpatrick, "The use of international human rights norms to combat violence against women" in R. Cook ed., *Human Rights: National and International Perspectives* (1994), p.532, argues that articles 2, 3, 6, 11, 12 and 16 of the Women's Convention relate to violence against women.

[21] The Committee on the Elimination of Discrimination against Women (CEDAW).

[22] General Recommendation 19 (11th Session, 1992) UN Doc. CEDAW/C/1992/L.1/Add 15 (1992).

[23] para. 9.

[24] para. 24(b).

[25] para. 24(t)(i).

[26] UN General Assembly Official Records (GAOR), 48th Session, February 23, 1994, UN Doc.A/Res/48/104 (1994) [hereinafter referred to as "the Violence Declaration"].

The Beijing Declaration and Platform for Action,[27] which identifies violence against women as one of its "critical areas of concern", lists a number of actions to be undertaken by governments. This list specifies the following actions, amongst others:

"Adopt and/or implement and periodically review and analyse legislation to ensure its effectiveness in eliminating violence against women, emphasising the prevention of violence and the prosecution of offenders; take measures to ensure the protection of women subjected to violence, access to just and effective remedies, including compensation and indemnification and healing of victims, and rehabilitation of perpetrators."[28]

The guidelines set out in the Beijing Platform are noteworthy in that they concretise the general duties referred to in the Women's Convention as well as in the Violence Declaration. In the Southern African context, similar guidance is provided by the Addendum to the Southern African Development Community (SADC) Declaration on Gender and Development[29] on the prevention and eradication of violence against women and children.[30] The Addendum (*inter alia*) requires SADC members to review and reform the criminal laws and procedures applicable to cases of sexual offences, to eliminate gender bias and ensure justice and fairness to both the victim and the accused.

The cumulative effect of constitutional provisions and international human rights norms is to impose a clear obligation on the South African state to re-examine and reform current sexual assault law. This duty should be carried out in the context of the overarching imperative to prevent, investigate, punish and compensate for acts of sexual assault against women. It is therefore not enough to simply "reform" the law: the objective of reform measures should fit into the paradigm demarcated by the Constitution and international human rights law.

This reading is borne out by the recent judgement of the South African Constitutional Court in *S v. Baloyi*.[31] In this matter the Court was called on to determine the constitutionality of section 3(5) of the Prevention of Family Violence Act of 1993.[32] In reaching the conclusion that the section concerned

---

[27] UN GAOR, U.N. Doc.A/Conf.117/20 (recommended to the UN General Assembly by the Committee on the Status of Women on October 7, 1995) [hereinafter referred to as "the Beijing Platform"].
[28] para. 124(d). See also paras 124(c) and (i).
[29] The SADC Declaration on Gender and Development was signed by the SADC Heads of State or Government on September 8, 1997.
[30] This Addendum was signed on September 14, 1998 and forms part of the Declaration.
[31] *S. v. Baloyi* 2000 (1) SACR 81 (CC).
[32] Act 113 of 1993. Section 3(5) prescribed the procedure to be followed at an inquiry into the alleged breach of an interdict in terms of the Prevention of Family Violence Act. The provi-

does not offend against the Constitution, Sachs J. notes that the State is under a series of constitutional mandates, which include the obligation to deal with domestic violence: to protect both the rights of everyone to enjoy freedom and security of the person and to bodily and physical integrity, and the right to have their dignity respected and protected, as well as the defensive rights not to be subjected to torture and not to be treated or punished in a cruel, inhuman or degrading way.[33] He adds that in enacting the relevant legislation, the legislature was also acting in compliance with South Africa's international obligations.[34]

CURRENT POSITION REGARDING SEXUAL ASSAULT

South African criminal law does not have a "specific" statute dealing with sexual assault. Instead, the relevant legal rules are to be found in the common law (as developed by precedent)[35] as well as in the provisions of general legislation such as the Criminal Procedure Act.[36] The rules of procedure and evidence (as well as the substantive definitions of offences) largely owe their origin to the Anglo-American tradition; while some of these rules have been amended in recent times,[37] a number of the legal principles applicable to sexual assault still closely resemble their antiquated historic antecedents.[38]

There can be little argument that the current profile of sexual assault in South Africa is highly disturbing, not only in terms of the high levels of these offences but also in terms of their specific violent nature.[39] Where reported

---

sion had been declared invalid by the court *a quo* for placing a reverse onus of proving absence of guilt on a person charged with breach of a family violence interdict. In doing so, s. 3(5) conflicted with the presumption of innocence; this limitation of the right to be presumed innocent could not be constitutionally justified. It should be noted that the provisions of the Prevention of Family Violence Act dealing with protective interdicts have subsequently been repealed by the Domestic Violence Act 116 of 1998.

[33] para. 11.

[34] para. 13. Sachs J. lists obligations incurred under the Universal Declaration of Human Rights, the Declaration on the Elimination of Violence Against Women, the Convention on the Elimination of Discrimination Against Women [*sic*] and the African Charter on Human and People's Rights.

[35] For example, the definitions of rape, indecent assault and *crimen injuria* derive from common law. In addition, certain rules of evidence (such as the rule admitting evidence from the person to whom the victim first reported the assault) also owe their origin to common law.

[36] Act 51 of 1977. For example, s. 227 regulates the admissibility of evidence on the victim's previous sexual history.

[37] For example, s. 227 of the Criminal Procedure Act. Protective measures for the testimony of vulnerable witnesses have been enacted in ss 158 and 170A of the Criminal Procedure Act.

[38] See in this regard L. Fryer, "Law versus prejudice: views on rape through the centuries" (1994) 7 S.A.C.J. (1994) 60–77.

[39] A criminological analysis shows that the nature of sexual assault in South Africa resembles sexual assault committed against women in situations of armed conflict. (Personal communi-

incidents of sexual assault result in prosecution, these cases are generally char-acterised by very low conviction rates.[40]

Advocates of victims' rights have long suggested that a re-examination of both substantive and adjective law is an essential measure to address sexual assault in South Africa.[41] In this context, it is significant that the South Afri-can Law Commission has recently undertaken an extensive review of the law relating to sexual assault. This inquiry, which had its origin in 1996, originally focused on sexual offences committed against children,[42] but the Commis-sion's mandate was broadened in July 1999 to also include sexual offences against adults.[43] The Commission has divided its investigation into three com-ponents: the first to examine substantive law; the second to look at issues of procedure and evidence; and the third to focus on commercial sex work and pornography.

The Commission published its first discussion paper on substantive law in August 1999.[44] This paper contains a number of interesting proposals, most notably an incisive reconceptualising of the offence of rape. The Commission proposes that the current offence of rape as defined in common law (namely "unlawful intentional sexual intercourse by a man with a woman without her consent")[45] be replaced with a statutory offence that prohibits the unlawful and intentional of an act of sexual penetration with another person.[46] An act of sexual penetration is prima facie unlawful if it takes place under coercive circumstances. A non-exhaustive list of "coercive circumstances" is proposed.[47]

---

cation with Ms Lillian Artz, chief researcher at the Gender, Law and Development Project, Institute of Criminology, University of Cape Town on January 31, 2000.)
[40] See B. Pithey *et al.*, *Legal Aspects of Rape* (unpublished paper commissioned by the Deputy Minister of Justice, 1999), p. 3. The authors calculate that only 10.84 per cent of cases re-ported in the Western Cape in January–June 1998 resulted in conviction.
[41] See *e.g.* D. Hansson, "Working Against Violence Against Women" in S. Bazili ed., *Putting Women on the Agenda* (1991), pp. 185–186; C. Hall, "Rape: The Politics of Definition" (1988) 67; K. Ross, "An Examination of South African Rape Law" in *Women, Rape and Violence in South Africa* (Community Law Centre, 1993), pp. 12–15; M. Reddi, "A Feminist Perspective of the Substantive Law of Rape" in S. Jagwanth *et al.* ed., *Women and the Law* (1994), p.159; P. Singh, "Protection from violence is a right" in S. Liebenberg (ed.), *The Constitution of South Africa from a Gender Perspective* (1995), pp.136–137.
[42] The investigation was originally titled "Sexual Offences by and against Children". However, the Commission decided to limit the investigation to sexual offences against children in the light of the co-existence of an investigation on juvenile offenders. See South African Law Commission, *Discussion Paper 85 Sexual Offences: The Substantive Law* (1999) [hereinafter referred to as "Discussion Paper"] at para. 7.2.1.
[43] Discussion Paper at para. 7.4.2.
[44] See n.41 above.
[45] Burchell and Milton, *op. cit.* at p. 487.
[46] See Discussion Paper at para. 9.4.7.1–9.4.7.3.
[47] See para. 9.4.7.4. The proposed list includes, amongst others, circumstances where there is any application of force, where the complainant is under the age of 12 years, where there is an abuse of power of authority, or where a person's mental capacity is affected to the extent that he or she is unable to appreciate the nature of an act of sexual penetration, or is unable to resist

In addition to the substance of the recommendations, which (if accepted at parliamentary level) would bring South African law in line with similar changes recently effected in comparable jurisdictions as well as developments in international law,[48] the basic approach taken by the Commission is also to be commended. In a chapter entitled "Underlying Principles",[49] the Commission examines the norms developed in terms of international law and the Constitution, and develops a set of principles for the management of sexual offences based on these norms.[50] These principles include, for example, the notion that victims should have the right to legal representation in civil, criminal and administrative proceedings.[51] The Commission notes that these principles should underlie all reform.[52]

The publication of the results of the second component of the inquiry, dealing with procedure and evidence, is eagerly awaited. One hopes that the paper, in addition to examining issues such as bail, rules of evidence and sentencing in relation to sexual assault, will also include a serious re-appraisal of the accepted rules regarding the role of the victim of sexual offences in criminal proceedings.[53]

It is, however, important to bear in mind that the reform of legal provisions is merely one dimension of a composite picture. The success or failure of such reform will ultimately be determined by judicial interpretation. Unfortunately, a close observation of the interpretation of the Criminal Law Amendment Act[54] in relation to sentencing in rape cases indicates cause for concern.[55] This Act introduced provisions to the effect that where an accused is convicted of a "listed" offence, the court is bound to impose a certain minimum sentence.[56] There is, however, an exception to this general rule: where the court is satisfied that "substantial and compelling circumstances" exist, a departure from the mandatory minimum is allowed.[57] The legislature provided no statutory guidelines as to the contents of the phrase "substantial and compelling circumstances", and left the term open to judicial interpretation. The construction placed on this term in two recent judgments gives pause for thought.

---

the commission of such an act, or is unable to indicate his or her unwillingness to participate in such act.
[48] See Pithey *et al., op. cit.* at pp.26–28.
[49] Chapter 2 of the Discussion Paper.
[50] para. 8.4.2.
[51] Principle 8(e) as set out in Para. 8.4.2.1.
[52] para. 8.4.4.2.
[53] See in this regard the recommendations put forward by Pithey *et al.* (*op. cit.*) at pp. 46-47.
[54] Act 105 of 1997.
[55] See in this regard generally H. Combrinck, N. Naylor and H. Galgut, *Comments: Discussion Paper 91* (unpublished submission to the South African Law Commission on Discussion Paper 91: A New Sentencing Framework, 2000).
[56] See ss. 51(1) and 51(2).
[57] See s. 51(3)(a).

In *S v. Mahamotsa*,[58] the accused had been convicted of raping two women under the age of 16 years. In considering sentence, Kotze J. held that the following constituted a "substantial and compelling circumstance" for departure from the prescribed minimum sentence of life imprisonment:

> "Although there was intercourse with each complainant more than once, this was the result of the virility of a young man still at school who had intercourse with other school pupils against their wishes, and, note, school pupils who had previously been sexually active. . . . Where one is dealing with school pupils, and where, in addition, it appears that the two girls concerned had already had intercourse before, one really shouldn't lose perspective, especially not in relation to the first count, which dealt with a complainant who had in any event been naughty a few days earlier and had intercourse with someone else."[59]

A similarly startling conclusion was reached in *S v. Abrahams*,[60] where Foxcroft J. found that the fact that the particular offence had been committed in a family context constituted "substantial and compelling circumstances" allowing for a departure from a sentence of life imprisonment. *In casu*, the accused had been convicted of raping his daughter (who was under the age of 16 years at the time of the incident).

These views stand in stark contrast to clear statements from the Supreme Court of Appeal affirming women's right to freedom from violence. In *S v. Chapman*,[61] Mahomed C.J. made the following statement:

> "The Courts are under a duty to send a clear message to the accused in rape cases, to other potential rapists and to the community that the Courts are determined to protect the equality, dignity and freedom of all women, and they will show no mercy to those who seek to invade those rights."[62]

The intrusion of subjective views on the effectiveness of well-intended legislative measures, as encountered in the *Mahamotsa* and *Abrahams* judgments, bears out the experience in other jurisdictions, where the potentially salutary effect of legal reforms was obstructed by judicial and prosecutorial interpretation. A study of law reform enacted in Michigan, USA,[63] showed that the

---

[58]Unreported, July 28, 1999, Case No 29/99, Free State Provincial Division of the High Court.
[59]Our translation from the Afrikaans judgment.
[60]unreported, September 20, 1999, Cape Provincial Division of the High Court.
[61]1997 (3) S.A. 341 (S.C.A.).
[62]p. 345.
[63]The reformative provisions introduced a single offence category of "criminal sexual assault" to replace forcible rape, assault with intent to rape and indecent liberties. See Pithey *et al.* (*op. cit.*) at p. 27.

"new" provisions did not have a major impact on report or arrest rates, and had only a limited impact on prosecution practices and trial outcomes.[64] However, research has also shown that even though the statute in question no longer made reference to "consent" as an element of the offence, in practice this has remained the key issue in many rape trials. A large proportion of judges, prosecutors and defence lawyers considered that, even under the new law, it was still absolutely essential for the prosecution to establish the victim's lack of consent.[65]

We therefore argue that it is essential for the formulation of new legislation on sexual assault to clearly state that such provisions measures should be interpreted within the framework of the right to freedom from violence.[66]

Such guidance should also include reference to other rights in the Bill of Rights, for example the right to dignity.[67] In its recent judgment in *S. v. Cornelius*,[68] the Cape Provincial Division of the High Court[69] noted that the rights of the accused to a fair trial (*in casu* specifically the right to adduce and challenge evidence) may be limited in order to protect the right to dignity of the complainant. In this matter, the unrepresented accused, charged with rape, had subjected the complainant to offensive cross-examination lasting for an excessively long period of time. The court remarked (*obiter*) that the fairness of the appellant's trial would not have been affected in any way had the offending questions been investigated and then ruled inadmissible.

CONCLUSION

"Ultimately, rape law reform is an intellectual exercise. It is an exercise performed in the hope that attitude will follow action."[70]

A question that becomes unavoidable at this point is the practical concern of whether the reform of sexual assault law will serve to change the incidence of sexual assault in South Africa. On a simplistic level, the answer to this ques-

---

[64] See S.A.L.C. Discussion Paper at para. 9.4.6.6.2.6.

[65] J.C. Marsh, A. Geist and N. Caplan, *Rape and the Limits of Law Reform* (1982), pp. 50–52.

[66] Such a "reminder" is not unique in the South African legislative context. For example, s. 3(1)(a) of the Promotion of Equality Act 4 of 2000 requires the Act to be interpreted so as to give effect to "the Constitution, the provisions of which include the promotion of equality through legislative and other measures designed to protect or advance persons disadvantaged by past and present unfair discrimination". See in this regard also s. 4 of this Act, which sets out guiding principles for the adjudication of proceedings instituted in terms of the Act as well as for the application of the Act.

[67] See s. 10 of the Constitution.

[68] 1999 J.D.R. 0145 (C).

[69] *Per* Donen A.J.

[70] C.T. Byrnes, "Putting the focus where it belongs: *mens rea*, consent, force and the crime of rape" (1988) *Yale Journal of Law and Feminism* at 280.

tion would have to be in the negative. It would be naïve, if not dangerous, to assume that law reform in itself will stem the time of violence against women. Legal provisions and their practical application within the criminal justice system form part of a closely interlinked lattice of structural responses to violence against women, and in order to ensure that the criminal justice system responds more appropriately, law reform should consequently be accompanied by a "safety net" of legislative and policy measures to secure the proper implementation of new provisions.[71]

There can be no doubt that such measures (including, for example, prosecutor-led investigations and specialist police units), will have resource and budgetary implications, and the drafting of new legislation cannot be insulated from practical limitations. However, we argue that the South African government should dispense with the facile (and, by now, overused) excuse of a lack of resources, and take the budgetary demands of addressing sexual assault into consideration in its overall allocation of resources.[72] This is not a matter of altruism or political goodwill; the government must take on this responsibility if it desires in any seriousness to comply with the demands implicit in the constitutional recognition of the right to freedom from violence.

---

[71] See in this regard the measures aimed at monitoring of implementation contained in s. 18 of the Domestic Violence Act.
[72] Para. 124(p) of the Beijing Platform calls on governments to allocate adequate resources within the government budget for activities related to the elimination of violence against women. See also Article 4(h) of the Violence Declaration.

SENTENCING PRACTICE IN IRELAND

A Focus on the Concepts of Minimum and Mandatory Sentencing

GENERAL PRINCIPLES OF SENTENCING

The common law tradition of sentencing places its emphasis upon the need to ensure the exercise of judicial discretion, subject only to the statutory maximum provided for the offence, and to the right of appeal to a higher court. The legislature sets a maximum penalty, but generally does not seek to impose minimum or mandatory sentences, nor to determine any guiding policy upon which sentencing practice should be based.

On the positive side, this means that the particular circumstances of the offender and his or her capacity for rehabilitation may be taken into account by the sentencing judge. However, it also means that while some judges may sentence according to rehabilitative principles, others may reject those principles and sentence the offender on the basis of other considerations.

Within the common law tradition, sentencing practice thus tends not to be guided by a single rationale. The exercise of judicial discretion is generally unstructured, so that the sentencing decision may be seen to represent an 'instinctive synthesis' of the offence, the characteristics of the offender and the past experience of the sentencing judge.[1]

Enlightenment thinkers such as Beccaria, upon whose ideas the penal codes of many European and African jurisdictions were modelled, advocated an alternative to this instinctive practice of sentencing. They believed that the sentencing decision should always be subject to one stated policy or model, so that punishment would be 'the minimum possible in the given circumstances, proportionate to the crime, and determined by the law.'[2]

This emphasis on the need for proportionality of punishment is today identified with the retributive approach to sentencing, or in its modern guise, the 'just deserts' theory. It is premised upon the classical view that punishment is

---

[*] LL.B., LL.M., B.L., Barrister, Reid Professor of Criminal Law, Criminology and Penology, Trinity College Dublin.
[1] Victorian Court of Criminal Appeal, in *R v. Williscroft* [1975] V.R. 292.
[2] Beccaria C., *On Crimes and Punishments* (Cambridge University Press, 1995), p.113 (first published 1764 as *Dei Delitti e Delle Pene*).

justifiable as the natural response to crime, and that it acts as a form of public denunciation of criminal behaviour. This approach presumes that individuals are rational actors whose decisions to commit crime will be influenced by the relative likelihood of punishment. Above all, the penalty must be proportionate to the offence.

The just deserts model has now been adopted as a basis for sentencing policy in many jurisdictions.[3] However, other approaches to sentencing may also be identified, based on the principles of rehabilitation, deterrence, incapacitation or restitution. It is not proposed to dwell upon the respective merits of each of these sentencing models here, but a brief explanation of the main features may be helpful.[4]

In short, retributive theories focus upon the degree of culpability of the offender, whereas the rehabilitative approach takes into account the potential for his or her reform. The deterrent model seeks to prevent future offending generally, while the incapacitative model aims to prevent recidivism by the individual offender. The most recently developed model, that of restitution, is associated with principles of restorative justice, whereby the offender is expected to make reparation to the victim for harm done.

MAXIMUM SENTENCES

The traditional legislative practice in common law jurisdictions has therefore been to adopt a discretionary approach to sentencing, by prescribing a maximum penalty for each offence. This is seen as the best method of distributing sentencing power between the legislature and the courts. Despite the theory, in many jurisdictions statutory maxima have come to bear no relationship to the actual sentence imposed in practice.

The Canadian Commission[5] found that 'maximum penalties as they currently stand have little impact upon the sentences handed down by judges and only serve to confuse the public'. Indeed, judges in England and Wales are advised that the maximum sentence of imprisonment provided for a particular offence should be reserved only for the worst examples of that offence likely to be encountered in practice. Moreover, in considering 'worst examples', the sentencer should have regard to cases actually encountered, rather than unlikely or hypothetical examples; in practice, maximum sentences are rarely handed down, and in practice never where the defendant has entered a plea of guilty.[6]

---

[3] For example, in England and Wales under the Criminal Justice Act, 1991.
[4] See, for example, A. Ashworth, "Sentencing" in M. Maguire, R. Morgan and R. Reiner ed., *The Oxford Handbook of Criminology* (Oxford, Clarendon Press, 1994), pp. 819-60.
[5] Canadian Sentencing Commission, *Sentencing Reform: A Canadian Approach*, 1987, pp. 199-200.
[6] D. Thomas, *Current Sentencing Practice* (London, Butterworths, 1999), p. 501.

This judicial practice is reflected in the Irish experience. Although the maximum penalty for burglary is 14 years' imprisonment, 28% of those imprisoned for burglary in 1988 received sentences of between one and two years, and 35% received sentences of between two and three years; no sentence exceeded 10 years in length.[7] As a result of these findings, the Law Reform Commission recommended in 1993 that a review of the set of maximum penalties should be carried out, in order to re-scale the levels in accordance with modern practice.

Minimum and Mandatory Sentences

If judges do not use the statutory maxima provided, legislators in many jurisdictions may develop a distrust of judicial discretion in sentencing. Thus, they may begin to provide for minimum or mandatory sentences for particular offences. The difference between the two types of sentence is as follows.

Minimum sentences of imprisonment are generally provided where the legislature wishes to ensure that offenders serve a particular determinate period of time in custody. They are mandatory in that they provide for a basic length of imprisonment, but they allow some judicial discretion in determining the precise extent of the sentence beyond that minimum length of time, although they may be imposed together with a prescribed maximum level. Thus, the judge's discretion is limited by the given statutory parameters.

Mandatory sentences, by contrast, leave no discretion to the sentencing judge. Rather, the stated penalty attaches automatically once the defendant is convicted. The judge generally has no role in determining the extent of the sentence. Such penalties may be indeterminate (such as the mandatory life sentence for murder that applies in Ireland) or determinate (where, for example, a defendant must be disqualified from driving for 12 months on a conviction for drunk driving in England).

Both minimum and mandatory sentences may be seen to serve the function of incapacitation, but they also carry a denunciatory function, in that their introduction is based upon the need to express strong public disapproval of certain conduct. They are also often justified by reference to their perceived deterrent effect. Such sentences are generally introduced, however, for political reasons: because of legislative distrust of the judiciary and of judicial discretion in sentencing, often because it is perceived to be exercised in a manner too favourable to the offender.

The stated justifications for imposing either type of sentence have received trenchant judicial and expert criticism in different jurisdictions. The Law Commission of India in their 14th Report stated that: "there can be no rule of gen-

---

[7] Law Reform Commission Consultation Paper on Sentencing (1993), p. 301.

eral application laying down a specific *quantum* of punishment that should be inflicted in the case of a particular offence." The Commission concluded that the legislature had introduced minimum sentences because there appeared to be "a feeling that courts seldom award sentences which would have a deterrent effect, particularly in certain types of offences, which are necessary to be dealt with sternly in the interests of society." [8]

The Canadian Law Reform Commission, similarly, concluded that 'experience does not show that [minimum sanctions] have any obvious special deterrent or educative effect. Other problems arise in denying judges discretion to select the appropriate sanction or the length of a prison term in individual cases. For one thing circumstances vary so greatly from case to case that an arbitrary minimum may be seen as excessive denunciation or an excessively long period of separation in the light of the risk and all the circumstances... Similar criticisms could be made of a sentencing provision that denies judges the power to choose between a custodial and a non-custodial sentence.'[9]

Because minimum sentences may prevent the sentencer from imposing a sentence which he or she believes genuinely reflects the seriousness of the offending behaviour, they may be seen to offend against the cardinal principle of desert theory, that of proportionality.

Mandatory sentences have been criticised by Howard,[10] among others, on similar grounds. He concluded that "it is impossible at the legislative level to foresee and provide in adequate detail either for the multitudinous variety of circumstances under which serious crimes are committed or for the sometimes considerable differences of personality, background and intelligence between people who commit them. What is virtually certain is that legislatively imposed fixed penalties for serious crimes will require the frequent intervention of executive clemency."

Apart from the principled arguments against minimum and mandatory sentences, on a more pragmatic level, experience shows that statutes providing for such sentences are often ineffective, since they meet with resistance at many levels within every criminal justice system. In England in the eighteenth and early nineteenth centuries, there was a huge increase in the number of capital offences. In 1,819, 220 offences carried a mandatory death penalty (most were offences against property).

Yet although large numbers of people were charged with these offences and many convicted, surprisingly small numbers were actually executed (21 a year in the 1780s; 53 a year in the 1790s). O'Malley suggests that this was due

---

[8] Law Commission of India 14th Report, Vol II, pp. 838-41.

[9] Law Reform Commission of Canada, *Criminal Procedure: Control of the Process* (1975), p. 24. In 35 years, every Canadian Commission which addressed the role of mandatory minimum penalties recommended the same thing – that they should be abolished.

[10] Howard, "An Analysis of Sentencing Authority in Reshaping the Criminal Law" *Essays in Honour of Glanville Williams* (Glazebrook, 1978), pp.408-409.

to the practice of jury nullification (*i.e.* juries refusing to convict where they knew a mandatory death penalty applied). Other factors were the courts' adoption of stringent procedural rules preventing conviction, and the extensive use of the Crown prerogative to pardon those who were sentenced to death.[11]

More recently, the American experience of mandatory sentences has shown a similar effect. Drugs and firearms offences have routinely attracted mandatory penalties in the last 20 years in the US; some states apply such penalties to rape and other offences of violence. They have always been popular at a political level, but the experience has been different in practice. With the introduction of mandatory sentences, enormous power is conferred upon prosecutors, who hold the defendant's fate in their hands, since they may decide to charge a lesser offence with a discretionary penalty. Where a mandatory penalty applies, juries are reluctant to convict, and police practice may even alter.

In Massachusetts, for example, where a one-year minimum sentence was introduced for anyone convicted of carrying a firearm, it was found that police became more selective about whom they frisked, so the number of arrests actually decreased.[12] One might conclude therefore that the legal process develops its own effective 'immune system' when mandatory sentences are introduced. One study of the effect of such sentences even showed the number of defendants who entirely avoided a conviction rose from 53.5% in 1974 to 80% in 1976.[13]

Across different jurisdictions, the offence for which a mandatory penalty is most frequently imposed is that of murder. The penalty of life imprisonment is frequently mandatory upon a conviction for murder. Statute may make the ancillary requirement that the offender serve a particular minimum period of time; in some jurisdictions the trial judge may recommend that a certain minimum be served, but in most jurisdictions there is no legislative or judicial role in determining the length of the life sentence. Rather, the release of the offender is at the instance of the executive.

This feature of the indeterminate mandatory sentence provides another argument against the use of such sentences. Because of these and other criticisms, the New South Wales Legislature abolished the mandatory nature of the life sentence for murder in 1982, as did that of Victoria in 1986. Both jurisdictions did so at least partly because they doubted the appropriateness of the length of sentence being determined in private by the executive rather than in public by a judge.

However, if the mandatory penalty for murder is abolished, so that life

---

[11] O'Malley, *Sexual Offences: Law, Policy and Punishment* (Dublin, Round Hall Sweet & Maxwell, 1996), pp 397-398.

[12] Federal Sentencing Reporter, *The Chasm between the Judiciary and Congress over Mandatory Minimum Penalties* Vol 6, No. 2 (Sept.-Oct., 1993).

[13] Carlson, *Mandatory Sentencing: The Experience of Two States* (Washington DC, National Institute of Justice, 1982).

imprisonment becomes instead the maximum sentence, then the distinction between the offences of murder and manslaughter becomes less clear. Various approaches to this problem have been identified. The option adopted in New South Wales, for example, as in Botswana, has been to retain the murder/manslaughter distinction, but to allow sentencers a more restricted discretion in sentencing murderers.

In other words, the presumption that a particular sentence will be imposed for murder remains, unless extenuating circumstances apply. The experience in New South Wales since the removal of the mandatory penalty for murder has been encouraging in this respect; the murder rate has not increased. This might be seen to confirm Tonry's view that "the enactment of mandatory penalty laws has either no deterrent effect or a modest deterrent effect that soon wastes away."[14]

MINIMUM AND MANDATORY SENTENCES – LAW AND PRACTICE IN IRELAND

Minimum sentences

Statutory minimum sentences are not a common feature of modern Irish criminal statutes, although in the past they have been introduced into some legislation, usually because 'it was felt that sentencers might not take a sufficiently serious view of the offences.'[15] For example, under the Regulation of Railways Act 1868 it was made an offence for a railway company to provide knowingly a special train to take parties to prize-fights or to stop an ordinary train to accommodate parties for that purpose at any station not an ordinary station. The fine applied had to be a minimum of £200 and a maximum of £500.

In some older statutes, minima were imposed in combination with a maximum (as in the case of certain offences in the law of Botswana, for example). To name one instance, the Larceny Act 1861 provided for terms of penal servitude for any term not exceeding seven years and not less than three years.

The only minimum sentence of imprisonment in Irish law still in existence is that of 40 years for capital murder (*i.e.* of a garda or prison officer in the course of duty) or treason, as provided for in section 3 of the Criminal Justice Act 1990. This appears to have been introduced specifically for its perceived deterrent effect. During the debate on the relevant provision, the Minister for Justice said: 'we have a largely unarmed Garda Force whose only protection from those with murderous intent is the statutory protection we can afford them by way of a penalty with deterrent effect.'[16]

---

[14]Tonry, "Judges and Sentencing Policy: the American Experience" in Munro and Wasik ed., *Sentencing, Judicial Discretion and Training* (London, 1992).
[15]Law Reform Commission Consultation Paper, *op. cit.*, p. 47.
[16]*Dáil Debates*, June 12, 1990, Col. 2023.

In practice, this minimum period of 40 years is treated for the purposes of remission as if it were a determinate sentence. Once the appropriate deduction for remission is made, a person convicted of capital murder or treason must expect to serve at least 30 years. Temporary release may not be granted until this minimum period has expired, except for "grave reasons of a humanitarian nature".[17]

Despite the Minister's stated view, in its review of minimum sentences the Law Reform Commission found no clear evidence that such sentences serve any useful purpose at all, not being justifiable according to a just deserts or retributive approach. The Commission concluded that any minima still in operation "are, generally, a relic of bygone days", and should be abolished.[18]

Mandatory sentences

The only provision for a mandatory sentence of imprisonment in Irish law is contained in section 2 of the Criminal Justice Act 1990, which provides that "a person convicted of treason or murder shall be sentenced to imprisonment for life." This section creates an indeterminate sentence, with no judicial input in deciding on the length of time to be served. The executive alone determines when the offender is to be released. The continued existence of this provision has been subject to strong academic criticism.[19] The Law Reform Commission has also suggested that mandatory sentences may breach the *audi alterem partem* requirement, since they deprive judges of the opportunity to hear evidence that might lead to mitigation.

In *Deaton*, the Supreme Court confirmed the exclusivity of the judicial role in the selection of punishment in ruling a section of a customs statute unconstitutional because it allowed the Revenue Commissioners to decide which of two penalties should be imposed on a person convicted of certain customs offences.[20] However, the implication of the decision was that the legislature could prescribe mandatory punishment, but the judiciary alone are entitled to select punishment, where there is a selection to be made. Since *Deaton*, the courts in Ireland have only once had an opportunity to confront head-on the constitutional status of mandatory sentences or penalties.

This was in *Cox v. Ireland*,[21] a Supreme Court decision striking down section 34 of the Offences Against the State Act, 1939. The section had re-

---

[17]T. O'Malley, *Sentencing Law and Practice* (Dublin, Round Hall Ltd, 2000), p. 286.

[18]Law Reform Commission, *op cit*, p. 309. For a critique of the Commission's analysis, see U. Ni Raifeartaigh, "The Law Reform Commission Consultation Paper on Sentencing" (1993) *Irish Law Times*, p. 103.

[19]See for example, T. O'Malley, "Sentencing Murderers" (1995) 5 *Irish Criminal Law Journal* 31-66, or A. Ashworth, "Reforming the Law of Murder" [1990] Crim L.R. 75.

[20]*Deaton v. Attorney-General and the Revenue Commissioners* [1963] I.R. 170

[21][1992] I.R. 503.

quired that anyone convicted of a scheduled offence by the Special Criminal Court would be banned from employment in the public sector for a period of seven years. Referring to the mandatory nature of the disqualification, the Court said:

> "This is so even though [the person convicted] might be in a position to establish, not his innocence of the particular offence charged, but the fact that his motive or intention in committing it, or the circumstances under which it was committed, bore no relation at all to any question of the maintenance of public peace and order or the authority or stability of the State."

O'Malley writes that in this statement may be found "the germ of an argument against the constitutional validity of stringent mandatory sentences".[22] The Court was essentially confirming, as it has done more explicitly elsewhere, that a penalty imposed should reflect not just the circumstances of the offence, but also those of the offender.

Mandatory sentences for summary offences have not generated the same debate in Ireland as the mandatory sentence for murder. However, they have far greater effect for a greater number of people. The Road Traffic Act 1961, for example, provides for 15 offences (including driving while intoxicated, dangerous driving etc.) for which a court must make a "consequential disqualification order".

For example, on a first conviction for driving while intoxicated, an offender must be disqualified for a minimum period of two years. For a second or subsequent offence, a minimum disqualification period of four years applies. In relation to some types of charge, such as dangerous driving, the court may choose not to impose any disqualification for a first offence where "special reasons" apply (*e.g.* if the offender needs to drive for his/her work).

Particulars of all consequential orders must be endorsed on the licences of all convicted persons. When the Law Reform Commission came to review this area, they found that all the judges of the District Court were opposed to mandatory sentences, in particular to the mandatory endorsement of a driving licence for the offence of careless driving.

Law reform

Ultimately, the Irish Law Reform Commission in its report recommended that both minimum and mandatory sentences should be abolished. The Commission noted the absence of any sentencing guidelines for Irish judges. They recommended that non-statutory guidelines should be introduced, based upon

---

[22] O'Malley, *Sentencing Law and Practice, op. cit.*, p. 101.

the just deserts approach, so that sentences would be consistent and severity would be measured in proportion to the seriousness of the offending behaviour. This itself would depend upon two factors; the degree of harm caused or risked by the offender, and his or her level of culpability. The Commission took the view that such an approach would not allow for the retention of minimum or mandatory sentences.

To date, the Irish legislature has not taken up the challenge of developing sentencing guidelines, despite the Law Reform Commission's strong recommendation. But, in spite of the Supreme Court indication that a doubt exists over the constitutionality of the mandatory sentence, legislation has recently been introduced providing for a mandatory 10-year sentence in respect of certain drugs offences.[23] Section 4 of the Criminal Justice Act 1999 provides, however, that the minimum 10-year period will not apply where there exist "exceptional and specific circumstances relating to the offence, or the person convicted of the offence, which would make a sentence of not less than 10 years imprisonment unjust in all the circumstances". The judge, in deciding if such circumstances apply, may have regard to a number of matters, including whether a guilty plea was entered and at what stage it was entered.

In fact, what has really been introduced is not so much a scheme of mandatory sentencing but rather a type of "presumptive sentencing" approach.[24] Had it not been for the insertion of this discretionary proviso, the Supreme Court might well have had an opportunity to consider expressly the constitutionality of mandatory sentences. But it appears from practice that the "exceptional and specific circumstances" clause is being used by judges to render the so-called mandatory sentence ineffective.

It is to be hoped that the Irish legislature does not go any further by adopting the suggestion made in recent years by some victims' groups that mandatory sentences be introduced for rape and incest. While such a measure might receive strong public support, on pragmatic grounds it would be unlikely to work, judging by the US experience. Such sentences should be opposed on the principled ground that there may always be exceptional rape or sexual assault cases in which, owing to particular circumstances, a non-custodial or short custodial sentence should be imposed, rather than the "immediate and substantial" custodial sentence which is the norm for such offences in Ireland at present.[25]

---

[23] The Criminal Justice Act 1999.
[24] O'Malley, *op. cit.*, p. 102.
[25] Rape must generally warrant such a sentence, according to the Supreme Court in *DPP v. Tiernan* [1988] I.R. 250. The majority of those sentenced to prison for rape are sentenced for periods in excess of five years. However, in *People (DPP) v. McCormack* (April 10, 2000), the CCA held that despite the defendant's conviction for aggravated sexual assault and attempted rape, a custodial sentence was not warranted given the extenuating circumstances of the convicted person. The Court re-affirmed the established principle that the sentence im-

MINIMUM AND MANDATORY SENTENCES – THE PRACTICE IN THE U.S.,
ENGLAND AND WALES

The catchphrase "three strikes and you're out" has gained notoriety world-wide in recent years. It describes the laws introduced in many US states following a 1993 Washington state referendum mandating life sentences for third-time felons. For example, in California courts are obliged to sentence offenders to 25 years' imprisonment without parole on their third felony conviction. In one particularly notorious case, a man with prior convictions was sentenced to 25 years' imprisonment for stealing a slice of pizza.[26] Commenting on this experience, the Prison Reform Trust said: "Offences do differ markedly in their gravity and circumstances: offenders have greater or lesser culpability and show greater or lesser remorse. Mandatory sentences do not allow for such distinctions. They are a denial of justice, reducing sentencing to a rubber stamp exercise."[27]

In England, the use of mandatory minimum penalties was confined to murder and drunk driving until very recently. Murder carried a mandatory life sentence under the Murder (Abolition of the Death Penalty) Act 1965, and a 12-month disqualification period is consequential upon a conviction for drunk driving. The actual length of time served for murder is up to the Home Secretary. But, in practice, the trial judge writes to the Home Secretary through the Lord Chief Justice indicating his or her view as to how long the offender needs to serve to meet the requirements of retribution and deterrence in the case. This is known as the "tariff" or "penal element". The Home Secretary is not obliged to accept this tariff, but recent figures show that he or she interferes in very few cases, only five per cent in one study.[28] Thus some element of judicial discretion is retained in devising the penalty for offenders convicted of murder.[29]

However, the retention of the mandatory penalty for murder has been subject to much criticism in England, just as in Ireland. The House of Lords Select Committee on Murder and Life Imprisonment concluded in 1989 that it should be abolished. This recommendation has not been adopted, nor does it appear to be politically popular.[30]

---

posed must be commensurate not alone with the facts of the offence, but with the particular circumstances of the offender.

[26]Williams, *The Independent*, March 4, 1995.

[27]Prison Reform Trust, *Lessons from America; Automatic Life Sentences: The California Experience* (1996).

[28]Clarkson and Keating, *Criminal Law, Text and Materials* (4th ed., London, Sweet & Maxwell, 1998), p.638.

[29]The average served for a life sentence in England and Wales is 12-14 years; *ibid.*, p. 725.

[30]House of Lords, Report of the Select Committee on Murder and Life Imprisonment (Session 1988-89, H.L. Paper 78), 1989, paras 108B-118. For a recent political response, see The Government Reply to the First and Second Reports From the Home Affairs Committee Session 1995-96, *Murder: The Mandatory Life Sentence* (1996, Cm. 3346).

Judges are given some guidance in determining sentence by the Criminal Justice Act 1991, which gives effect to the principle of just deserts, stating that sentences should be commensurate with the seriousness of the offence. The Act allows an exception whereby dangerous violent and sexual offenders may be sentenced to longer than normal terms of imprisonment; this provision is in conflict with the stated guiding principle of proportionality.

More serious inroads on the principle of proportionality have been made by the Crime (Sentences) Act 1997. This Act provides for the first time that three types of offenders are liable to mandatory or minimum sentences if they have previous convictions. First, dealing with violent and sexual offenders, where a person who already has a conviction for a "serious offence" is convicted of another "serious offence", a life sentence must be imposed unless there are "exceptional circumstances". Secondly, where a person with two convictions for trafficking class-A drugs is convicted a third time for a similar offence, a court must impose at least seven years' imprisonment unless specific circumstances would render such a sentence unjust. Thirdly, where a person is convicted a third time of domestic burglary, the court must impose at least three years' imprisonment, again unless it would be unjust. These provisions are aimed at being both a general deterrent and a means of incapacitating the persistent or dangerous offender.

Clarkson and Keating argue that this new Act means that sentencing in England and Wales is now based upon a "philosophical mish-mash". The guiding principle for determining severity is still based on desert principles, but the exceptions, based upon grounds of incapacitation and deterrence and thus allowing sentences in excess of those permissible under the concept of desert, are assuming an ever-increasing importance.[31]

COMMENT ON A SOUTHERN AFRICAN EXPERIENCE: MINIMUM AND MANDATORY SENTENCES IN BOTSWANA

The Penal Code for Botswana does not indicate an overall policy guiding sentencing practice in Botswana. It would appear that, as in Ireland and in other common law jurisdictions, a relatively wide judicial discretion is maintained.

Sections 25-33 of the Penal Code deal with punishment of offenders. Section 27(2) provides that a person convicted of an offence punishable with imprisonment for life or any other period may be sentenced for any shorter term. This sets out clearly the general principle of judicial discretion, to be applied where the statute provides only for a maximum penalty. Section 33 further provides that when no punishment is specifically provided for an offence, it

---

[31] Clarkson and Keating, *op. cit.*, p. 70.

shall be punishable with imprisonment for a term not exceeding two years, or with a fine, or both.

There is no mention of minimum sentences as a concept in this section of the Code, but it appears that minimum sentences are imposed in relation to a few specified offences, although the more usual approach is to apply only a maximum penalty for each offence. There are also some examples of mandatory sentences. A mandatory death penalty is prescribed by sections 34 and 35 (for treason and related offences) and section 203 (for the offence of murder). However, on a conviction for treason, where "extenuating circumstances" apply, the court may impose instead a sentence of between 15 and 25 years imprisonment.

A more significant proviso relates to convictions for murder. Under section 203(2), the court may impose "any sentence other than death" upon someone convicted of murder, again where it is of the opinion that "extenuating circumstances" apply. The court must in such cases take into consideration the "standards of behaviour of an ordinary person of the class of the community to which the convicted person belongs" (section 203(3)). Greater judicial discretion than in Ireland is thus retained in cases of murder.

However, stricter parameters again are placed on the exercise of judicial discretion in sentencing for sexual offences, under the amendments to sections 142-147 introduced in 1998. Under these provisions, varying minimum sentences are prescribed for the offences of rape, attempted rape, abduction for immoral purposes, and unlawful carnal knowledge of minors. Higher minima are provided where a person convicted of rape or unlawful carnal knowledge of a minor has tested positive for the Human Immunodeficiency Virus (HIV), and higher again where the person is proved, on a balance of probabilities, to have been aware of his HIV-positive status.

Sections 141 and 142 provide for a minimum 10-year sentence for those convicted of rape, up to a maximum of life imprisonment. Aggravated rape, defined as rape attended by violence resulting in injury to the victim, carries an increased minimum penalty of 15 years' imprisonment. A person convicted of either rape or aggravated rape who is found to be HIV-positive is subject to a minimum of 15 years' imprisonment, increased to 20 years if it is proved that he was aware of his HIV-positive status. Sentences for rape may not run concurrently with any other sentence/s imposed on the offender. Attempts to commit rape under section 143 carry a minimum penalty of five years' imprisonment, and again a maximum of life.

Unlawful carnal knowledge of a minor (under 16 years) is dealt with in section 147, which provides for a 10 year minimum sentence, increased to 15 or 20 years if the offender is HIV-positive, and if he was aware of his status at the time of the offence.

No extenuating circumstances can be applied to reduce the minimum sentence applicable for these crimes under the recent amendments. In *State v.*

Rebagago, the accused had pleaded guilty to rape and been committed from the Magistrates Court to the High Court for sentence under section 295 of the Criminal Procedure and Evidence Act. The High Court held that he would thus become the "first victim" of the new law. Rebagago was HIV-positive, although the Court ruled that it could not have been proved on a balance of probabilities that he was aware of his status. Thus, he was sentenced to the minimum prescribed period of 15 years' imprisonment.[32]

This case demonstrates the harsh nature of the minimum penalty, particularly so where the convicted person is HIV-positive and so is unlikely to survive the full duration of the minimum prison sentence. The minimum penalty amendments were presumably introduced to reflect justifiable public concern about the extent to which crimes of rape are being perpetrated, and perhaps because of rising levels of reported rape. The increased minimum applicable when the defendant is HIV-positive must reflect the increased harm which the victim of the rape will potentially suffer as a result of the offender's act. However, the application of the minimum penalty in a case where the offender has pleaded guilty, and was not aware of his HIV-positive status at the time of the rape, seems unduly severe.

But the norm in sentencing remains in Botswana, as it is in Ireland, in accordance with the tradition of the discretionary model; the majority of offences carry only a statutory maximum, but judicial discretion is otherwise unfettered by the legislature.

CONCLUSION

The use of minimum and/or mandatory penalties in different jurisdictions is and has always been a controversial issue. The efficacy of such penalties in preventing future offending is dubious; the extent to which they may even be enforced in any criminal justice system may be doubted. The strongest justification for their use may be for the purpose of public denunciation. But it is argued that they should have no place in a legal system committed to the just deserts model, the principle of proportionality, and a belief in the potential for rehabilitation of individual offenders.

A structured sentencing policy, designed to provide guidance for judges and thereby aiming to reduce disparity, but without unduly fettering the discretion of the sentencing judge where particular extenuating circumstances apply, would be an infinitely preferable approach to the development of a sentencing policy in any jurisdiction.

---

[32] *State v. Chester Rebagago* (High Court at Francistown, December 16, 1998).

IMPLICATIONS OF THE TRADE AND DEVELOPMENT CO-OPERATION AGREEMENT WITH SPECIFIC REFERENCE TO THE JUSTICIABILITY OF ECONOMIC RIGHTS IN A MUNICIPAL FRAMEWORK: THE SOUTH AFRICAN AND EUROPEAN POSITION

PATRICIA LENAGHAN (LOTTERING)*

Introduction

Trade by its mere nature is a commodity that affects the lives of everyone. There is no doubt that market liberalisation provides major gains overall, reaching an increasing number of people every day. The participants and the beneficiaries of the trade arena, therefore, are individual people. Market liberalisation, however, is achieved by means of multilateral trading regimes, of which the participating parties are the contracting States.

The European Union (E.U.) has participated on a large scale in the creation of a multilateral trading regime, both on an international and a regional/individual level.

The Trade and Development Co-operation Agreement (TDCA), entered into between the E.U. and South Africa on March 24, 1999, is an example of an individually-negotiated multilateral trading regime. The TDCA has as its primary focus the establishment of a developmental free trade area. For the TDCA to be justly effective and to prevent the resulting benefits from being undermined, these rights need to be enforceable, not only by the contracting parties, but also by the individuals to whom these rights are advantageous. There is little point in having international agreements granting advantages if there is no procedure for enforcing the resulting rights from these agreements that give rise to the benefits.

The aim of this paper is to emphasise, by means of a comparative analysis, the dissimilarity between the protection afforded to nationals of South Africa as opposed to nationals of a member state of the E.U., in so far as the protection of economic rights arising from the TDCA are concerned. This will be illustrated by posing the following questions:

---

* Lecturer, Law Faculty, University of the Western Cape.

Firstly, the distinction regarding the justiciability of "international rights" within a municipal framework will be explored:

- The European Court of Justice (ECJ) has by means of interpretative measures held international agreements entered into by the European Commission on behalf of the E.U.[1] to be directly applicable within the E.U., consequently bestowing rights on an individual, justiciable in their own municipal courts.

- However, South Africa requires ratification and incorporation of international agreements into national legislation. The consequence is that international agreements are not applicable within a municipal framework until Parliament has acted upon them.

Before focusing attention on the justiciability of these internationally created economic rights, a brief overview of the respective commercial policies of the E.U. and South Africa will be presented.

EUROPEAN UNION

Commercial policy

The international level

On the international level, the E.U. has been a central member of the General Agreement on Tariffs and Trade (GATT), which supervised global trade rules, and has played a key role in various negotiations reducing trade barriers. The most ambitious of these negotiations was the Uruguay Round, which resulted in a substantial liberalisation of international trade and the creation of a stronger supervisory body to replace GATT – the World Trade Organisation (WTO).

The regional/individual level

On a regional level, mutually advantageous commercial concessions form the cornerstone of many of the bilateral agreements the E.U. has negotiated with countries on a regional or individual basis. The external commercial policy of the E.U. however, is mainly regulated in accordance with international structures such as the WTO. The E.U. will, however, negotiate regional or individual agreements where justifying circumstances exist. Justifying circumstances could include pre-accession agreements[2] or agreements entered into as a means of development co-operation.[3] The E.U.'s relationship with

---

[1] With regards to the so-called exclusive competencies of the E.U.
[2] As a means of paving the way for accession.
[3] The relationship of the E.U. to the African, Caribbean and Pacific (ACP) countries in terms of

South Africa in the form of the TDCA is a direct result of South Africa's exclusion from the Lomé Convention[4] – the E.U.'s developmental support vehicle to the rest of Africa.

LEGEAL STATUS OF EXTERNAL COMMERCIAL POLICY ENTERED INTO BY THE
EUROPEAN UNION

Direct applicability

"Direct applicability" refers to the way in which community law immediately becomes part of the national legal system. Under general principles of international law, it is necessary for norms to enter a national legal system. This can be accomplished either by transferring the measure into national law, or by adopting the act into a national legal system. Provisions of European Community law are, however, held to be directly applicable without the need for implementing measures. The E.U. has the external competencies to enter into international agreements outside the Community, such as trade agreements, for example those under Article 133(3),[5] which then constitute Community Acts, forming part of its legal order. According to Article 300(7),[6] international agreements concluded by the E.U. are binding on the Community and its Member States and become an integral part of E.U. Law.[7] The E.U. has to act within the limits of its powers. Therefore, the provisions of these international agreements have to fall within the ambit of the exclusive competencies of the E.U.[8] Provisions falling outside this ambit will be not be considered to form an integral part of E.U. Law. The conclusion of an agreement incorporating provisions outside of the ambit of exclusive competencies will give rise to a so-called mixed agreement. Ratification of the resulting international agreement by the different Member States will be a prerequisite for direct applicability of those provisions falling outside the field of exclusive competence.[9]

Direct effect

It is unclear whether the Treaty framers meant the phrase "directly applicable" to include the endowing of individuals with rights they can enforce in their

---

what is now the Cotonou Convention comes to mind. The system of trade preferences granted by the EU to the ACP states, with no duty of reciprocity, but way of derogation from the rules governing world trade (WTO).

[4] Now replaced by the Cotonou Convention.

[5] Consolidated version of the Treaty establishing the European Union (Amsterdam Treaty) [TEC Consolidated version].

[6] TEC.

[7] See Case 181/73 *Haegeman v. Belgium*, [1974] E.C.R. 449, paras 2 to 6.

[8] Article 5 TEC.

[9] The TDCA entered into between the E.U. and South Africa is a so-called "mixed agreement".

own national courts. The European Court of Justice (ECJ)[10] has indeed interpreted the phrase in this way.

In contrast with other international organisations, the E.U. has developed a system of norms that bind each of the Member States, without the need for national implementing measures in their domestic systems.[11] Consequently, the E.U. represents a departure from the traditional *intergovernmental* nature of the international legal order. This development was brought about by the interpretative influence of the ECJ. This illustrates a rather different approach from that governing the domestic treatment of norms of international law between states.

Apart from the primary provisions[12] and the secondary sources of E.U. law,[13] other sources of Community law include, *inter alia,* international agreements entered into between the European Commission, acting on behalf of the E.U., and the contracting state. The Community has the external competencies to enter into international agreements outside the E.U., for example trade agreements under Article 133(3),[14] which then constitute Community Acts and form part of its legal order.

A question arises about the legal effect of such agreements: are these international agreements seen as traditional international agreements binding only upon the states that have signed them and having no effect upon the individual? Or are they acts of the E.U., directly effective and enforceable by individual litigants when sufficiently clear, and containing an unconditional obligation which does not depend on a further act of implementation?[15]

The ECJ held that international agreements can, "in certain instances" be directly effective. In *Hauptzollampt Mainz v. Kupferberg*[16] the court held that Article 21(1) of the Free Trade Agreement with Portugal (before Portugal had joined the E.U.) was directly effective, since the condition was clear and unconditional. Moreover, the court held that certain provisions of the Lomé Convention were directly effective.[17] Accordingly, the Court has readily accepted the direct effect of the co-operation agreements concluded with third countries, as long as the conditions that grant the rights are sufficiently clear and unconditional.

---

[10]Case 26/62 *Algemene Transporten Expeditie Onderneming van Gend en Loos v. Nederlandse Administrasie der Belastingen* [1963] E.C.R. 1.

[11]Paul Craigh, Grainne de Burca, *EU Law Text Cases and Materials* (2nd ed., Oxford, 1998), p.163.

[12]TEC.

[13]s. 249 of the TEC. The primary and secondary sources of Community Law will not be discussed in the ambit of this paper, as the focus of this paper is the so-called international agreements entered into the E.U. and other States.

[14]TEC.

[15]See Case 270/80, *Polydor Ltd v. Harlequin Record Shop Ltd.,* [1982] E.C.R. 329 at 347.

[16]Case 104/81 [1982] ECR 3641, [1983] 1 C.M.L.R. 1.

[17]Case 469/93, *Amministrazione delle Finaze dello Stato v. Chiquita Italia* [1995] E.C.R. I–4533.

The TDCA is considered by the E.U. to be a "mixed"[18] agreement in terms of its own rules and procedures. Most of it is considered an E.U. agreement, and consequently an integral part of E.U. law. Part of it,[19] however, would have to be ratified by each Member State. The question arises as to the direct applicability and direct effect of the provisions of the TDCA that *are* within the field of exclusive E.U. competency.

Will these provisions be held to be directly effective as was the case in *Hauptzollampt Mainz v. Kupferberg*? It would appear that the ECJ would be willing to grant direct effect to the provisions that create rights for individuals, if these provisions are sufficiently clear, precise and unconditional. Consequently individuals in the E.U., regardless of their nationality, could claim protection of these rights within their own municipal courts.

Supremacy

The ECJ[20] has held that the legal order created by the founding treaties of the European Communities established an entirely new legal system, different in nature from international law. No reference was made to the constitution of any particular Member State. Consequently, differing constitutional approaches amongst the Member States regarding the primacy afforded to international treaties is avoided. The constitutional orders of some of the Member States do not easily accommodate the principle of supremacy. Moreover, supremacy relies on being implemented in the municipal courts of the Member States, not merely by the ECJ. The amplification of the principle of supremacy within the framework of the ECJ is relatively uncomplicated. However, the incorporation into the municipal courts proves more problematic. This difficulty is particularly evident in circumstances where it is felt that E.U. law could be in conflict with a Member State's own Constitution.[21]

---

[18]In so far as the provisions agreed upon pertain to the expressed competencies of the E.U. in terms of the founding treaties, and other provisions falling outside the scope of the E.U. competency.

[19]Mostly provisions on trade related aspects, pertaining to issues outside the competency of the European Community.

[20]Case 6/64 *Costa v. ENEL* [1964] E.C.R. 585.

[21]In *Internationale Handelsgesellschaft mbH v. Einfuhr- und Vorratstelle für Getreide und Futtermittel* [1974] 2 C.M.L.R. 540, the Court held that the protection of fundamental rights in the German Constitution would prevail over E.U. law in the event of conflict, as the transfer of legislative power to international organisations could not cover the transfer of power to amend an "*inalienable essential feature*" of the German Constitution. The German Federal Court challenged measures that exceed the constitutional limitations of a particular member state for exceeding E.U. competence. Changes in the E.U. law since this decision regarding the protection of fundamental human rights and democracy resulted in the Bundesverfassungs-gericht ruling in the *Re Wüssche Handelsgesellschaft* [1987] 3 C.M.L.R. 225 *[Solange II]*, in which it was held that "*so long as*" the European Communities ensure the effective protection of fundamental human rights substantially similar to the protection afforded by the Constitu-

SOUTH AFRICA

Commercial policy

The international/regional/individual level

South Africa is a party to various international agreements with regards to international trade:

- as an original contracting party to GATT and a member of the WTO;

- as a qualified partner of what is now the Cotonou Convention[22];

- on a regional level as a member of the Southern African Customs Union (SACU)[23] and the Southern African Development Community (SADC)[24];

- as a party to the Trade and Development Co-operation Agreement.[25]

Relationship with the European Union

South Africa's relationship with the European Union rests on two pillars.

- It is a qualified member, in conjunction with other African, Caribbean and Pacific (ACP) countries, of the Cotonou Convention. The Cotonou Convention is the successor of the Lomé Convention,[26] which expired in February 2000. It has amended the principles of Lomé to involve non-state actors, NGOs, civil society and the private sector.[27] Moreover, appreciation of the fact that sustainable development requires effective economic diversification[28] has led to the realisation that a gradual introduction of regional trading partnerships compatible with WTO rules[29] is imperative

---

tion, the Federal Constitutional court would no longer exercise its discretion to decide on the applicability of secondary Community legislation. Secondary Community legislation refers to legislation passed in accordance with Art. 249 of the TEC and would therefore not include international agreements.

[22] Renewal of the Lomé Convention, agreed upon February 3, 2000, and signed in Benin on June 23, 2000.

[23] This is a customs union between South Africa on the one hand and Botswana, Lesotho, Namibia and Swaziland on the other. The SACU trade framework provides for a free movement of goods between the members and a common external tariff (CETT).

[24] The SADC is a broader regional association, which has a membership of 14, including the five countries of SACU.

[25] For the purposes of this paper emphasis will be placed only on the relationship between SA and the E.U.

[26] The system of trade preferences granted by the E.U. to the ACP states, with no duty of reciprocity, by way of derogation from the rules governing world trade (WTO).

[27] Appreciating the fact that trade affects the lives of individuals and not merely States.

[28] Despite generous preferences, most ACP countries remain heavily dependant on the export of a few primary commodities, which are faced with declining prices.

[29] For example, the TCDA.

- It is party to the bilateral Trade and Development Co-operation Agreement, covering all aspects excluded in terms of the Cotonou Convention.

The Trade and Development Co-operation Agreement[30]

The TDCA was concluded in October 1999. In addition to establishment of a asymmetrical, differentiated, developmental[31] free trade area (FTA), the TDCA covers various areas of co-operation.[32] The FTA will be established within a 10- to 12-year transitional period.[33] Negotiations on promoting free trade are based on certain central principles:

- banning discrimination (so that no one is given concessions);

- ensuring equal treatment of local and imported goods on domestic markets;

- progressively providing easier access to other markets.

The lowering and dismantling of trade barriers also means that traditionally sheltered sectors will be forced to face up to stiffer competition. As a result, both partners are allowed to exclude certain products from the FTA in order to protect economically vulnerable sectors.[34] The FTA has the objective of establishing free trade, but excludes certain highly sensitive products in a summarised "negative list". The negotiators are confident that the TDCA meets the requirements of the WTO and the provisions of GATT, which state that free trade must cover "a substantial level" of trade in all areas. The TDCA will cover 90 per cent of current trade between the E.U. and SA, asymmetrically applied. Consequently the TDCA will substantially cover all trade.[35] However, it will respect sensitive sectors on both sides.[36] Agriculture remains a sensitive area for the E.U., in spite of the high subsidies enjoyed by European farmers in terms of the Common Agricultural Policy (CAP). The E.U. agreed to liberalise approximately 61 per cent of agricultural imports from South Africa. In addition, tariff quotas will be granted for certain agricultural prod-

---

[30] As the Cotonou Convention has a limited impact regarding trade in SA, only the TDCA will be discussed in this paper.
[31] With Europe opening its market more quickly and more substantially over a 10- to 12-year period.
[32] Development co-operation, political dialogue, social and cultural co-operation, financial assistance, economical co-operation.
[33] With Europe opening its markets more rapidly than South Africa.
[34] Europe: set aside – beef, sugar, maize; partial liberalisation – substitute cereals, dairy, fruit, vegetables and wine. South Africa: set aside – beef, sugar, automotive; partial liberalisation – certain automotive tyres, textiles, footwear, chemicals.
[35] Europe will liberalise up to 95 per cent of its markets and South Africa will open up 86 per cent to European imports.
[36] See n.34 above.

ucts, making up 13 per cent of agricultural trade with the E.U.[37] Over 74 per cent of South African agricultural products will thus enjoy some form of relief from tariffs. The E.U., perennially protective of its agricultural sector, has excluded 26 per cent of South Africa's agricultural exports from the negotiations, inclusive of the partial liberalisation by means of a special "tariff quota" system on cereals, processed fruit, cut flowers, dairy products and wine. Several of the agricultural products that are included in the tariff phase down are "back loaded", meaning that the tariffs will only be phased down at the end of the 10-year period. This highly disadvantageous restriction on South African agricultural exports to Europe is further exacerbated by the threat of CAP-subsidised European agricultural products flooding South Africa and its SACU partners. Perhaps, a better approach would have been to obtain a more favourable Generalised System of Preferences (GSP) ensuring preferred trade access of South African products to the E.U. as enjoyed by other producers of similar products. The E.U. has not considered it necessary to give South Africa preferential access for the above-listed products given their already strong presence in the E.U. market despite the tariff barriers.

The implementation of the TDCA strongly symbolises South Africa's return to the international community. The E.U. is South Africa's main trading partner, accounting for 40 per cent of its imports, 30 per cent of its exports and more than 50 per cent of direct investment. Furthermore, the TDCA will be beneficial for regional economic development in Southern Africa. South Africa required that every aspect of the agreement be tested against any possible harm it could do to, or benefits it could have for the member countries of SACU (Botswana, Lesotho, Namibia and Swaziland), as well as the broader-based SADC.[38]

For the TDCA to be justly effective and to prevent the resulting benefits from being undermined, these rights need to be enforceable, not only by the contracting parties, but also by the individuals to whom these rights are advantageous. There is little point in having international agreements that grant advantages if there is no procedure for enforcing the resulting rights and thus ensuring the benefits.

---

[37]The E.U. has offered quotas for cheese, flowers, wine (a duty-free tariff quota of 32 million litres), fruit juices and canned fruit.

[38]The members of SADC are Angola, Botswana, the Democratic Republic of the Congo, Lesotho, Malawi, Mauritius, Mozambique, Namibia, the Seychelles, South Africa, Swaziland, Tanzania, Zambia, and Zimbabwe.

LEGAL STATUS OF EXTERNAL COMMERCIAL POLICY ENTERED INTO
BY SOUTH AFRICA

Direct applicability

Section 231 of the South African Constitution requires the parliamentary ratification[39] and incorporation[40] into municipal law of international agreements, with the exception of international agreements of a "technical, administrative or executive nature".[41] The meaning of these terms is uncertain. This is not the only ambiguity contained in the provisions of section 231. A further vagueness is constituent in the wording of section 231(4),which provides for provisions of a treaty that are "self-executing". Accordingly, "self-executing" provisions of a treaty, if approved by parliament and consistent with the Constitution and an Act of Parliament, form an integral part of the municipal law despite not being incorporated into municipal law. International agreements are therefore considered part of the municipal system once ratified and implemented by legislation or if self-executing.

The courts will therefore have to decide whether a treaty is "self-executing" in the sense that existing law is adequate to enable the Republic to carry out its international obligation of the agreement, without further legislative action.[42] This is not the only interpretative exercise that will have to be undertaken by the courts. The provisions of the treaty will only be part of the municipal legal system if consistent with the Constitution as well as other acts of Parliament. Consequently, the court will have to identify if the provisions of a international agreement are in accordance with domestic law.

The position in terms of section 231 heralds two main obstacles for an individual wishing to claim protection of the rights afforded in terms of an international agreement:

- ratification and subsequent incorporation thereof into municipal legislation; or alternatively

- interpretation of the provision as a "self-executing" provision that is consistent with the Constitution and other acts of Parliament.

Government departments are required to scrutinise treaties for conflict between the provision of the treaty and domestic law prior to their submission to Parliament. Subsequently, these departments are hesitant to present treaties unless they were absolutely certain that there is no conflict. This results in

---

[39] s. 231(2).
[40] s. 231(4).
[41] s. 231(3) of the Constitution Act 108 of 1996.
[42] J. Dugard, *International Law a South African Perspective* (2nd ed., 2000), p. 58.

tremendous delays, prior to the presentation of a treaty to Parliament for ratification.

An individual will not be able to directly rely on the provisions of the
TDCA until it is incorporated into the municipal legal system unless the provision is found to be "self-executing" and consistent with domestic law. In
most instances, the trade agreements have not been enacted into municipal
law. Consequently, unless these provisions are construed as self-executing,
these agreements will not be justiciable before the municipal courts.[43] No
general guidelines are given as to when a provision will be "self-executing"
and each case will have to be decided on its own merit. Similarities are to be
found in the requirements of "self-executing" as required in terms of section
231 and the requirements[44] laid down by the ECJ regarding the direct effectiveness of Community law. The South African courts have, however, not yet
laid down a test for their prerequisites for determining whether a provision is
a "self-enacting" provision of a treaty. Furthermore, it would appear that the
TDCA necessitates "some review of the legislative implications of the agreement", particularly in "trade related" areas such as intellectual property law,[45]
preventing the possibility of an individual claiming that these provisions are
"self-enacting" and accordingly directly applicable.

Failing incorporation of the TDCA by parliament, the question arises as to
whether an individual will have recourse to the provisions of the TDCA by
means of indirect interpretative measures as provided for in terms of the Constitution. Section 39(1) requires that the court is under the obligation to consider international law in the interpretation of the Bill of Rights. However, in
the interpretation of other legislation, section 233 requires that the court must
prefer any reasonable interpretation that is consistent with international law.
No judicial clarity exists as to how the court will approach the question as to
the measure of the court's recourse to agreements such as the TDCA, as a
means of interpretation.[46] In practice, many provisions of these international
agreements are reflected in legislation,[47] complicating the question as to
whether such agreements will be justiciable as part of the municipal law in the
event of no further action taken by parliament.

As illustrated, the position of an individual within the South African municipal framework seeking protection of a right in terms of an international
agreement such as the TDCA is at a disadvantage when compared to the protection afforded to national or residents of a Member State of the E.U. The

---

[43] *ibid.* at p. 352.
[44] Requirements that the provision is sufficiently clear and precise and unconditional.
[45] Davies, *Seminar Report –South African Business and the European Union in the context of
the New Trade and Development Agreement* (Konrad Adenhauer Stiftung), p. 39.
[46] J. Dugard, *International Law a South African Perspective* (2nd ed., 2000), p. 61.
[47] See amendments introduced by the Intellectual Property Laws Amendment Act 38 of 1997,
reflecting the TRIPS agreement.

ECJ has by means of a broad interpretation interpreted the provisions of international agreements to be directly applicable. Moreover, the requirements for direct effect have been broadly construed. The ECJ interpretation has been in favour of an effective application. The South African position is, however, dotted with obstacles and subject to interpretation, without any parameters as to the basis of the courts decision. Consequently the South African position lacks clarity and the resulting benefits from the TDCA are being undermined.

CHALLENGES

In a question of trade relations between South Africa and the E.U.,[48] the possibility exists that a transaction may be addressed by different legislative provisions of international agreements. In so far as the application of one provision to the transaction rather than another may affect the interests of the parties differently, there is potential for dispute.[49]

The TDCA determines that the agreement is to be administered by the Cooperation Council to be established by the parties. In the event of dispute, each party may refer the matter to the Co-operation Council, which may settle the dispute by means of a binding decision. The agreement contains provisions for arbitration by the WTO. This right of referral is, however, excluded regarding a right and obligation in terms of the WTO, unless both parties agree to refer such an issue for arbitration.[50] These provisions are, however, only available to the contracting parties and consequently only the E.U. or South Africa, not individual citizens, can access these dispute resolution mechanisms.

In the event of a national from the E.U. being negatively affected, such an individual would have recourse to his or her own municipal courts, as the provisions of the TDCA are directly applicable and consequently directly effective as discussed above. As a result of the principle of direct effect, the rights resulting from the TDCA could be relied upon by the individual and therefore assertively enforced.

The position in South Africa appears less promising. As the TDCA has not yet been ratified by Parliament, and this is unlikely to happen in the foreseeable future, South Africans cannot directly approach their municipal court and claim protection of the benefits resulting from the TDCA. The incapacitated individual will have to rely on the state to enforce his or her rights. This

---

[48] Both of which are members of the TDCA and WTO.
[49] Art. 4(1) of the TDCA provides: "The European Community and the Republic of South Africa agree to establish a FTA in accordance with the provisions of this Agreement and in conformity with those of WTO".
[50] Article 104 (10) of the TDCA.

disadvantage is further magnified in the event of the resulting harm being caused by the state's failure to act.

CONCLUSION

We live in a world characterised by uneven and unequal relations between the developed countries of the North and the developing countries of the South. Trade relations continue to reflect these uneven power relations. Trade negotiations between the E.U. and South Africa once again revealed the tension between economically unequal partners with distinctly different agendas. Negotiations identified various key areas of dispute.[51] The E.U. in particular remains protectionist in sectors where developing countries currently enjoy comparative advantages, such as agriculture. The list of agricultural product wholly excluded from the TDCA amounts to 26 per cent. This disadvantage is further emphasised by the advantage held by European farmers as a result of their products benefiting from the subsidies in terms of the Common Agricultural Policy (CAP).

The inequality between the TDCA partners has been revealed not only in the overt forms of discrimination practised against South Africa by the E.U., but in covert ways too. For the TDCA to be really effective and to prevent the expected benefits from being undermined, these rights need to be enforceable, not only by the contracting parties, but also by individuals. There is little point in having international agreements granting advantages if there is no mechanism for ensuring that those who should benefit do benefit. As discussed above, the provisions of the TDCA are directly effective and enforceable by individuals in a municipal framework within the E.U. South African citizens, on the other hand, would have to rely on the supervisory protection of the state, and would have no recourse in the event of the state failing to act to ensure compliance with the rights resulting from the TDCA.

---

[51] Market access for South African agricultural products; tariff dismantling in the industrial sector; rules of origin; competition policy, parallel agreement on wines and spirits; and fisheries.

OPEN DEMOCRACY LEGISLATION – IMPLEMENTATION POLICIES AND POSSIBILITIES[1]

ESTELLE FELDMAN*

"[Freedom of Information (FOI)] has inherent characteristics which limit its impact. It is a form of accountability that governments automatically dominate, even if they do not fully control it. The duty of enforcement is up to citizens. The individual citizen engages through the Act with agencies which are practised at dealing with requests. Collective action is largely precluded, and applications are made on an individual basis. FOI is not a procedure whereby success by one applicant necessarily increases access to like material for all. It operates on the basis that citizens must rely upon their government to agree to the terms of its being policed. Governments must be relied upon to record decisions and reasons, and to produce them when requested. FOI is founded upon distrust in government, yet it does not escape the need to trust government."[2]

In 1997 a Freedom of Information Act was passed in Ireland. It was a full year before it was implemented. During this period personnel in public bodies were engaged in intensive training for the anticipated demands of a vocal citizenry. Since the implementation of the Act in April 1998 there have been many interesting disclosures leading to a better-informed public debate. Openness and transparency is beginning to permeate government. The thrust of this paper describes some of these developments and implementation issues. However, in order to set a context for a South African audience, an attempt has been made to describe some recent developments in South Africa of a related nature, namely Open Democracy legislation. The forbearance and tolerance of the South African audience is sought in advance in the hope that the views of this Northern hemisphere outsider living at the other side of the world are not too out of place.

---

* Research Associate, School of Law, Trinity College, Dublin.
[1] This paper further develops research first published in Martin and Feldman, "Access to Information in Developing Countries" (Transparency International Berlin 1998). Also an Internet publication: www.transparency.de/documents/work-papers/martin-feldman/index.html
[2] Terrill, "The Rise and Decline of FOI in Australia" McDonald and Terrill eds., *Open Government, Freedom of Information and Privacy* (MacMillan Press, London, 1998), p. 111.

Three pieces of Open Democracy legislation have been passed in the Republic of South Africa in 2000 in accordance with the requirements of the 1996 Constitution. These are the Promotion of Access to Information Act,[3] the Promotion of Administrative Justice Act[4] and, most recently, the Protected Disclosure Act.[5] This paper seeks to assess some of the implementation issues that may be faced primarily by reference to the Freedom of Information regime in Ireland.

The South African Promotion of Access to Information Act (POAIA) is the key piece of legislation. The language in which it is drafted is clear, a heartfelt comment from one having to negotiate the obfuscation of the Irish Freedom of Information Act.[6] It incorporates best theoretical practice in terms of its emphasis on accessibility and its rejection of the blanket of exemptions incorporated in many other regimes. However, it is most unusual in one respect.

Generally, access to information legislation is considered to refer to information held by the government of a state and by bodies who have some contractual or other direct relationship with the government. This Act gives effect not only to the constitutional right of access to any information held by the State, but also to access to any information that is held by another person and that is required for the exercise or protection of any rights. This arises from sections 8 and 32(1)(b) of the Constitution, which refer to the horizontal application of rights.[7] The right of access may be limited to the extent that the limitations are reasonable and justifiable in an open and democratic society based on human dignity, equality and freedom as contemplated in section 36 of the Constitution.[8] More specifically, the objects clause of the Act notes that the right is subject to justifiable limitations including, but not limited to, limitations aimed at the reasonable protection of privacy, commercial confidentiality and effective and efficient good governance;[9] and the right must be exercised in a manner which balances that right with any other rights, including the rights in the Bill of Rights in Chapter 2 of the Constitution.[10] The Act seeks, generally, to promote transparency, accountability and effective

---

[3] No. 2, 2000.

[4] No. 3, 2000.

[5] No. 26, 2000.

[6] The Irish Law Reform Commission's *Consultation Paper on Statutory Drafting and Interpretation: Plain Language and the Law* (1999) notes that as a matter of principle "legislation should be as comprehensible as is possible to the ordinarily well-educated individual" (para. 5.42 at 109). Far from qualifying for this positive description, the Irish Freedom of Information Act more aptly fits within the category of "dismal opacity" complained of in legislative drafting by Keane J., now Chief Justice (quoted at 63). This is all the more ironic given that the long title of the Act is specifically directed at "members of the public" to enable them obtain access to information.

[7] As noted in the POAIA Preamble.

[8] *ibid.*

[9] POAIA, s. 9(b)(i).

[10] POAIA, s. 9(b)(ii).

governance of all public and private bodies. To this end, it seeks to empower and educate everyone: first to understand their rights in terms of the Act in order to exercise their rights in relation to public and private bodies; secondly, to understand the functions and operation of public bodies; and thirdly, to effectively scrutinise and participate in decision-making by public bodies that affects their rights.[11]

According to the definitions section of the Act, "private body" means: (a) a natural person who carries on or has carried on any trade, business or profession, but only in such capacity; (b) a partnership which carries or has carried on any trade, business or profession; or (c) any former or existing juristic person. It excludes a public body.[12]

Such a definition appears to have no limits and seems completely open-ended. Furthermore, the responsibilities of the private body to respond to requests are in most instances a word-for-word replication of the duties placed on a public body. For example, section 34(2)(f) requires the head of a private body to disclose a record "about an individual who is or was an official of a public body and which relates to the position or functions of the individual, including, but not limited to (i) the fact that the individual is or was an official of that public body; (ii) the title, work address, work phone number and other similar particulars of the individual; (iii) the classification, salary scale or remuneration and responsibilities of the position held or services performed by the individual; and (iv) the name of the individual on a record prepared by the individual in the course of employment."

While there seems nothing unreasonable about such information being released in relation to a public servant who is, after all, paid from the public purse, section 63(2)(f) applies exactly the same statutory obligation to a private body. It is suggested that this raises serious issues in relation to the balance between the right to information, the right to privacy and the right to freedom of trade, occupation and profession. With regard to the right to privacy, the Constitutional Court has stated that "it is the compulsion to respond to particular questions about oneself and one's activities, for example, which could lead to an infringement of one's right to personal privacy. Before this stage is reached a person's privacy is not compromised".[13]

This balance of rights was not raised by the Open Democracy Campaign Group in their formal submission on the implementation of the Act, although they have recommended permanent and long-term exemptions from the publication of a section 51 information manual for traders and small businesses.[14]

Nowhere within the Act does there appear to be a requirement of proxim-

---

[11] POAIA. s. 9(e).
[12] POAIA. Chapter 1.
[13] *Bernstein v. Bester* [1996] 4 L.R.C. 528 *per* Ackermann J. at 564.
[14] http://www.pmg.org.za/bills/ODCG.htm; POAIA. s. 14 refers to the public body requirement.

ity between the requester and the private person. By that it is suggested that there is some causal link between a "private body" as described in the Act and an employee or an ex-employee, a customer, or a neighbour of the business, including, for instance, someone who lives many miles away but is dependant for his or her water on the same resource as the "private person". In the absence of such a requirement there is a danger that a business competitor may engage in a series of requests in order to be disruptive.

There seems no doubt that the granting of these broad and open-ended rights to information arises from the disregard of rights that occurred during the apartheid regime. However, it is respectfully suggested that other branches of law may provide a more appropriate avenue for redress. This is particularly the case in a situation where the right of appeal of the refusal for an information request is essentially confined to the courts.

The Promotion of Administrative Justice Act (POAJA) gives effect to the right to administrative action that is lawful, reasonable and procedurally fair, and to the right to written reasons for administrative action.

> "The importance of ensuring that the administration observes fundamental rights and acts both ethically and accountably should not be understated. In the past, the lives of the majority of South Africans were almost entirely governed by labyrinthine administrative regulations which, amongst other things, prohibited freedom of movement, controlled access to housing, education and jobs and which were implemented by a bureaucracy hostile to fundamental rights or accountability."[15]

According to the preamble, the purpose of the Act is to promote efficient administration and good governance and to create a culture of accountability, openness and transparency in the public administration or in the exercise of public power or the performance of a public function, by giving effect to the right to just administrative action. Essentially the Act provides for judicial review of administrative action by a court or a tribunal.[16]

The Protected Disclosures Act (PDA)[17] makes provision for procedures in terms of which employees in both the private and public sectors may disclose information regarding unlawful or irregular conduct by their employers, or other employees in the employ of their employers, and for the protection of employees who make a disclosure that is protected in terms of the Act.[18] The

---

[15] *President of the RSA v. SARFU* [1999] S.A.C.L.R. LEXIS 21 *per curiam* at para. 133.

[16] POAJA, s. 6. Section 7 provides that until rules of procedure are implemented, all proceedings for judicial review must be instituted in a High Court or in the Constitutional Court.

[17] At the time of writing the approved text of the Public Interest Disclosure Act was not yet posted to the South African Government's website, so that information is taken from a copy of the official Bill.

[18] Bill, synopsis.

Act is modelled on the U.K. Public Interest Disclosure Act 1998. It is an intention of the U.K. Act to promote a culture whereby wrongdoing will be disclosed within an organisation insofar as is possible. The South African Act proposes very specifically to create a culture in which employees will disclose information of crime and other irregular conduct in the workplace in a responsible manner, and generally to promote the eradication of crime and other irregular conduct in organs of state and private bodies. While this last piece of legislation is an integral part of Open Democracy legislation, it has no specific reference to the administrative functions of the State as the other two Acts do.

There is a strong public perception that the United States has one of the world's most open and transparent systems of government.[19] However, since 1981 President Reagan used a variety of devices to lessen the impact of the freedom of information legislation on the administration and extended the range of immunities from disclosure. According to Birkinshaw, a European academic, who has written extensively on the topic:

> "[t]hese developments were achieved by a variety of instruments, some involving Congressional legislation such as the Paperwork Reduction Act 1980, which was passed under the Carter administration, the CIA Information Act 1984 and the 1986 FOIA Reform Act. Other devices included Executive Orders and internal directives. The curtailing of FOI rights has been accompanied by a growing tendency to executive secrecy in the USA."[20]

However, Birkinshaw is careful not to over-sensationalise or exaggerate the position.

> "I have listed the above as a corrective to the commonly held assumption that everything is open or freely available in the USA. That is not the case. If we accept that government ought to behave responsibly, part of that responsibility must be to protect that which, in all our interests, must be properly safeguarded. Events in the USA may or may not be disproportionate to the legitimate attainment of that objective. But two points must be made. Most of the efforts to enhance protection have not taken place through law, but by executive and administrative action. . . . Further, the resort to secrecy reflected badly on the standing of President Reagan and upon his management of executive affairs in so far as secrecy was seen to counter the requirements of accountability."[21]

---

[19] See generally Feldman, "Access to Information . . . Theory, Law and Practice", a paper prepared for the Trinity College Dublin School of Law South African Study Tour, 1999.
[20] Birkinshaw, *Freedom of Information: The US Experience Studies in Law* (Hull University, 1991), p. 5.
[21] *ibid.* at p. 9.

A recent publication in Britain, Open Government, Freedom of Information and Privacy,[22] reviewed the access to information provisions in a number of other common law countries. A constitutional policy expert highlighted the difficulties that are now being experienced at the national or federal level in countries that have had access legislation since the early 1980s, particularly at the nexus between the right to personal information and the right to privacy.

> "The main hinge between FOI and privacy lies in the definition of personal information. It is a fundamental definition for privacy legislation which determines its scope. It is a key exemption provision in FOI legislation which may protect from disclosure personal information about third parties. Whether privacy is the dominant value will depend on the breadth of the definition of personal information, whether its release is subject to any public interest test and by whom the definition is interpreted."[23]

Australia, which introduced a Freedom of Information Act in 1982, appears to be avoiding the conflict between regimes. The Privacy Act of 1988 is subordinate to the freedom of information legislation to the extent that the remedies available under this legislation must be exhausted before the Privacy Commissioner will entertain a complaint of denial of access.[24] In Canada, 1982 also saw the introduction at federal level of both an Access to Information Act and a Privacy Act, each enforced by a Commissioner. As a consequence the public is confused as to which regime is appropriate for a request for personal information and apparently, administrators are sometimes equally confused. Moreover, there is institutionalised conflict between the Information Commissioner and the Privacy Commissioner.[25] New Zealand is experiencing similar difficulties. Again in 1982, the Official Information Act was introduced, enforced by the Ombudsman. However, in 1991 a Privacy Commissioner was established and the 1993 Privacy Act removed the right of access to personal information from the 1982 Act and re-enacted it with the usual privacy protection principles. The first Privacy Commissioner has had a very high profile and as his rulings are sometimes at odds with those of the Ombudsman, the seed of institutional conflict are emerging.[26] Freedom of information observers are remarking on the chilling effect that the Privacy Act is beginning to have on freedom of information disclosures and on information policy generally.

With regard to Australia in the same publication, an Australian expert on

---

[22] McDonald and Terrill, *op. cit.*
[23] *ibid.*, Hazell, *Balancing Privacy and Freedom of Information*, p. 80.
[24] *ibid.* at p. 72.
[25] *ibid.* at p. 71.
[26] *ibid.* at p. 72.

information policy who has worked with government is by no means as sanguine. He notes that the considerable political support present at the introduction of freedom of information has declined, a key factor in undermining freedom of information. Bureaucratic support for access has always been mixed, with senior officials almost always opposed. All reviews have recommended more openness, while almost all amendments have restricted access. Furthermore, recommendations of committees that have proposed related areas of openness including legislation to protect whistleblowers have not been followed.[27]

The Canadian federal legislation on access to information is strongly criticised by an information and privacy expert. Comparing the United States, which has over 30 years' experience with freedom of information, and Canada, he concludes that the U.S. has not solved many of the problems apparent in the Canadian federal system. However, the United States has the attitude that the legislation is growing and developing in continuous support of their democracy, a spirit and intent he finds missing in Canada. "It seems that after passing an FOI statute, parliamentarians have succumbed to collective amnesia about information rights, while officials at all levels have, at their best, given lip-service to the letter of the law but little inspired leadership for open and accountable government."[28]

As recently as 1994/1995, the Information Commissioner pointed out that "'guided by often hostile ministers and a foot-dragging bureaucracy', the federal government has often indulged in the business of managing exceptions to access as opposed to promoting genuine openness in its activities".[29] There have been a number of high-profile incidents centred on attempts to thwart access to government information through destroying or tampering with records. These include altering the records of peace-keeping activities in Somalia by the Department of National Defence in 1995. The following year a senior manager in Transport Canada ordered the destruction of all copies of an audit report to ensure the suppression of criticism of departmental management.[30] In 1996 it was discovered that in the 1980s records of the Canadian Blood Committee were destroyed so that the information would not become public and be used in any legal actions involving tainted blood and blood products.[31]

Recommendations for change include creating a statutory obligation for public bodies to establish mechanisms for providing access to information without the need for a freedom of information request and that, where appropriate, they should actively disseminate information. Legislation should include the principle that pricing of government information for purposes of

[27] *ibid.*, Terrill, *The Rise and Decline of FOI in Australia, op. cit.*, p.111.
[28] *ibid.*, Gillis, *Freedom of information in Canada*, p. 158.
[29] *ibid.* at p. 150.
[30] *ibid.* at p. 149.
[31] *ibid.* at p. 156.

public access would not normally exceed the cost of dissemination of the information, so that there are no unfair restrictions to government information on the basis of cost.[32]

A senior public servant in New Zealand makes no mention of the tensions between access to information and privacy. She notes that the Official Information Act was only one in a series of changes designed to create greater transparency and accountability. It reflected part of a general culture change occurring at many levels in New Zealand society, away from secrecy towards greater openness. The Act has enhanced accountability and the openness ensuing from its implementation may have improved the quality of advice and of decision-making.

"Public servants are always aware that the advice they provide may be released under the Official Information Act and be scrutinised by a range of interested – and potentially critical - parties."[33] The New Zealand access regime did not give the public general rights of access but required enabling criteria to be applied and interpreted flexibly by civil servants. Potentially this gives considerable power to the civil service in deciding what information to withhold. The States Services Commission carried out intensive training for all public servants when the Act was introduced to make them aware of their obligations and responsibilities. Combined with public confidence in the enforcing authority, the Ombudsman, these two factors were critical to the Act's smooth implementation.

One other side of open government is to achieve wider participation in decision-making. To achieve this, information needs to be made available and interpreted to the general public or special interest groups in a form that enables them to express opinions or take action. The media have a major responsibility to discover information and to disseminate it objectively in a way that will throw light on government. The New Zealand experience is that there have been some difficulties for journalists in obtaining information about key decisions in a timely fashion.[34] However, the Ombudsman's Annual Report for 1996 notes that newspaper reports regularly refer to information having been obtained under the Act. "We consider this an encouraging sign because the media thereby show that the Act does work to get access to official information. This helps the public to understand the key purposes of the Act and how it can be used effectively."[35]

This use by the media has been the experience of the Irish regime since its introduction.[36] What is of most interest in the contribution of the two Irish

---

[32] *ibid.* at p. 161.

[33] *ibid.*, Aitken, *Open Government in New Zealand*, pp. 117-142, at 136.

[34] *ibid.* at p. 134.

[35] *ibid.* as quoted at p. 134.

[36] Media requests under the Freedom of Information Act have led to significant public debate on such issues as the manner in which parliamentarians' expenses are used; the extent and nature

civil servants to this published debate on privacy and freedom of information, is their frank and informative assessment of the lessons learned during the implementation of the Freedom of Information Act 1997 they helped steer through the legislation and reflect that the single critical factor they overlooked is that freedom of information was a change process, not just a legislative matter.

> "In a democracy profound change such as FOI requires a lot of time for consultation and information-giving across parliamentary, administrative and public forums. . . . This was a learning experience, not just for others but also for ourselves. Their perspectives and concerns helped us crystallise issues and develop our thinking. However this process of telling, selling and learning meant a daily struggle to ensure that time was actually spent on progressing the legislation itself.
>
> Because of the nature of the legislation and its lack of congruence with existing culture and practice there were strong reservations about the measure. These found expression in a number of ways: outright opposition on the grounds that FOI was unworkable; a view that it was not in the public interest that it should apply in a particular area; assertions to the effect that FOI proposals were highly laudable but required far greater consideration and development before matters could proceed further; and official silence, complemented by discreet efforts to build alliances against the measure."[37]

Three key factors contributed to smooth the implementation of the cultural change in the Irish public service from secrecy to freedom of information. As with the New Zealand experience, access to information was introduced as part and parcel of much wider changes in an effort for greater openness and accountability in government. Perhaps, as a consequence, there was in place an informal network across the senior levels of administration who were well-informed and highly effective in encouraging wider support. However, deemed of vital significance was "ongoing direct access to officials abroad who had practical experience of FOI for over a decade and a half, and were able rapidly to provide answers to many hard questions."[38]

In contrast to the South African Open Democracy legislation, it could be considered that the regime on access to information in Ireland falls far short of

---

of information made available to the public about schools by the Department of Education; the behind-the-scenes decision-making processes regarding major planning decisions and the drafting of certain pieces of legislation. *The Guardian* newspaper, which is at the forefront of the campaign for freedom of information in the U.K., has included several news stories of interest to the British public based on material released by request to Irish public bodies under the Irish Act.
[37] *ibid.*, Kearney and Stapleton, *Freedom of Information Legislation in Ireland*, p.177.
[38] *ibid.* at p. 178.

the theoretical best practice for such legislation.[39] There is no express constitutional right to information and the provisions of the Freedom of Information
Act 1997[40] include numerous exemptions, wide discretionary powers and allow for Ministerial certificates of exclusion without recourse to the appeal
mechanism of the Information Commissioner. Nevertheless, it was noted after
just one year in full operation that the system seemed to be having a real result
in opening up a hitherto secretive public service.[41]

This change in policy toward release of information is very much in line
with Ireland's obligations as a member of the European Union. The Irish legislative system is subject to a multitude of directives and judgments of the
European institutions at the highest level.[42] In 1994, a Code of Conduct an-
nexed to Decision 94/90/ECSC laid down as a general principle, subject to
express exceptions that "[t]he public will have the widest possible access to
documents held by the [European] Commission and the Council." Most recently, a decision of the European Court of Justice stated that that Code was
adopted "with the aim of making the Community more transparent, the transparency of the decision-making process being a means of strengthening the
democratic nature of the institutions and the public's confidence in the administration." In this judgment the Court of First Instance held that a Community
regulation that imposed restrictions on the dissemination of information could
not prevail over the Community's general policy of openness in regard to the
disclosure of information.[43]

Additionally, decisions of the European Court of Human Rights (ECHR)
are authoritative and will become binding after the adoption into Irish jurisprudence of the European Convention on Human Rights. In this regard, while
Goodwin v. United Kingdom[44] related primarily to freedom of the press, the
judgment, which reiterated the Court's 1992 judgment in *Sunday Times v. United
Kingdom*,[45] contains a very clear interpretation of Article 10 of the European
Convention on Human Rights relating to information:

---

[39] It should be noted that judicial review by the Irish High Court and review by quasi-judicial
tribunals such as the Irish Ombudsman are well-established and highly effective in ensuring
the principles of natural justice and rights of procedural correctness as envisaged by the Promotion of Administrative Justice Act. With regard to whistleblower protection, as of yet the
only statutory provision is the Protections of Persons Reporting Child Abuse Act 1998. See
generally Feldman, *Whistleblower Protection: Comparative Legal Developments* 17:17 (1999)
ILT 264 at 265.

[40] The Act and any Regulations can be accessed on an Internet site maintained by the Information Commissioner at http://www.irlgov.ie/oic/foi.htm.

[41] See further Feldman, "Access to Information . . . Theory, Law and Practice", *op. cit.*

[42] See for instance Council Directive 90/313/EEC of June 7, 1990 on the freedom of access to
information on the environment.

[43] *JT's Corporation v. Commission of the EC* Case T–123/99. Judgment October 12, 2000 as
reported in *The Times*, October 18, 2000.

[44] (1996) 22 E.H.R.R. 12.

[45] (1992) 14 E.H.R.R. 229.

"Freedom of expression constitutes one of the essential foundations of a democratic society; subject to paragraph 2 of Article 10, it is applicable not only to 'information' or 'ideas' that are favourably received or regarded as inoffensive or as a matter of indifference, but also to those that offend, shock or disturb. Freedom of expression, as enshrined in Article 10, is subject to a number of exceptions which, however, must be narrowly interpreted and the necessity for any restrictions must be convincingly established."[46]

In this judgment the ECHR also stated the relationship between its role and that of the individual state.

"The [Convention organs'] task, in exercising [their] supervisory jurisdiction, is not to take the place of the competent national authorities but rather to review under Article 10 the decisions they delivered pursuant to their power of appreciation. This does not mean that [their] supervision is limited to ascertaining whether the respondent State exercised its discretion reasonably, carefully and in good faith; what [they have] to do is to look at the interference complained of in the light of the case".[47]

Of course, if access to information is to operate effectively, it should not be necessary to appeal any decisions through national courts, let alone at the supranational level. The costs of this are prohibitive and the timescales involved are likely to render the information useless if and when it is accessed.[48] What is required is a non-secretive public service. In the case of Ireland, the Freedom of Information Act was introduced at a time when the Strategic Management Initiative, a radical reform of the Civil Service, had already been initiated. In the words of the Information Commissioner in his first annual report, "the Act has an important contribution to make to public service reform. If it is used effectively by requesters and operated conscientiously by public servants, it has the potential to bring about significant improvement in

---

[46] *Goodwin v. United Kingdom* (1996) 22 E.H.R.R. 12 at para. 60a.
[47] *ibid.* at para 60d.
[48] In this regard it is interesting to note that the South African legislation relies solely on the Court. To an outsider it seems strange that no role is envisaged for the traditional forms of leadership. It is acknowledged that during the apartheid regime all institutions, including the courts, betrayed their constituents' trust in some respect. However, as has been noted in the Discussion Document Towards A White Paper on Traditional Leadership and Institutions: "Traditional leaders ruled over the members of their tribes as kings-in-council and according to the principles of African democracy and accountability" (Department of Provincial and Local Government April 11, 2000 at 10). This would appear to be a valuable and inexpensive mediation forum for access to information. It is hoped to delve deeper into this topic based on preliminary discussions begun with academics from both the University of Western Cape and the University of Westville-Durban.

the overall standard of public administration."[49]

Any law, no matter how well intentioned requires implementation. Where the law is going to effect the operations of government and its administration at every level, such implementation requires considerable training. Little attention has been paid by legal commentators to the training aspect of laws imposing duties to provide information. Legal objectives are not made effective by simply placing words on paper. Skill and expertise are required, as well as financial resources.[50]

Irrespective of the oversight regime, the significance of training should most definitely not be underestimated. This has already been noted in the New Zealand experience. In Ireland during the lead-in period, *i.e.* a 12 month period prior to the full implementation of the Act, there was extensive training for personnel in the public bodies affected by the new legislation to include implementation of and training in new methods of filing, in retrieval of files and in dealing with requests under the Act. Training is an on-going process resulting in a depth of openness and transparency in relation to almost all public bodies, which is unexpected given their former secrecy.

No matter how good the training, an independent oversight regime is necessary to monitor freedom of information legislation. The Irish solution was to take the existing Office of the Ombudsman and appoint the incumbent as Information Commissioner also. The Director of the Office of the Ombudsman also performs the function of Director of the Office of the Information Commissioner and the support staff is common to both functions. A hallmark of the Irish Ombudsman's function is a patient and intensely thorough investigative culture combined with a pervasive and persuasive capacity for encouraging settlement between a complainant and a public body.

It can be noted that there are significant differences in the statutory role and responsibility of each Office, not least of which is the confusion for the general public that some bodies that now come within the Information Commissioner's ambit remain outside the purview of the Ombudsman. Moreover, the Information Commissioner's decisions have binding effect, subject solely to an appeal to the High Court on a point of law.[51] This is in contrast to the Ombudsman, whose recommendations need not be accepted.

The operational investigative staff differ between the two Offices and each performs a different statutory function. Nevertheless, without any evident difficulty apparent to the outside world, the Information Commissioner's staff have maintained the extraordinary level of competence and concern for best practice in public administration that has been developed through the exercise of the Ombudsman's function.

---

[49] Annual Report of the Information Commissioner 1998, Government of Ireland at p. 1. Also on the Internet at http://www.irlgov.ie/oic.

[50] Birkinshaw, *op. cit.*, p. 10.

[51] Unusually, there is no appeal from the High Court to the Supreme Court.

As the accountability and transparency of the freedom of information regime takes a deeper and firmer hold on the Irish public service, it becomes even more evident to the close observer that the thrust for implementing the Freedom of Information Act in an open and easily accessible manner may be attributed to the incumbent, Mr Kevin Murphy. His annual reports as Ombudsman are exercises in public service courtesy, thoroughness and common sense. This same trend also permeates his annual reports as Information Commissioner and, indeed, every publication of his office.

The first complete year of the operation of the Freedom of Information Act saw increased use of the Act, with over 11,000 requests being made to public bodies, compared to 3,700 the previous year. Such a level of use compares well with the experience in other jurisdictions. Not surprisingly, the increased use is reflected in a significant increase in the number of cases accepted for review by the Information Commissioner which, at 443, is up from 179 in 1998. Since the Act was not in operation for the full 12 months of 1998, a better indication of the increased workload of the Office is the fact that the average number of cases accepted for review on a monthly basis has still increased by over 60 per cent since 1998. As the Act is gradually extended to encompass other bodies the number of applications for review is expected to increase.[52] Of the cases accepted for review, 374 related to a decision by a public body to refuse access to records and the majority of cases related to personal information.

The Information Commissioner completed 141 reviews during the year. In 19 cases he varied the decision of the public body and in a further 39 cases a settlement was reached. In 54 cases he affirmed the decision of the public body. Four appeals against his decisions have been heard by the High Court to date.

An immediate judgment delivered in July affirmed the Information Commissioner's decision of how to interpret whether pre-commencement documents were necessary to understand the substance or gist of documents accessible under the Act.[53] Of the remaining three reserved judgments, two are expected to be delivered at the commencement of the forthcoming law year.

The first of the judgments on an appeal to the High Court was delivered in December 1999.[54] The Department of Agriculture and Food, both at first in-

---

[52] Annual Report of the Information Commissioner 1999, Government of Ireland at p. 4.

[53] *Salve Marine v. Information Commissioner* (unreported, Kelly J., *Irish Times*, July 20, 2000). Unlike the South African legislation, which in general does not permit any date restriction on access to a record, the Irish Act only applies to records created after the commencement of the Act in April 1998, with the exception of personal information.

[54] *Minister for Agriculture and Food v. Information Commissioner* (unreported, High Court, December 17,1999). For the complete judgment, see Information Commissioner's website. For a fuller analysis of this judgment, see the Information Law section in Byrne and Binchy eds., *Annual Review of Irish Law 1999* (Round Hall Sweet and Maxwell, 2000).

stance and on internal review, had refused a request to grant full access to his personnel files to a member of the Department's staff.[55] The refusal was based on section 6(6)(c). On review by the Information Commissioner, the public body sought additional reliance for refusal of access on grounds of exemption (law enforcement and public safety[56] and information obtained in confidence[57]). The Information Commissioner decided to grant fuller, although still incomplete, access to the requested records, but held that parts of some records were exempt from disclosure on the grounds of legal professional privilege. O'Donovan J. varied the Commissioner's decision and granted total access to the requester.

The most important issue raised by this case is a consideration of the nature of the statutory appeal on a point of law to the High Court under section 42(1) of the Freedom of Information Act and, as a consequence, the nature of the review that the Information Commissioner is empowered to take under section 34. The learned judge was highly critical of the manner in which the Information Commissioner conducted his review, both in examining the records at issue and in permitting the Department to rely on additional grounds for refusal of access to those it had relied on initially.

In questioning the Information Commissioner's right to examine records and permit the introduction of new grounds, O'Donovan J. would seem to be denying that section 34 is authorising an appeal *de novo*. Such an approach is at odds with the provisions of the Act.

On review the Commissioner may exercise the same powers as the head of the public body. The substantive terms of section 34(2) are identical to the equivalent terms of section 14(2). The head of the public body may review a decision and following that review may, as he or she considers appropriate, affirm or vary the decision or annul the decision and, if appropriate, "make such decision in relation to the matter as he or she considers proper".

However, the writ of the Commissioner is far wider than that. Section 37 confers extraordinary powers of search and entry on the Commissioner for the purposes of the review. This is not confined to summoning witnesses and examining documents. For the purposes of both a section 34 review, the matter at issue in the instant case, or a section 36 oversight investigation of any particular public body or bodies, section 37(2) empowers the Commissioner to "enter any premises occupied by a public body". This independent power is not subject to the grant of a judicial warrant. Finally, section 37(6) allows that

---

[55] There are exceptions to the rule on personal information, one of which is that members of staff of public bodies may be refused access to their personnel records created before April 21, 1995. As regards records created earlier, s. 6(6)(c) provides that access to these may be refused if such a record "is not being used or proposed to be used in a manner or for a purpose that affects, or will or may affect, adversely the interests of the person."
[56] s.23.
[57] s.26.

the procedure for conducting a review or investigation under the Act "shall be such as the Commissioner considers appropriate in the circumstances of the case".

It is hardly possible that the Oireachtas (Parliament) granted such robust and untrammelled powers to the Commissioner, and such latitude in the performance of his function, with the intention that a section 34 review by the Information Commissioner was anything but *de novo*.

In addition, section 34(8) provides that relevant persons in relation to a proposed review "may make submissions (as the Commissioner may determine, in writing or orally or in such other form as may be determined) to the Commissioner in relation to any matter relevant to the review and the Commissioner shall take any such submissions into account for the purposes of the review". Moreover, if the Commissioner considers, in relation to the original decision to refuse access or to the internal review, that the statement of the reasons for the decision to refuse are inadequate, the Commissioner "shall direct" the head concerned to furnish "any further information in relation to those matters that is in the power or control of the head". As a creature of statute, the Commissioner is also obliged to take account of the Act's objects, as specified in the preamble, that the provision of access to information must be consistent with the public interest to the greatest extent possible. Cumulatively, therefore, it seems that the plain intention of the statute is that the Commissioner, in conducting a review, is obliged to consider, indeed request and consider, any additional information or reasons that might justify a decision to refuse access, lest the public body concerned has not sufficiently protected the public interest.

In conclusion, it is worth noting that the Irish Act is directed at "any member of the public" and the onus is on the public body to justify non-disclosure. What a sad reflection on the Irish public service and some senior members' attitude to the spirit of the Act that of the four appeals to the High Court, two have been taken in the name of Government Ministers desirous of maintaining the secrecy of the information they hold.

CONSTITUTIONAL GUARANTEES AND FREEDOM OF TESTATION IN SOUTH AFRICAN LAW

FRANÇOIS DU TOIT*

Introduction

South Africa's new constitutional dispensation necessitates a re-appraisal of traditional private law institutions. Such re-appraisal is occasioned by the ostensible direct horizontal operation of applicable constitutionally guaranteed rights contained in the Bill of Rights (Chapter 2) of the Constitution of the Republic of South Africa.[1] The view that the South African Constitution indeed allows for the direct horizontal application of appropriate rights is principally founded upon sections 2 and 8 of the Constitution. Section 8(1) provides in this regard:

> "The Bill of Rights applies to all law, and binds the legislature, the executive, the judiciary and all organs of state."

Woolman, a strong proponent of the direct horizontal operation of applicable constitutionally guaranteed rights, observes with regard to section 8(1)[2]:

> "The section makes express the application of the Bill of Rights to *all law* and to all action of the *judiciary*. We can assume that all law encompasses common-law disputes between private parties. If any legal dispute is left uncovered by subjecting all law – and thus the entire body of common law – to direct application, then subjecting *all* judicial actions to constitutional review should fill that space. And so we would appear finally to have unqualified, direct horizontal application."

Constitutional guarantees therefore impact (at least potentially) upon the relationships (and hence also litigation) between private parties in the realm of the common law. The constitutional obligation on South African courts to de-

---

* Senior Lecturer, Department of Private Law, University of the Western Cape.
[1] Act 108 of 1996.
[2] In Chaskalson *et al.*, *Constitutional Law of South Africa* (1996), pp. 10–57.

velop the common law in order to give effect to a constitutionally guaranteed right[3] or to limit such a right[4] is indeed a difficult and unenviable task, particularly in areas of private law where private autonomy has traditionally reigned supreme. In this regard the law of testate succession distinguishes itself as arguably *the* area of private law where the personal inclinations, convictions and idiosyncrasies of the individual traditionally enjoy not only legal recognition but also protection. Such recognition and protection is embodied in the principle of freedom of testation or testamentary freedom.

FREEDOM OF TESTATION

Freedom of testation is recognised as one of the founding principles of the South African law of testate succession. This principle prescribes that a testator is free, subject to certain limitations, to dispose of his/her assets in a will in any manner he/she deems fit. In *Crookes v. Watson*, Van den Heever J.A. declared in this regard:

> "Since testation has become unfettered, the testator is not obliged to benefit any person in his will, and if he does, he is at liberty to condition and restrict the benefits which he confers in any manner he pleases. In interpreting and putting into effect the provisions of a will the testator's wishes are of paramount importance."[5]

Freedom of testation is further acknowledged in South African law by virtue of the fact that private ownership is recognised as a founding principle of South African property law. Ownership exercised over assets by an owner in his/her private capacity entitles such an owner to dispose freely of those assets, also upon death. The acceptance of private ownership as a principle of property law therefore facilitates the legal recognition of both private succession and freedom of testation. De Waal correctly points out in this regard:

> "[T]hat ownership embraces, in principle, the right to dispose of the property owned (the *ius disponendi*) is indeed one of the basic tenets of the South African law of property. The power to dispose of one's property ... includes disposal upon death by any of the means recognised by the law, including a last will."[6]

Section 25(1) – the property clause – of the South African Constitution now

---

[3] s. 8(3)(a) of the Constitution.
[4] s. 8(3)(b) of the Constitution.
[5] (1956) 1 S.A. 277 (A) 298A–B.
[6] In Rautenbach *et al.*, *Bill of Rights Compendium* (1998), 3G8.

also provides a constitutional guarantee of private ownership:

> "No one may be deprived of property except in terms of law of general application, and no law may permit arbitrary deprivation of property."

Despite the absence of express reference in section 25(1) to private ownership, private succession and freedom of testation, it is generally accepted that these are indeed guaranteed by the property clause. De Waal *et al.* argue convincingly that "property" for purposes of section 25(1) carries its traditional "common law meaning":

> "'Property' for purposes of s. 25 should therefore be seen as those resources which are generally taken to constitute a person's wealth, and which are recognised and protected by law. Such resources are legally protected by private law rights – [*inter alia*] real rights in the case of physical resources. . . ."[7]

The property clause of the South African Constitution therefore implicitly guarantees private ownership, private succession and freedom of testation. In this regard it corresponds to a large extent, particularly as far as its legal effect is concerned, with article 14(1) of the German *Grundgesetz* (Basic Law):

> "Ownership and the law of succession are guaranteed. Their content and limitation are determined by the laws."[8]

THE LIMITATION OF FREEDOM OF TESTATION

Freedom of testation in South African law is by no means absolute or entirely unfettered. Limitations, both under common law as well as in terms of statute, are placed upon free testamentary disposition in South African law. For the purpose of this contribution, the limitation of particular relevance dictates that a testamentary provision which is to be regarded as *contra bonos mores* or which militates against the legal convictions of the community or public policy may be invalidated by a court.[9]

The manner in which the legal convictions of the community or public policy was judicially employed in the past to limit freedom of testation in South African law is somewhat contentious. This is particularly true with regard to so-called testamentary faith and race clauses, in other words, condi-

---

[7] *Bill of Rights Handbook* (1999), pp.403–405.
[8] Translated from the original German.
[9] Corbett *et al.*, *The Law of Succession in South Africa* (1980), p.81.

tional testamentary bequests which, under penalty of forfeiture of benefits, require adherence to a given religion or the conclusion of a marriage within a given religious or racial group. The legal position in South African law with regard to such clauses necessarily requires re-evaluation in view of horizontally operational constitutional guarantees of freedom of religion (section 15 of the South African constitution) and equality (section 9 of the South African Constitution).

TESTAMENTARY FAITH AND RACE CLAUSES

The seminal decision on testamentary faith and race clauses in South African law is that of the Appellate Division five decades ago in *Aronson v. Estate Hart*.[10] *In casu* a testator provided for the forfeiture of benefits should a beneficiary "marry a person not born in the Jewish faith or forsake the Jewish faith". The Appellate Division found this provision to be valid and enforceable. The court arrived at this decision under the guidance of social considerations, in particular that a testator should be allowed to protect his/her descendants (as testamentary beneficiaries) against the perils of an injudicious change of religion and the dangers of a "mixed" marriage. Greenberg J.A. declared in this regard:

> "[A] person who is a reasonable, honourable, law-abiding and patriotic citizen may well fear that a marriage between what can conveniently be described as a Jew and a non-Jew will tend as far as the spouses are concerned to increase the tensions and stresses, ordinarily to be expected between them, to such an extent as to lead to irreconcilable differences; in the case of the children of such a marriage he may equally be apprehensive of the unsettling effect on them of the inner conflicts which may leave then rudderless and adrift on the sea of life. He may also fear that that they may fall between two stools and be acceptable to neither section. I know of no principle in law which would make it contrary to public policy for him to attempt (according to his rights) to safeguard his descendants against these perils."[11]

Van den Heever J.A. decided in similar vein:

> "There is nothing immoral or against public policy in a Jew remaining true to the faith of his fathers and a [testamentary] condition that he shall not marry a person of another religion is conducive to happy marriages."[12]

---

[10](1950) 1 S.A. 539 (A).
[11] *ibid.* at 546.
[12] *ibid.* at 567.

The decision was criticised almost immediately on the ground that it permitted a testator to use patrimonial means to exert influence on the private life and personal choices of a beneficiary (in modern constitutional parlance, it allowed a testator to compromise constitutionally guaranteed rights of a beneficiary through patrimonial means). Hahlo formulated his objection to the *Aronson* decision in this regard as follows:

> "The question is whether it is contrary to our notions of propriety that a testator should be allowed to use the power of the purse to force his descendants for one, two or more generations to profess a faith which they may no longer hold and to refrain from following the dictates of their hearts in the choice of a mate if such choice happens to conflict with the ideas of their deceased ancestor."[13]

It is submitted that this criticism provides an appropriate basis for the formulation of a new approach in South African law to testamentary faith and race clauses in view of constitutional guarantees.

TESTAMENTARY FAITH AND RACE CLAUSES: A NEW APPROACH IN VIEW OF CONSTITUTIONAL GUARANTEES

Comparative research reveals that Hahlo is by no means alone in his criticism of testamentary provisions that are employed by testators to "rule from the grave" and to direct the personal and intimate choices of testamentary beneficiaries. In both common law and civil law jurisdictions, not only have similar objections been raised but the view has also been expressed that such provisions should indeed be treated with caution and might readily be regarded as militating against the legal convictions of the community or public policy.

In English law the famous decision on a Jewish faith and race clause by the House of Lords in *Clayton v. Ramsden* immediately comes to mind.[14] Lord Russell describes the effect of the provision (which required marriage in the Jewish faith) *in casu* as follows:

> "[T]his is a case in which the testator has sought ... to direct the lives of his children from the grave ... [and] ... to control his daughter Edna's choice of husband."[15]

Lord Atkin observes with regard to this clause:

---

[13](1950) *South African Law Journal* 240.
[14][1943] 1 All E.R. 16.
[15]*ibid.* at 17.
[16]*ibid.* at 17.

"For my own part I view with disfavour the power of testators to control from their grave the choice in marriage of their beneficiaries and should not be dismayed if the power were to disappear."[16]

This view is shared in the civilian tradition by the German author Brox with regard to testamentary provisions aimed at the exercise of influence in the private lives of testamentary beneficiaries. He declares:

"A testator may not attribute material benefit to a decision which, according to general opinion, has to be arrived at free from the influence of others and with regard to which material considerations ought to play no part."[17]

It is submitted that the South African Constitution in general and the Bill of Rights in particular can be viewed broadly as an embodiment of prevailing societal legal convictions and public policy norms in this country. The horizontal operation of constitutionally guaranteed rights accepted, it stands to reason that the ideals of religious freedom and equality should direct a court when deciding on the legal tenability of testamentary faith and race clauses employed by testators to exert the kind of influence referred to above.

This will inevitably result in the classic judicial balancing act with regard to competing constitutional rights – the constitutionally guaranteed testamentary freedom of the testator (which is by definition premised upon personal preference and choice, even discrimination in the wide sense of the word) will have to be weighed against the constitutionally guaranteed right to freedom of religion and/or equality of the beneficiary. Such a balancing exercise must of course be undertaken in compliance with the provisions of the general limitations clause (section 36) of the South African Constitution, subsection (1) of which provides as follows:

"The rights in the Bill of Rights may be limited only in terms of a law of general application to the extent that the limitation is reasonable and justifiable in an open and democratic society based on human dignity, equality and freedom, taking into account all relevant factors, including–

(a) the nature of the right;

(b) the importance of the purpose of the limitation;

(c) the nature and extent of the limitation;

(d) the relationship between the limitation and its purpose;

(e) less restrictive means to achieve the purpose."

[17] *Erbrecht* (1998), p.172. Translated from the original German.

It is submitted that the factors listed for consideration in terms of section 36(1) allow a court to limit either the testator's freedom of testation on the one hand or the beneficiary's freedom of religion or right to equality on the other, only with due cognisance of the facts of each case. That such is the *modus operandi* required is supported by ample authority from common law as well as civil law legal systems. With regard to the former, Kitto J. decides in the Australian case of *Trustees of Church Property of the Diocese of Newcastle v. Ebbeck* with regard to a testamentary forfeiture clause that required a change of religion on the part of a beneficiary's spouse:

> "[I]t is not difficult to believe that in some cases the offer of a legacy to one spouse on condition that the other will renounce an existing religious adherence may lead to discord between them. But whether it will, and to what extent it will, must depend [on the particular circumstances] of every case."[18]

The Dutch author Van den Burght expresses a similar view in his commentary on the statutory provision with regard to the limiting effect of the good morals on testamentary freedom in the Dutch Civil Code:

> "The usual examples of [testamentary] conditions which conflict with good morals are conditions to enter into marriage or not to enter into marriage, to re-marry or not to re-marry, to adhere to a given religion or to convert to a different religion. One can never say in the abstract that any of these conditions are immoral. Everything depends on the circumstances. . . . One must ascertain in every given instance whether the purport of the condition is to exercise undue control."[19]

The following factors (in addition to those listed in the general limitations clause) should, it is submitted, also be taken into account when a court evaluates the facts of each case:

(a) The intention of the testator and the general scheme of his/her will – is the relevant testamentary provision an attempt by the testator to actively exert influence in the private life or with regard to personal choices of a beneficiary (which influence might in appropriate instances conceivably be labelled as an attempt to unfairly discriminate against an instituted beneficiary), or is it an attempt to distinguish (on the basis of justifiable individual preference and choice) between beneficiaries?

---

[18] [1960] 104 C.L.R. 394 at 417.
[19] *Het Nederlandse Burgerlijk Wetboek* (1997), pp.77–78. Translated from the original Dutch.

(b) The interest of the testator in the attempted exercise of influence in the private life of a beneficiary – a justifiable objective on the part of the testator (in other words, an objective founded upon sound social, economic, political or philosophical grounds) might in appropriate circumstances afford protection to a testator's freedom of testation and so warrant the infringement on a beneficiary's rights. In the absence of such an objective, the testator's attempt to "rule from the grave" and the resultant infringement on a beneficiary's rights, might well be labelled as contrary to public policy.

(c) The extent to which the beneficiary's interests are affected by the relevant testamentary provision – a court might look more favourably upon an attempt to exercise influence in a limited or prescribed context, while less so in the case of unlimited interference in the private life of a beneficiary.

(d) The individual beneficiary's willingness to abide by the testamentary directive and hence, in essence, to forfeit the exercise of certain constitutionally-protected rights in favour of a testamentary patrimonial benefit.

CONCLUSION

The law of testate succession in general and testamentary freedom in particular provide a challenging arena for the interplay between private autonomy and constitutionally founded public policy norms. The obligation on South African courts to perform the requisite judicial balancing between testamentary freedom on the one hand and competing constitutional rights such as religious freedom and equality on the other, undoubtedly renders a constitutional challenge on freedom of testation with regard to testamentary faith and race clauses one of the most interesting, yet controversial, issues that the South African judiciary will be called upon to resolve.

SOME UNANSWERED QUESTIONS IN IRISH DEFAMATION LAW

WILLIAM BINCHY*

INTRODUCTION

The law of defamation is in a state of ferment internationally. Courts and leg-islatures have re-assessed the traditional principles of the law in the light of contemporary values regarding freedom of speech, the role of the media, the accountability of those in public life and the role of the jury in assessing dam-ages awards. The trend has been largely in one direction: towards reducing the scope of liability and reducing the quantum of damages awards.

In Ireland, these trends have yet to establish themselves clearly. Ireland's membership of the European Union[1] and its adherence to the European Con-vention on Human Rights, as well as broader cultural and economic influ-ences, are likely to lead to changes largely similar to those that have taken place in other jurisdictions.

Two particular aspects of Irish defamation law have generated consider-able controversy in recent times. These concern the scope of the defence of privilege for defamation by the media and the question of damages as a rem-edy for defamation. Before embarking on that discussion, it may be useful to sketch the constitutional dimension.

The Constitutional dimension

The starting point of our analysis is Article 40.6.1°i of the Constitution, where by the State guarantees liberty for the exercise, subject to public order and

---

* Regius Professor of Laws, Trinity College Dublin.
[1] Ireland became a member of the European Communities in 1972. A constitutional amendment was required. Further constitutional amendments were occasioned by the Single European Act of 1987 and the Maastricht Treaty of 1992. The European Court of Justice, in Case C–68/ 93 *Sheville v. Presse Alliance* [1995] E.C.R. I–415 has prescribed jurisdictional options for victims of defamation in the European Community: they may sue either in the state where the publisher is established, for all the damage caused by the defamatory publication, or in any state where injury to reputation occurred, but only for the injury sustained in that state: see Kennedy, *Defamation Across National Borders: Suing the Foreign Defendant*, in Recent Developments in Defamation and Contempt of Court: A Practical update, Trinity College Dublin, January 23, 2000; Vick & Macpherson, "Anglicising Defamation Law in the Euro-pean Union", 36 Va. J. of Int'l. L. 933 (1996).

morality of:

> "The right of the citizens to express freely their convictions and opin-
> ions.
>
> The education of the public opinion being, however, a matter of such
> grave import to the common good, the State shall endeavour to ensure
> that organs of public opinion, such as the radio, the press, the cinema,
> while preserving their rightful liberty of expression, including criticism
> of Government policy, shall not be used to undermine public order or
> morality or the authority of the State.
>
> The publication or utterance of blasphemous, seditious, or indecent mat-
> ter is an offence which shall be punishable in accordance with law."

The qualified language of this guarantee appears to have discouraged the courts
from a liberal interpretation of its scope. It is hard to disagree with the assessment of my colleague Eoin O'Dell that "... this section has failed to develop
very meaningful protection for speech, especially in comparison with the protection accorded in other jurisdictions".[2] One reason for this restraint is that
the Constitution, in Article 40.3.2°, protects a countervailing value: the right
to one's good name. The courts have on more than one occasion[3] referred to
this protection of reputation as the constitutional basis for the defamation action. They have not gone so far, however, as to say that the existing calibration
of the competing rights of speech and reputation is the only one that has a
constitutional justification. On the contrary, they have indicated that there is a
fairly broad margin of appreciation within which the legislature may make
choices without falling foul of the Constitution. In *Hynes-O'Sullivan v.
O'Driscoll*[4] Henchy J., rejecting the defendant's argument that a belief (or
perhaps only a reasonable belief) on the part of the defamer that the person to
whom the defamation was published had an interest or duty to receive it should
give rise to the defence of qualified privilege, expressed the opinion that:

> "the suggested radical change in the hitherto accepted law should more

---

[2] O'Dell, "When Two Tribes Go to War: Privacy Interests and Media Speech" in *Law and the
Media* (McGonagle ed., 1997, p.271. See further O'Dell, "Does Defamation Value Free Expression? The Possible Effect of New York Times, Sullivan on Irish Law" [1990] D.U.L.J.
50; Frazier, "Liberty of Expression in Ireland and the Need for a Constitutional Law of Defamation" 32 And. J. of Transnat'l L. 391 (1999).

[3] See, *e.g.*, *Barrett v. Independent Newspapers Ltd* [1986] I.R. 13 (Sup. Ct., *per* McCarthy J.,
dissenting), *Kennedy v. Hearne*, [1988] I.R. 481 (High Ct., Murphy J.), *Hynes & O'Sullivan
v. O'Driscoll* [1988] I.R. 436. (Sup. Ct.) *(per* Henchy and McCarthy JJ.) *Foley v. Independent
Newspapers (Ireland) Ltd.*, [1994] 2 I.L.R.M. 61 (High Ct., Geoghegan J.) (Circuit Appeal).

[4] [1988] I.R. 436 (Sup. Ct.).

properly be effected by statute. The public policy which anew formulation of the law would represent should more properly be found by the
Law Reform Commission or by those others who are in a position to
take a broad perspective as distinct from what is discernible in the tun-
nelled vision imposed by the facts of a single case. That is particularly
so in a case such as this, where the law as to qualified privilege must
reflect a due balancing of the constitutional right to freedom or expression and the constitutional protection of every citizen's good name. The
articulation of public policy on a matter such as this would seem to be
primarily a matter for the legislature."

In *Foley v. Independent Newspapers (Ireland) Ltd.*,[5] Geoghegan J. took a still
more passive stance on the relationship between the Constitution and the law
of defamation. It is worth quoting his remarks in full:

"Counsel for the defendants, apart from relying on the ordinary common
law defence of fair comment calls in aid also Article 40.6.1.i of the Constitution. He has referred me to authorities indicating that the traditional
law of contempt of court has been affected by that constitutional provision and he argues that the law of libel may also be affected by it. Even
if that submission as a general proposition is correct any consideration
of that constitutional provision would have to be balanced by consideration of Article 40.3.2, which requires that the State shall by its laws
protect as best it may from unjust attack and in the case of injustice done
vindicate the good name of every citizen. As far as this particular case is
concerned, I am satisfied that once that balancing is done the plaintiffs
entitlement to succeed under the ordinary laws of libel is unaffected."

Defamation by the media

Over the past few decades and particularly in the last five years or so, there
has been a major international debate as to the proper scope of defamation
where the subject matter is political or, more broadly, involves public figures
and where the media are involved. There is no necessary connection between
these themes, but it is striking how they coalesce in discussion. The debate has
taken place against a background of rights-language, contained in constitutions, international conventions and human rights initiatives. Those (including the media) who advocate freedom of speech have wrested the high ground
from the champions of a person's good name.

The landmark decision was that of the United States Supreme Court in

---

[5] [1994] 2 I.L.R.M. 61 at 67 (High Ct.) (Circuit Appeal).
[6] 376 U.S. 254 (1964).

New York Times v. Sullivan,[6] holding, on First Amendment grounds, that those who criticise public figures, basing their charges on false factual assertions, are exempt from liability in defamation save where the particular defamed public figure can prove actual malice – knowledge that the statement is false or reckless disregard as to its truth or falsity.

The New Zealand Court of Appeal, in *Lange v. Atkinson*,[7] has taken a somewhat similar approach: protection is afforded to false statements regarding political matters, even in the absence of reasonable care, provided the defendant is not motivated by ill-will and is not seeking to take improper advantage of the occasion of publication. The High Court of Australia has been more circumspect: it requires the defendant to establish reasonable care on its part in order to avail itself of the privilege.[8]

No recent Irish decision has addressed the scope of media privilege in defamation. The traditional approach was that the media were not generally protected by qualified privilege as there was not normally a reciprocal interest or duty as between the media and their readers, viewers or listeners to impart and receive, respectively, false communications. Exceptions relating to fair reporting of parliamentary debates, judicial proceedings, public meetings and so on were dealt with primarily by express statutory provisions.

One has to look to recent developments in England to find guidance as to how Irish courts will probably be called on to address the issue in a future case. The House of Lords made a subtle contribution to the debate on the matter in *Reynolds v. Times Newspaper Ltd*.[9]

The litigation was rooted in Irish political controversy. In November 1994, Mr Albert Reynolds resigned as Taoiseach (Prime Minister) and leader of the Fianna Fáil party following a political crisis. The Fianna Fáil/Labour coalition Government came under pressure as a result of delay that had occurred in the processing of the extradition from the Republic to the North of Ireland of a priest charged with paedophile offences there. Tensions had developed between the Taoiseach and the Tanaiste (Deputy Prime Minister), Mr Dick Spring, where Mr Spring felt that he was not kept fully informed as to what was happening. The Sunday after Mr Reynolds's resignation, the defendants published an article on the matter, which failed to give Mr Reynolds's version of the events. Mr Reynolds sued the publishers, the editor and the author for libel, alleging that the sting in the article was that he had deliberately and dishon-

---

[7] [1998] 3 N.Z.L.R. 424 (C.A.), analysed by Tobin, "Political Discussion, Freedom of Expression and Qualified Privilege: Lange & Atkinson" (1999) 7 Torts L.J. 32, *New York Times v. Sullivan* and its progeny have influenced courts in other Commonwealth jurisdictions: see *Rajogopal v. State of T.N.* [1994] 6 S.C.C. 632 (Indian Supreme Ct., applying "reckless disregard for truth" test in respect of defamation of public officials). See further Docherty, "Defamation Law: Positive Jurisprudence" (2000) 13 Harv. Human Rts. J. 263, at pp. 276-278.
[8] *cf. Lange v. Australian Newspapers Ltd.*, 189 Comm. L. R. 520 (High Ct. of Austr., 1992).
[9] [1999] 4 All E.R. 609.

estly misled the Dáil (Parliament), the Cabinet and especially Mr Spring. At trial the jury rejected the defence of justification, but found that there was no malice on the part of author and, extraordinarily, awarded no damages. The judge substituted an award of a penny, and in a subsequent dispute over costs he held that the defendants were not entitled rely on the defence of qualified privilege. Mr Reynolds appealed, alleging misdirections to the jury, and the defendants cross-appealed on the question of qualified privilege. The Court of Appeal allowed Mr Reynolds' appeal and ordered a retrial. On the issue of the qualified privilege, it ruled that the defendants would not be entitled to rely on the qualified privilege defence in the view of the circumstances of the publication. The defendants appealed, claiming that libellous statements made in the course of political discussion should automatically attract qualified privilege. The question also arose as to whether the Court of Appeal had been correct in introducing, in addition to the traditional "duty-interest" test, a "circumstantial test", to determine whether qualified privilege exists.

The House of Lords rejected the argument that the common law should develop "political information" as a generic category of information which would always attract qualified privilege irrespective of the circumstances. To do so would fail to protect adequately the individual's reputation to the level necessary for the well-being of a democratic society. Moreover, it was not possible rationally to distinguish between "political information", which the defendants argued should attract qualified privilege, and other serious matters of public concern where no automatic privilege was to apply. In determining whether a privileged occasion exists, the House of Lords gave a vote of confidence for the common law approach, which addressed the question of qualified privilege in a flexible way taking all the circumstances of the case into account. The Court of Appeal was wrong, according to the House of Lords, in elevating these factors into a separate and additional test in determining whether the occasion was privileged. The circumstances must be weighed up when the duty/interest is being considered; there is not an additional "circumstantial test" one has to address after the duty/interest criteria is considered.

To recognise "political information" as automatically attracting qualified privilege would not give due recognition to the individual's reputation in balancing this interest against the right to freedom of expression. If such a privilege existed, then the onus would be on the plaintiff to show malice, a task that would be very difficult, if not impossible, especially when it was recognised that the common law protected the media's right to protect its sources. In the absence of discovery, the individual plaintiff would be at an unacceptable disadvantage, nor would altering the onus of proof assist matters.

Lord Nicholls, who delivered the leading speech, observed:

"I have been more troubled by Lord Lester's [counsel for *Times Newspapers*] suggested shift in the burden of proof. Placing the burden of proof on the plaintiff would be a reminder that the starting point today is freedom of expression and limitations of this freedom are exceptions. That has attraction. But if this shift of the onus were applied generally, it would turn the law of qualified privilege upside down. The repercussions of such a far-reaching change were not canvassed before your Lordships. If this change were applied only to political information, the distinction would lack a coherent rationale. There are other subjects of serious public concern. On balance I favour leaving the onus in its traditional place, on him who asserts the privilege, for two practical reasons. A newspaper will know much more of the facts leading up to publication. The burden of proof will seldom, if ever, be decisive on this issue."[10]

What then are the circumstances which a court ought to take into consideration when applying the duty/interest test to determine whether a privileged occasion exists? In a crucial passage, Lord Nicholls stated:

"Depending on the circumstances, the matters to be taking into account include the following. The comments are illustrative only. (1) The seriousness of the allegation. The more serious the charge, the more the public is misinformed and the individual harmed, if the allegation is not true. (2) The nature of the information, and the extent to which the subject matter is a matter of public of public concern. (3) The source of the information. Some informants have no direct knowledge of the events. Some have their own axes to grind, or are being paid for their stories. (4) The steps taken to verify the information. (5) The status of the information. The allegation may have already been the subject of an investigation which commands respect. (6) The urgency of the matter. News is often a perishable commodity. (7) Whether comment was sought from the plaintiff. He may have information others do not possess or have not disclosed. An approach to the plaintiff will not always be necessary. (8) Whether the Article contained the gist of the plaintiffs side of the story. (9) The tone of the article. A newspaper can raise queries or call for an investigation. It need not adopt allegations as statements of fact. (10) The circumstances of the publication, including the timing.

This list is not exhaustive. The weight to be given to these and any other relevant factors will vary from case to case."[11]

---

[10]*Reynolds v. Times Newspapers Ltd*, above, at 624. In the USA, where *Sullivan* prevails, extensive discovery is available to the plaintiff which helps to balance the interests more fairly. See Lord Nicholls in *Reynolds* at 622-3.
[11]*ibid.*, at 626. In *Grassi v. W.I.C. Radio Ltd.*, 49 C.C.L.T. (2d) 65, at 93 (Br. Col. Sup. Ct., 2000), Lysyk J. quoted this passage from Lord Nicholl's speech. Whilst not specifically en-

In the *Reynolds* case itself, the Lords were very much influenced by the fact that in such a hard-hitting article which made serious allegations against Mr Reynolds by name, no mention was made of Mr Reynolds's own explanation to Parliament. This left the impression on English readers that Mr Reynolds had given no explanation. "An article which fails to do so (*i.e.* give gist of plaintiffs explanation) faces an uphill task in claiming privilege if the allegation proves to be false and the unreported explanation proves to be true".[12] In the absence of this information, the serious allegations presented as statements of facts were not information that the public had a right to know and the publication was not one that should in the public interest be protected by privilege. Essentially, in determining whether the occasion was privileged, the courts should consider whether both sides of the story had been presented to the public. Failure to give the plaintiff's version of the facts could easily result in a decision denying privilege to the occasion.

Although the House of Lords decision is merely persuasive, it is likely that the Irish courts would consider that it strikes an appropriate balance in the matter. It is probable in view of the language of Article 40.6.1°i of the Constitution that the Irish courts would regard an appeal that to recognise "political information" as a generic category of information automatically attracting qualified privilege as involving a step too far, tipping the scales unconstitutionally against the individual's right to his reputation. It is worth noting that in *Reynolds* the House of Lords indicated that in general there should be a reluctance to stifle unduly the freedom of the press:

"In general, a newspaper's unwillingness to disclose the identity of its sources should not weigh against it.

Further, it should always be remembered that journalists act without the benefit of the clear light of hindsight. Matter which are obvious in retrospect may have been far from clear in the heat of the moment. Above all, the court should have particular regard to the importance of freedom of expression. The press discharges vital functions as a bloodhound as well as a watchdog. The court should be slow to conclude that a publication was not in the public interest and, therefore, the public had no right to know, especially when the information is in the field of political discussion. Any lingering doubts should be resolved in favour of publication."[13]

The media should be pleased with the *Reynolds* decision. When one examines closely Lord Nicholl's 10-point formula, it actually gives the media very con-

---

dorsing it, he sought to distinguish the facts of the case before him from those specified by Lord Nicholls.

[12] [1999] 4 All E.R., at 627, *per* Lord Nicholls.

[13] *ibid.* at 626, *per* Lord Nicholls.

siderable latitude. If a newspaper reporter asks the person about whom the paper is to run a story for comment on it, gives him or her plenty of opportunity to do so and publishes what he or she has to say, the ultimate falsity of the allegations will stand a good chance of being clothed with the cover of qualified privilege. The defence for the media is, in essence, one of due care and moderation. This is a completely new development, though it is presented in *Reynolds* as being rooted in traditional principles relating to qualified privilege.

Damages: the roles of judge and jury

The question of damages in defamation litigation has proved highly controversial in recent years.[14] The traditional approach has been to give the jury substantial leeway in making an award. The reason – which has perhaps become somewhat occluded in much contemporary discussion – is that defamation is rooted in community values. The trial judge's role is to ensure that the jury adjudicates only on communications that are *capable* of being characterised on defamatory but, within that broad limitation, the jury, as representative of the community, makes the decision as to liability.[15] Equally, the jury has the task of quantifying the damage to the plaintiff's reputation in monetary terms[16] with some guidance from the trial judge but not to the extent of having specific figures mentioned in the judge's direction.

Over the past decade, there has been a veritable assault on this approach. Several factors are involved. Some particularly high awards against media defendants by British juries provoked a strong media campaign to rein in the damages for defamation. This campaign extends well beyond the alleged frailty of jury decision-making, however, since it encompasses the broader argument

---

[14]Fleming, *The Law of Torts* (8th ed., 1998), pp.657-663.

[15]Thus, in *Quigley v. Creation Ltd.*, [1971] I.R. 269 at 272, Walsh J. observed:

  "Basically, the question of libel or no libel is a matter of opinion and opinions may vary reasonably within very wide limits. When a jury has found that there has been a libel, this court would be more slow to set aside such a verdict then in other types of actions and it would only do so if it was of opinion that the conclusion reached by the jury was one to which reasonable men could not or ought not have come. . . . In defamation, as in perhaps no other form of civil proceedings, the position of the jury is so uniquely important that, while it is for the judge to determine whether the words complained of are capable of a defamatory meaning, the judge should not withhold the matter from the jury unless he is satisfied that it would be wholly unreasonable to attribute a libellous meaning to the words complained of."

[16]cf. *Barrett v. Independent Newspapers Ltd.*, [1986] I.R. 13, at 35 (Supreme Ct., *per* McCarthy J.):

  "The law reports abound with judicial tributes to the particular respect [for] a jury in libel actions . . . Walsh J.['s] . . . observations [in *Quigley v. Creation Ltd* [1971] I.R. 269 at 272] apply no less to the assessment of damages than they do to the issue of libel or no libel."

that the media are unduly restrained by the basic principles of defamation law on such matters as the onus of proof, strict liability and the limits of the defence of qualified privilege.

Apart from these broader concerns, there is a discernible patrician disdain among the British judiciary for the capacity of members of juries to understand the value of money once the sums involved are beyond their day-to-day experience[17]: this has led to greater specificity in directions by trial judges in defamation cases[18] and the increasing willingness to include references to amounts of awards in earlier cases that have received the blessing of the appellate courts.

A third factor should be noted. This is the European dimension. Speaking broadly, there is no tradition in continental European jurisdictions of awarding high sums in defamation cases. Defamation is treated differently in civil law countries, with less emphasis on damages and much more on other processes, including the criminal law and remedies involving retraction.[19] Juries play only a limited role in civil litigation in these countries. Moreover, compensation for personal injuries is also far less extensive in these countries than it is in common law jurisdictions, particularly Ireland, where damages levels are high. Bearing these substantial differences in mind, it was relatively easy to predict that the European Court of Human Rights might not look with complete favour on high awards in defamation cases by juries acting with little specific guidance from the trial judge as to what would be an appropriate amount.

Earlier Irish authorities

The Irish courts have made it plain that juries are not given a completely free hand when deciding the quantum of damages in defamation cases. On the

---

[17]Thus, in *Sutcliffe v. Pressdam Ltd* [1991] I Q.B. 153, where the jury made an award £600,000 general damages, Donaldson M R observed (at) that he could:

"not believe that the jury appreciated the true size of the award which they were making. This is understandable. Despite the inflation which has occurred in the post-war years, sums of money of £100,000 or more, and in many cases less, still lack the reality of the £ 1 coin or the £5 note. In the lives of ordinary people they are unlikely ever to intrude except in the form of the nominal sale or purchase price of a house. . . . What is, I think, required is some guidance to juries in terms which will assist them to appreciate the real value of large sums."

In *Rantzen v. Mirror Group Newspapers* (1986) *Ltd* [1994] Q.B. 670, the Court of Appeal upheld the trial judge's direction to the jury, which advised the jury to relate the amount awarded in damages to "what [money] can buy a house, a car or a holiday".

[18]*cf. Rantzen v. Mirror Group Newspapers* (1986) *Ltd.*, above, *John v. MGN Ltd* [1996] 2 All E.R. 35.

[19]See Vick & Macpherson, "Anglicising Defamation Law in the European Union" 36 Va. J. of Int'l L. 933, at 952ff (1996), Arnold Nicholson, "Re Libel: A Case Study in English Defamation Law" 18 Wisconsin Int'l L. J., at 6-8 (2000).

contrary, they have insisted that juries act on the principle of proportionality, taking into account *(inter alia)* the relative gravity of the charge made against the plaintiff.

The *locus classicus* is contained in Henchy J.'s judgment in *Barrett v. Independent Newspapers Ltd.*,[20] where the Supreme Court struck down as excessive a jury award of £65,000 damages in favour of a politician about whom a journalist had written that, in the immediate aftermath of an unsuccessful "push" against Taoiseach Charles Haughey at Leinster House (the parliamentary building), the politician had "leaned over and pulled at my beard and said 'You thought you'd dance on his grave'."

Henchy J. stated:

> "In a case such as this in which there is no question of punitive, exemplary or aggravated damages, it is the duty of the judge to direct the jury that the damages must be confined to such sum of money as will fairly and reasonably compensate the plaintiff for his injured feelings and for any diminution in his standing among right-thinking people as a result of the words complained. The jury have to be told that they must make their assessment entirely on the facts as found by them, and they must be given such direction on the law as will enable them to reach a proper assessment on the basis of those facts. Among the relevant considerations proper to be taken into account are the nature of the libel, the standing of the plaintiff, the extent of the publication, the conduct of the defendant at all stages of the case, and any other matter which bears on the extent of the damages. The fact remains . . . that the jury were not given any real help as to how to assess compensatory damages in this case. A helpful guide for a jury in a case such as this would have been to ask them to reduce to actuality the allegation complained of, namely, that in an excess of triumphalison at this leader's success the plaintiff attempted to tweak the beard of an unfriendly journalist. The jury might then have been asked to fit that allegation into its appropriate place in the scale of defamatory remarks to which the plaintiff might have been subjected. Had they approached the matter in this way, I venture to think that having regard to the various kinds of allegations of criminal, immoral or otherwise contemptible conduct that might have been made against a politician, the allegation actually complained of would have to come fairly low in the scale of damaging accusations. The sum awarded, however, is so high as to convince me that the jury erred in their approach. To put it another way, If £65,000 were to be held to be appropriate damages for an accusation of a minor unpremeditated assault in a moment of exhaltation, the damages proper for an accusation of some

---

[20][1986] I.R. 45 (Sup. Ct.)

leinous or premeditated criminal conduct would be astronomically high. Yet, a fundamental principle of the law of compensatory damages in that the award must always be reasonable and fair and bear a due correspondence with the injury suffered. In my view, the sum awarded in this case went far beyond what a reasonable jury applying the law to all the relevant considerations could reasonably have awarded."[21]

These observations made it clear that there is no judicial surrender to the vagaries of perverse juries. A criterion of objective proportionality must be applied by juries and failure by a trial judge to apprise them of this obligation may well render his or her charge to the jury legally defective. Moreover, the jury's tariff must be such as to keep the maximum sum for damages for the most serious libels within reason: if it is "astronomically high", that will not pass the scrutiny of the Supreme Court.

In *McDonagh v. News Group Newspapers Ltd.*,[22] the Supreme Court again favoured an approach based on objective proportionality. Here the jury had awarded £90,000 to the plaintiff, a practising barrister, who had represented the Irish Government at an inquest held in Gibraltar into the shooting dead of Mairead Farrell, Sean Savage and Daniel McCann, members of the provisional IRA, by members of the Special Air Service regiment of the British Army.[23] The Sun newspaper had published an article under the headline "Leftie Spies pack SAS Gib Inquest", which the jury found defamed the plaintiff in several respects, including allegations that he was a left-wing spy, that his report to the Irish Government on the inquest would be biased, that he sympathised with terrorist gangs, and that he was incapable of performing the duties for which he had been appointed by the Irish Government.

The Supreme Court dismissed an appeal against the quantum of damages. It seemed to Finlay C.J. that, though the figure was "probably at the top of the appropriate range", it was not so great that the Court should interfere. With regard to the allegation that the plaintiff was a sympathiser with terrorist causes, the Chief Justice was satisfied that "there are not very many general classifications of defamatory accusation which at present in Ireland, in the minds of right-minded people, would be considered more serious". To an extent, the seriousness might be somewhat aggravated by the fact that it was an accusation that had been made against a person who had a professional role in the

---

[21] *ibid.*
[22] Supreme Ct., November 23, 1993.
[23] The European Court of Human Rights subsequently held (by a majority) that Britain had violated the protection afforded by Article 2 of the Convention to the right to life: *McCann v. United Kingdom*, 324 E.C.H.R. (Ser. A) p. 214 (1995): see Irwin, "Comment: Prospects for Justice and the Procedural Aspect of the Right to Life under the European Convention on Human Rights and Its Application to Investigations of Northern Ireland's Bloody Sunday" (2000) 22 Fordham Int'l. L. J. 1822, at 1842-1846.

administration of justice. The other allegations, in their combined effect, constituted an extremely grave accusation of professional misconduct by the plaintiff.

The *De Rossa* litigation

We now must consider the crucial decision of the Supreme Court was in *De Rossa v. Independent Newspapers plc*,[24] in 1999. In that case, the plaintiff, the leader of the Democratic Left Party, had formerly been a leading member of the Workers' Party. The defendant published an article about the plaintiff's role in the Workers' Party, which the jury found to be defamatory of him in suggesting that he had been involved in, or tolerated, serious crime and had personally supported anti-Semitism and violent communist oppression. The jury awarded £300,000 damages. On appeal to the Supreme Court by the defendant against the quantum of damages, the appellant argued that the existing practice of allowing juries unguided discretion in their assessment of damages in defamation cases led to excessive and disproportionate awards and was contrary to the Constitution. Instead, it argued guidelines should be given to juries, including reference to the purchasing power of any contemplated award, comparison with personal injury damages awards and awards in previous libel cases, and the estimates of the trial judge and counsel, respectively, of the appropriate level of damages in the case before them. The appellant further argued that the Supreme Court was obliged, under common law and the Constitution, to subject large awards to a more searching scrutiny than formerly.

The new test proposed by the appellant was that favoured by the English Court of Appeal in *Rantzen v. Mirror Group Newspapers Ltd*,[25] namely, whether a reasonable jury could have thought that the particular award it made was necessary to compensate the plaintiff and to re-establish his or her reputation.

The Supreme Court, by a four-to-one majority,[26] rejected this argument and dismissed the appeal. Hamilton C.J., for the majority, expressed the view that "[t]here does not appear to be any conflict between Article 10 [of the European Convention on Human Rights] and the common law or the Constitution". Proportionality was the key principle and this was already well established in Irish case law on the subject of damages for defamation, notably in Henchy J.'s judgment in *Barrett*.[27]

The Chief Justice went on to state that neither the Constitution nor the

---

[24]Supreme Ct., July 30, 1999, analysed by Browne, "A Judgment that Chills Media's Zeal" *Irish Times*, August 4, 1999.

[25][1994] Q.B. 670 (C.A.).

[26]Hamilton C.J., Barrington, Murphy and Lynch JJ. concurring, Denham J. dissenting.

[27]*Supra.*

Convention required that the guidelines to be given to juries should be changed in the manner argued for by the appellant:

> "If the practice as outlined in *Rantzen* case and extended as outlined in *John's* case were to be followed, the jury would be buried in figures, figures suggested by counsel for both parties as to the appropriate level of damages, a figure from the judge representing his opinion as to the appropriate level of damages, figures with regard to damages made or approved by the Court of Appeal in previous libel actions and figures with regard to damages in personal injuries actions and at the same time be subject to the direction of the trial judge that it is not bound by such figures and must make up its own mind as to the appropriate level of damages.
>
> It is accepted by all that, even if the giving of such guidelines and figures were permissible, the jury would not be bound by such figures and was under an obligation to make up its own mind to the appropriate level of damages.
>
> I am satisfied that the giving of such figures, even though only by way of guideline, would constitute an unjustifiable invasion of the province or domain of the jury."

Hamilton C.J. was equally opposed to having the trial judge refer to awards in personal injuries litigation when directing the jury in defamation proceedings. The highly subjective element in assessing the damage to reputation made this comparison unhelpful, in his view.[28]

The Chief Justice stressed the individual character of each defamation case as a further reason why reference to awards in other defamation cases would not assist the jury's task:

> "Each defamation action has its own unique features and a jury in assessing damages must have regard to same: these include the nature of the libel, the standing of the plaintiff, the extent of the publication, the

---

[28]The relationship between damages for personal injuries and damage for loss of reputation is complex and controversial. It might at first be considered odd that loss of reputation should warrant greater maximum compensation than the worst physical injury imaginable, but there is no necessary *logical* connection between the two. Who is to say that to be falsely accused of being a child molester or a traitor or a racist is more or less serious in its impact than a broken spine? If the intuition is that the broken spine should warrant greater damages, is that an argument for bringing defamation damages down to the artificial level prescribed by the Supreme Court in *Sinnott v. Quinnsworth Ltd* [1984] I.L.R.M. 523, or for reviewing the adequacy of personal injury awards? The (somewhat crude) rationale for the *Sinnott* tariff surely has no necessary application to defamation cases.

conduct of the defendant at all stages and many other matters. These will
vary from case to case. Figures awarded in other cases based on different facts are not matters which the jury is or should be entitled to take
into account."

To retain the traditional guidelines for juries unaltered would not mean that
their discretion was limitless:

"[T]he damages awarded by a jury must be fair and reasonable having
regard to all the relevant circumstances and must not be disproportionate to the injury suffered by the injured party and the necessity to vindicate such party in the eyes of the public. A wards made by a jury are
subject to a right of appeal and, on the hearing of such appeal, the award
made by a jury is scrutinised to ensure that the award complies with
these principles."

Hamilton C.J. rejected the *Rantzen*[29] test for appellate tribunals on the basis
that it would remove from the jury award its "very unusual and emphatic sanc-
tity".[30] The correct test was that the appellate court could set aside an award
only when satisfied that it was so disproportionate to the injury suffered and
the wrong done that no reasonable jury would have made it.

    Applying that test to the facts of the case, the Chief Justice was satisfied
that the award should stand:

"To publish of any person words meaning that he or she was involved in
or tolerated serious crime and personally supported anti-Semitism and
violent Communist oppression would, if untrue, constitute the gravest
and most serious libel: it is hard to imagine a more serious one.

To publish such words in relation to the respondent, a politician dependant on the support of his constituents and his colleagues and at a time
when he was engaged in negotiations, as was well known to the appellant at the time of publication, which might lead to his participation in
Government, renders such publication more serious and grave, particularly when they might have interfered with his chances of participation
in such Government. The words published clearly affected the respondent's personal integrity and professional reputation."

Moreover, one of the most important facts in the assessment of damages was
the effect of the libel on the plaintiff's feelings. It was easy to imagine the hurt

---

[29] *Supra.*
[30] *Barrett v. Independent Newspapers Ltd* [1986] I.R. 13 at 19 (Supreme Ct., *per* Finlay C.J.).

and distress caused by allegations of the kind made by the appellant. The extent of the publication was very wide: the newspaper – *The Sunday Independent* – had a readership of over a million. No apology, retraction or withdrawal of the allegation had been made at any time. During the course of the proceedings, the respondent had been subjected to immensely long and hostile cross-examination by counsel for the appellant. Right to the very end of the trial the appellant had contested the right of the respondent to damages, and had challenged his motives in taking the action and his honesty and credibility.

Having regard to all these considerations, it appeared to Hamilton C.J. that the jury "would have been justified in going to the top of the bracket and awarding as damages the largest sum that could fairly be regarded as compensation".

Denham J., dissenting, favoured giving guidelines to the jury on the level of damages in defamation cases. They "would assist in [reaching] consistent and comparable decisions, which would enhance public confidence in the administration of justice". Information should be given to the jury of previous awards in libel cases made or affirmed by the Supreme Court. The jury should also be able to compare the value of what courts usually awarded to people in personal injury actions. In neither case was compensation a fully effective remedy:

> "The lame do not walk after an award of compensation. The defamed do not cease to have been defamed after an award of damages. An order of damages is an artificial form by which a court gives a remedy to an injured person.
>
> It is quite reasonable to have proportionality in the wider scheme of damages. Thus, a reference to a case which imposes a cap on general damages might be useful. However, rather than reference to general damages in catastrophic injury cases, where there may be issues of consciousness etc., the tariff for injures such as an eye, a leg or an arm may be helpful. It is entirely reasonable that there be a degree of uniformity, consistency, a sense of compatibility, of rationality, in the wider scheme of damages."

Denham J. considered that the appellate tribunal, in determining whether the jury's award was reasonable and proportionate, could also have resort to some guidelines on damage levels that had been given to the jury. As to the amount of damages awarded in the instant case, Denham J. referred to *McDonagh v. News Group Newspapers Ltd*,[31] whose facts involved "strong similarities" in the seriousness of the defamation allegations and the standing of importance

---

[31] Supreme Ct., November 23, 1993.

in the community which both plaintiffs shared. The award of £90,000 in
McDonagh had been considered by the Supreme Court to be at the top of the
permissible range. Even making allowance for the further aggravating ele-
ments in the instant case, Denham J. considered the award of £300,000 to be
so large as to be unsustainable.

The Supreme Court decision in *De Rossa* left the law in an unsatisfactory
state. The defendants have sought to have the case determined by the European Court of Human Rights. The outcome of that case is hard to predict and
the Supreme Court's analysis of the Convention was disappointingly summary. Hamilton C.J. offered no explanation for his bald assertion that "[t]here
does not appear to be any conflict between Article 10 [of the Convention] and
the common law or the Constitution". Nor did he explain how the exclusion of
guidance for juries as to the purchasing power of awards or as to what appellate courts had authorised and the existing, somewhat deferential, appellate
approach towards jury awards could be reconciled with what the European
Court of Human Rights said in *Tolstoy Miloslavsky v. United Kingdom.*[32] The
crucial passage from *Tolstoy* must be quoted *in extenso:*

> "The jury had been directed not to punish the appellant but only to award
> an amount that would compensate the non-pecuniary damage to [the
> plaintiff]. The sum awarded was three times the size of the highest libel
> award; previously made in England and no comparable award has been
> made since. An award of the present size must be particularly open to
> question where the substantive national law applicable at the time fails
> itself to provide a requirement of proportionality.
>
> In this regard it should be noted that, at the material time, the national
> law allowed a great latitude to the jury. The Court of Appeal could not
> set aside an award simply on the grounds that it was excessive but only if
> the award was so unreasonable that it could not have been made by sen-
> sible people and must have been arrived at capriciously, unconscionably
> or irrationally. In a more recent case, *Rantzen v. Mirror Group Newspa-
> pers Ltd.* the Court of Appeal itself observed that to grant an almost
> limitless discretion to a jury failed to provide a satisfactory measure-
> ment for lending what was 'necessary in a democratic society' for the
> purposes of Article 10 of the Convention. It noted that the common law
> – if properly understood – required the courts to subject large awards of
> damages to a more searching scrutiny than had been customary. As to
> what guideline the judge should give to the jury, the Court of Appeal
> stated that it was to be hoped that in the course of time a series of deci-

---

[32] 20 E.H.R.R. 442 (1995).

sions of the Court of Appeal, taken under section 8 of the Courts and, Legal Services Act 1990, would establish some standards as to what would be proper awards. In the meantime the jury should be invited to consider the purchasing power of any award which they might make and to ensure that any award they made was proportionate to the damage which the plaintiff had suffered and was a sum which it was necessary to award him to provide adequate compensation and to re-establish his reputation.

The Court cannot but endorse the above observations by the Court of Appeal to the effect that the scope of judicial control, at the trial and on appeal, at the time of the applicant's case did not offer adequate and effective safeguards against a disproportionately large award.

Accordingly, having regard to the size of the award in the applicant's case in conjunction with the lack of adequate and effective safeguards at the relevant time against a disproportionately large award, the Court finds that there has been a violation of the applicant's rights under Article 10 of the Convention."[33]

It is very hard to interpret this passage as offering support for a system that does not contain provision for guiding juries on the lines indicated in *Rantzen*.[34]

---

[33] *ibid.* at 472-473.

[34] In *De Rossa*, Hamilton C.J. quoted this passage and stated:

"It is clear from the foregoing that the primary reason for the court's decision was the size of the award and the lack of adequate and effective safeguards at the relevant time against a disproportionately large award. It recognised, however, that an award of damages must bear a reasonable relationship of proportionality to the injury to reputation suffered. The court gave approval to the guidance to be given to a jury as laid down by the Court of Appeal in *Rantsen's* case."

What is striking about this passage is that the Chief Justice clearly acknowledged that an element in the Courts' reasoning was the lack of adequate and effective safeguards *"at the relevant time"* (emphasis added) against a disproportionately large award. This lack had been remedied by the English Court of Appeal's judgment in *Rantzen*. An obvious question therefore arises. If Irish law endorses an approach which suffers from what the European Court of Human Rights has identified as involving a lack of adequate and effective safeguards, how can it be consistent with Article 10 of the Convention? It is true that the European Court of Human Rights, while endorsing the observations of the English Court of Appeal in Rantzen, restricted that endorsement, *expressis verbis*, to the Court of Appeal's finding that the then existing legal approach "did not offer adequate and effective safeguards against a disproportionately large award." *Pace* Hamilton C.H., it did not expressly "give approval to the guidance to be given to a jury as laid down by the Court of Appeal in *Rantzen's* case." Nevertheless, the import of the endorsement, especially its reference to "the above observations by the Court of Appeal" (which extended to a specific prescription as to what should replace the discredited legal approach), justify Hamilton C.J.'s conclusion that the endorsement carried with it a necessary implicit approval for the guidance to juries which the Court of Appeal prescribed. It would, of course, be open to a plaintiff to argue that this approval did not commit the Euro-

Whilst the Irish system can be defended on the basis that the jury's discretion is not untrammelled and that the principle of proportionality must underline its award and the appellate assessment of it, the fact remains that the trial judge's hands are tied in being prevented from translating an invocation to be sensitive to requirements of proportionality into offering practical examples of what has been held to be proportionate.

O'Brien: the issue revisited

The Supreme Court returned to the issue in *O'Brien v. Mirror Group Newspaper*.[35] In this case, the defendants published in one of their newspapers allegations that the plaintiff, "a well known and successful businessman",[36] had paid a Minister of the Government a bribe of £30,000 to secure the awarding of a radio licence, and that the plaintiff had secured the awarding of a mobile telephone licence in circumstances that gave rise to a suspicion of bribery or corrupt practices. The jury held that these allegations amounted to actionable defamation and awarded damages of £250,000.

The defendants appealed to the Supreme Court, contending that the damages awarded were excessive. They argued that the appropriate test for determining whether to set aside an assessment of damages was whether the assessment was one which a reasonable jury would have thought necessary to compensate the plaintiff and establish his reputation. Specifically, they claimed that the trial judge had misdirected the jury in failing to have referred (or allowed counsel to refer) to three matters which derived from the English decisions of *Rantzen* and John and which had already been canvassed thoroughly in *De* Rossa. These were the purchasing power of the award that the jury might be minded to make and the income it would produce; by way of comparison, the compensation scales in personal injury cases and previous libel awards made or approved by the Supreme Court; and the level of awards that counsel and the trial judge respectively considered to be appropriate. Counsel for the appellants argued that the rules of law or practice restraining counsel and the trial judge in defamation trials from offering guidance of this nature were inconsistent with the provisions of the Constitution. Finally, they asserted that the size of the award was an infringement with the defendants' right to freedom of expression, in breach of Article 40 of the Constitution and Article 10 of the European Convention on Human Rights.

Having regard to the *stare decisis* principle,[37] the defendants had a formi-

---

pean Court of Human Rights to the position that, in the precise approach favoured in *Rantzen* was the only one that would guarantee compliance with the requirements of Article 10.
[35] Supreme Ct, October 25, 2000.
[36] *Per* Keane C.J. at p. 1 of his judgment.
[37] *Cf. Attorney General v. Ryan's Car Hire Ltd* [1965] I.R. 642, *Mogul of Ireland v. Tipperary (North Riding) County Council* [1976] I.R. 260.

dable task in trying to persuade the Supreme Court to depart from *De Rossa,* only 15 months previously. This clearly proved too serious an obstacle for the majority. Keane C.J., Murphy and O'Higgins JJ. concurring, acknowledged that "a different view could legitimately be taken from that expressed by Hamilton C.J.,[38] in *De Rossa* but he had "no doubt that the fact of itself could not justify this court in overruling the decision".[39]

In the light of this, the appeal could not succeed on the ground that the trial judge had not followed the guidelines laid down by the Court of Appeal in *John* and had directed the jury as to the law in accordance with *De Rossa.*

The Chief Justice went on to consider whether the award should nonetheless be set aside as disproportionately high, having regard to the law laid down in *Barrett* and *De Rossa.* He thought it proper for the Court, "[no] doubt [exercising] a degree of caution,"[40] to make comparisons with earlier defamation awards that had reached the Court on appeal. The allegations in the instant case were undoubtedly seriously defamatory and justified the award of substantial damages:

> "However, the case must be approached, in my view, on the basis that the damages awarded are in the highest bracket of damages appropriate in any libel case. They are comparable to the general damages awarded in the most serious cases of paraplegic or quadriplegic injuries[41] and, relatively speaking are in the same bracket as the damages awarded in *De Rossa.* The libel, however, although undoubtedly serious and justifying the award of substantial damages, cannot be regarded as coming within the category of the greatest and most serious libels which have come before the courts".[42]

The instant case could be distinguished from *De Rossa* in several respects. The libel in *De Rossa* could not have been of a more serious character, alleging that the plaintiff had "supported some of the vilest activities of totalitarian regimes in the twentieth century and was personally involved in or condoned serious crime",[43] on any view this was a significantly more damaging and serious libel than the admittedly serious allegation against the plaintiff in the instant case. The circulation of the newspaper in *De Rossa's* case was well over seven times as large as in *O'Brien*. Mr De Rossa was more widely known to the public than the plaintiff in the instant case. Finally, there was a differ-

---

[38]p. 24 of Keane C.J.'s judgment.
[39]*ibid.*
[40]*ibid.* at p. 25.
[41]At present the judicial tariff for general damages in relation to injuries of this character is £250,000.
[42]p. 28 of Keane C.J.'s judgment.
[43]*ibid.*

ence in the manner in which the two proceedings had been conducted: in *De Rossa*, the plaintiff had been subjected to prolonged and hostile cross-examination, while in *O'Brien* the plea of justification had not apparently been seriously pressed and the cross-examination of the plaintiff had been gentle. On these grounds, Keane C.J. concluded that the award was disproportionately high and should be set aside. Denham, Murphy and O'Higgins JJ. concurred, on the issue of setting aside the award. There was thus a majority in favour of this course. Denham J. arrived at her conclusion by a route different from that of the Chief Justice. She considered it proper to revisit *De Rossa* on the basis of the importance of the questions whether Irish law was in breach of Article 10 of the European Convention on Human Rights and whether further information and guidance should be given to juries than had been countenanced in *De Rossa*. She reiterated the views that she had expressed in these issues in *De Rossa*. On the issue of the amount of the award she was in agreement with Keane C.J. that it was excessive.

Geoghegan J. differed from his colleagues on that issue, though he agreed with the Chief Justice that the Court should not entertain arguments to the effect that *De Rossa* had been wrongly decided. Geoghegan J. identified important differences between appeals in defamation cases and appeals from an award in personal injury litigation.

"In the case of personal injuries an appeal court can determine with some confidence what would be the range of awards which a reasonable jury (or, nowadays a reasonable judge) might make. This the appeal court can do because although every personal injury case is different from every other personal injury case there are also great similarities. A broken hip case relates to some extent at least to every other broken hip case. A loss of an eye case relates to some extent at least to every other case of loss of an eye etc. Members of the court from their experience at the Bar and/ experience as trial judges and indeed experience of previous similar appeals may with some confidence form a view as to what the legitimate spectrum of awards could be. In the case of a libel appeal however the appeal Court although it has to engage in the same exercise, it can only do so with diffidence rather than confidence."

The future for defamation law in Ireland

It is not easy to predict the future for defamation law in Ireland. It may be that the European Court of Human Rights will find that Irish law in relation to the process of arriving at an award of damages in defamation proceedings violates Article 10 of the Convention. In any event, the statutory incorporation of the Convention into Irish domestic law, subject to the provisions of the Constitution, may also act as a source of encouragement to the judiciary to be more sensitive to the requirements of Article 10.

The movement towards greater emphasis on the Convention's norms is not necessarily all in one direction, however. There is good reason to expect that Irish courts will place greater emphasis on the value of privacy[44] over the coming years. In that regard, we may yet find an interesting debate leading to an ultimate synthesis of the norms protected by Articles 8 and 10 of the Convention.[45]

---

[44] *Cf.* J. Casey, *Constitutional Law in Ireland* (3rd ed., 2000), 387-404, *Kennedy v. Ireland* [1987] I.R. 587.

[45] *Cf.* English, "Confidentiality and Defamation", Chapter 11 of R. English & P. Havers (eds.), *An Introduction to Human Rights and the Common Law* (2000).

SUBJECT INDEX